A Time for Every Purpose Under Heaven

An Exploration of Sacred History

A Time for Every Purpose Under Heaven

An Exploration of Sacred History

Rt. Rev. James D. Heiser, M.Div., S.T.M.

REPRISTINATION PRESS
MALONE, TEXAS

Published in 2012 by

Repristination Press
P.O. Box 173
Bynum, Texas 76631

www.repristinationpress.com

ISBN 1-891469-39-8

TABLE OF CONTENTS

INTRODUCTION.

The pages which follow are a humble attempt to explore a topic of nearly-limitless scope. How can one hope to adequately discuss that which is, by definition, unknowable, save in the hidden counsel of the all-knowing providence of God? That is, how can finite man speak of the whole span of the history of our race, let alone the purpose behind that history? Discussing the interaction of sacred history, secular history and myth, one must immediately concede the impossibility of saying more than a fraction of what must needs be said—and there is always the danger of saying much which is simply wrong. Those who have endeavored to reduce history to a system have simply revealed the impossibility of the task for human reason.

What follows, then, is not a system, but an exploration conducted in three parts. In the first portion, the task is to wrestle with some of the fundamental issues of the relationship of sacred and secular history to myth. The second portion is an evaluation of some of the more pernicious reigning myths of this modern age. The final portion is an exploration of aspects of the historical development of these myths.

It should be noted that no part of this work is actually a work of history, in the usual senses of that term. In certain regards, it is a prolegomena to historical study. The intellectual and ecclesiastical history of many of the ideas touched upon in these pages have been dealt with at great length in other books, many of which are referenced. The earnest reader is referred to them, with the present author hoping that they will elucidate those matters which can only be briefly touched upon in the current context.

We are all bound to live in time in this vale of tears, and the writing of this work has thus intruded upon the days which the author has been allotted for life with family, colleagues, and parishioners. They have all been quite gracious in accepting the frequent interruptions which the writing of this book has necessarily imposed. I can only express my gratitude to them for the care and support which they have provided time and again.

As for that which is found in these pages, the errors are mine alone, while the insights—such as may be found—are often those of others which I gladly communicate to you, with appropriate attribution, of course. Where there are flaws, I encourage you to improve upon that which has been set forth herein. As our brief sojourn in this world is witness to many shortcoming and failure rooted in our sinfulness, I ask that you receive that which is profitable, and kindly forgive that which falls short of my intentions.

+James D. Heiser, M.Div., S.T.M.
Bishop, The Evangelical Lutheran Diocese of North America
Pastor, Salem Lutheran Church (Malone, Texas)

Time and the Church—
An Exploration of Sacred,
Secular and Mythological
Conceptions of History

10

CHAPTER 1.
HISTORY—SACRED, SECULAR AND MYTHOLOGICAL.

hat is history? For many post-modern men—maltreated and miseducated by substandard pseudo-educators in the holding pens which society calls "public schools"—history is just a string of disassociated events which reduces to a catalog of 'one blasted thing after another.' Taught to avoid any awareness of a transcendent significance associated with any event and to simply become immersed in fleeting concerns, the cultivated ignorance of history has partially blinded its victims to the reality which surrounds them from before the moment of birth.

Our endeavor here, implicitly, is to defend the significance of history for men, in general, and for the Christian man, in particular. This is a task rendered virtually impossible due to a curious commingling of profound simplicity and immeasurable complexity in its content. History—in all the plenitude of meaning which permeates that word—is all caught up in the questions which are simultaneously transcendent and solipsistic. In our ever-shifting present moment, all of history is seen through our current hour and the fluctuations which that imminence implies. In this endeavor, the words which Herodotus—the "Father of History"—attributes to Xerxes may have some wisdom for the endeavors which follow: "I would much rather take a risk and run into trouble half the time than keep out of any trouble through being afraid of everything."[1] Where there are weaknesses in that which is presented, the fault is my own. But it is better to speak in promotion of virtue than to remain silent in the presence of vice, and the ignorance of history is the cultivation

---

1   Herodotus, *The Histories*, (New York: Penguin Books, 1972) p. 462 (Book 7.50)

of a plethora of ancient evils, *redux*. Thus what follows may be deemed a 'work in progress,' but one hopes that it is, in the end, progress.

In a sense, a defense of the study of history is a rather straightforward affair, because the questions posed in the course of such study are often universal. We are drawn to the study of history in its various forms because it helps to address the questions which are of most pressing significance to every human being: "*Who* am I?," "*Where* am I?," and "*When* am I—what *time* is it?" These questions are, of course, regularly used in a fashion which is quite mundane, but that does not vitiate the fact that they remain questions of central concern to man throughout his earthly existence. They are fundamental questions pertaining to the identity of man before the Triune God and his fellow man. I cannot entirely know *who* I am until I know *where* and *when* I am—that is, until I understand what I know of these things.

The mundane answers to the fundamental questions come rather easily, and exist at a level of concern which is, perhaps, ultimately personal. The Lord of heaven and earth assures us in Matthew 10:30: "But the very hairs of your head are all numbered," but such matters are probably only of concern to the Triune God and the individual in question.

At a higher level of inquiry, to know that I reside in the United States of America—more specifically, that I am a citizen of the State of Texas—living in the Year of our Lord 2012, which is the 223rd year of the ratification of the Constitution of this Republic, unveils layers of meaning which are more fully grasped for a knowledge of history in its various forms. *Who* I am, *where* I am, and *when* I am take on a deeper meaning.

But we may move to another layer still. To be a Confessional Lutheran in this age when the beginning of the Reformation is nearly five centuries past, living in a post-Christian culture, does not vitiate any of the points previously stated; rather, it enriches that which was already known, and allows for further integration of each individual within his various vocational circles.

However, each layer vastly expands the complexity of adequately addressing matters of historical significance pertaining to the basic questions. The circle of interaction of my history with that of other people—and, increasingly, people who are no longer living—renders each level of inquiry increasingly complex. The fundamental questions—"Who am I?," "Where am I?," and "What time is it?"—provide rather shallow replies at the lowest levels of inquiry, but such data are more easily ascertained. Each level higher requires a greater facility to grasp the enduring significance of the histories of other people. Finally, to reach the point of understanding oneself in the whole sweep of history is a point of perspective no less than divine. Only the Triune God understands the life of each individual in relationship to each and every other person in the whole span of history. Thus, our knowledge of history—and our place in it—is fragmentary and inherently imperfect, insofar as it is dependent on knowledge which originates in the reason and experience of men.

These different 'layers' contain within them points of contact with both that which men would deem 'secular' and 'sacred' history. As such, they offer themselves for comparison on similar points with men of previous ages. There is an inherent instinct that there are lessons to be learned from past events which can and should influence our own thoughts and actions. Thus the famous words of George Santayana, that those who ignore history are condemned to repeat it.[2] For example, one may

---

2   oft cited, but for our purposes, one may refer to Russell Kirk, *The Roots*

14

consider the example of the historian's labor in the writing of Herodotus (484–425 B.C.), who began his famous history with the explanation that "his *Researches* are here set down to preserve the memory of the past by putting on record the astonishing achievements both of our own and of other peoples; and more particularly, to show how they came into conflict,"[3] and concludes his work with an implicit admonition to his readers to consider well the type of civilization they construct for themselves:

> 'Since,' they said, 'God has given empire to the Persians, and among individuals to you, Cyrus, by your conquest of Astyages, let us leave this small and barren country of ours and take possession of a better. There are plenty to choose from—some near, some further off; if we take one of them, we shall be admired more than ever. It is a natural thing for a sovereign people to do; and when will there be a better opportunity than now, when we are masters of many nations and all Asia?'
>
> Cyrus did not think much of this suggestion; he replied that they might act upon it if they pleased, but added the warning that, if they did so, they must prepare themselves to rule no longer, but to be ruled by others. 'Soft countries,' he said, 'breed soft men. It is not the property of any one soil to produce fine fruits and good soldiers too.' The Persians had to admit that this was true and that Cyrus was wiser than they; so they left him, and chose rather to live in a rugged land and rule than to cultivate rich plains and be subject to others.[4]

Clearly Herodotus wanted his readers to understand that such a choice confronts each civilization: Do you desire the easy and prosperous life, or do you desire national power? The historian

of American Order, 3rd ed. (Washington, D.C.: Regnery Gateway, 1991) p. 9.
3   Herodotus, p. 42.
4   ibid., p. 624.

confronts us with an opportunity to examine our own choices, and to think about what kind of people *we* want to be. The lessons of history may be taught to us by means of analogies, but when properly constructed, the lessons are often hard to ignore.

Ultimately, however, each one of us lives in the history into which he has been born. One of the great temptations for the student of history is to develop a love for particular ages in preference for one's own time. But the world of past generations is further removed from us than are the stars in the heavens. José Ortega y Gasset once wrote that "It is the mission of history to make our fellow beings acceptable to us. ... To understand other people, I have nothing else to resort to than the stuff that is my life. Only my life has of itself 'meaning' and is therefore intelligible."[5] Ortega's emphasis was on a form of alienation which divides the generations, rooted in the fact that the man of another time remains beyond our influence; one cannot persuade dead men of the preferable character of your own prejudices over those of their generation:

> Past generations are past, not because, in an adventitious chronology, they are located in times that as such are past, but the other way around: the dead cannot come out of the days of yore that are past, and live over again in another time that is present, because their reality is essentially different from the reality of the present and consequently from me. Their being *forever* and *irretrievably* other than I distinguishes them from my mere "neighbor" and gives them a character of inexorable "remoteness" and "ancientness." The vision of the remote is irrevocably remote, the discovery of "ancientness," constitutes the historical perspective which therefore presupposes the realization of the radical otherness of former men.

---

5   José Ortega y Gasset, "Prologue to a History of Philosophy," in *Concord and Liberty,* (New York: W.W.Norton & Co., 1963) p. 92–3.

Whereas of my contemporary I always hope that he may at last become like me, I have in my intercourse with ancient man no other way of understanding him that to assimilate myself imaginatively to him—that is, to become that other man. The technique of such intellectual unselfishness is the science of history.[6]

But the study of history is not restricted to simply overcoming such alienation. For there is a certain romanticism to the virtual timelessness of past ages, as well. Just as the men of another time remain beyond our ability to refute and reform, so too, they are fixed, unchanging; in our own unsettled, mutable age the fixed character of the past can often feel preferable—a refuge from the warfare, intellectual and otherwise. However, that sensation is an illusion, for each age is marked by its own peculiar battles. And one of the battles of our age is for the veracity of history—both secular and sacred.

The distinction between that which is termed secular and sacred history is a delineation which is fundamental to our task at hand. In defining the distinction it is not sufficient to say that secular history deals with 'nonreligious' matters of human history, while sacred history treats of religious themes. The reign of Caesar Augustus is, for example, intimately connected to sacred history, as is observed by St. Luke the Evangelist. Even more recent events—consider the Reformation, for example—are given both a sacred and secular examination.

How, then, will we properly distinguish between secular and sacred history? In tracing the origins of order in the American Republic, one of the great conservative philosophers of the twentieth century, Dr. Russell Kirk, offered a distinction between sacred and secular history which provides us with a place to start:

---

6   ibid., p. 95.

But what we need to bear in mind, if we wish to grasp the connection between the experience of order in biblical times and the experience of order in in our own age, is that there exist two distinct forms of history: sacred history, and secular history. Sacred history consists of an account of mankind's experience with God; secular history consists of an account of mankind's experience in mundane affairs. The first form of history often can be expressed only through imagery—through parables, allegories, and the "high dream" of poetry. The second form of history, dealing with worldly events, tries to confine itself to such verifiable records and narrations as are available.[7]

The first portion of Kirk's distinction is quite serviceable, and conforms to our own assessment of the distinction between sacred and secular history. Sacred history does consist "of an account of mankind's experience with God"; likewise, secular history does consist "of an account of mankind's experience in mundane affairs." One might almost think of history in this sense as consisting of two tables: one between God and men, and the other between men. Rightly understood, sacred and secular history are distinct from each other, but not separate—in fact, events may even be common to both, and yet serve different purposes according to the way in which they are being viewed at the moment. Thus, for example, the Flood, the Exodus, the Babylonian Captivity, and the reign of Caesar Augustus are all events which have both sacred and secular significance, and to the extent that it is possible, a student of history is well-served by a careful study of that which may be known of such events according to both categories of history.

---

7   Russell Kirk, *The Roots of American Order,* 3rd ed. (Washington, D.C.: Regnery Gateway, 1991) p. 39.

18

Where Kirk's definition breaks down is in his further elaboration of the nature of the distinction between these two forms of history because he obscures the distinction between sacred history and mythology. Kirk was disinclined to believe in the secular historicity of events such as the account of Jonah, and drew a distinction between the "historical Moses" and "the Moses of Exodus."[8]

Here we must take issue with Kirk's use of the term "sacred history." Sacred history, as that term is understood within the Christian verity, cannot be used only in reference to "parables, allegories, and the 'high dream' of poetry"—far from it. As we shall explore at length later on, while it is true that the Scriptures of the Old and New Testament may not have been written with the intention of serving as a "history textbook" according to the canons of that field of study in the 20th and 21st centuries, nevertheless, the manifest intention of the authors—and the Author—of Holy Writ was that those historical events which are related in its pages are, in fact, a true record of actual events which transpired. The interactions of God's people with the Gentiles establishes links between established sacred and secular history throughout the biblical record. Indeed, the careful recitation of genealogies in the Old and New Testaments identifies a definite intention to relate literal events.

How then shall we describe or define sacred history? As a Christian, one may say that it is secular history from a divine perspective, or that it is secular history seen from the perspective of God's plan of salvation for fallen man. Historical events gain a greater significance when more of their meaning is thus discerned.

However, not all 'sacred histories' can be so defined. In fact, the 'sacred histories' of other religions are unabashedly

---
8   ibid., p. 38, 40–41.

expressed in the terms employed by Kirk—"only through imagery—through parables, allegories, and the 'high dream' of poetry." In such circumstances, one is dealing with "myth"—in a non-pejorative sense of that term. Mircea Eleade, a prominent expert on the nature and structure of myths, has defined them as follows:

> Myth narrates a sacred history; it relates an event that took place in primordial Time, the fabled time of the "beginnings." In other words, myth tells how, through the deeds of Supernatural Beings, a reality came into existence, be it the whole of reality, the Cosmos, or only a fragment of reality—an island, a species of plant, a particular kind of human behavior, an institution. Myth, then, is always an account of a "creation"; it relates how something was produced, began to *be*. Myth tells only of that which *really* happened, which manifested itself completely. The actors in myths are Supernatural Beings.[9]

However, such mythic events are not merely so remote from modern man as to belong to an inaccessible period of human time. In other words, it is not simply a matter of the events related in myth falling before a 'historical' time, so that men—having forgotten the literal events which transpired—make up a story to cover over a lacuna of human knowledge. The belief of adherents of myth is that the modern may participate in the mythic event by means of ritual. Thus, unlike events of secular and sacred history—which transpire at one given moment in time, and then recede—mythic events allow for ongoing participation. Again, in Eliade's words:

> We may note that, just as modern man considers himself to be constituted by History, the man of the archaic societies declares that he is the result of a certain number of mythical events. Neither regards himself as "given,"

9   *Myth and Reality*, (Long Grove, Illinois: Waveland Press, Inc., 1998) p. 5–6.

"made" once and for all, as, for example, a tool is made once and for all. A modern man might reason as follows: I am what I am today because a certain number of things have happened to me, but those things were possible only because agriculture was discovered some eight to nine thousand years ago and because urban civilizations developed in the ancient Near East, because Alexander the Great conquered Asia and Augustus founded the Roman Empire, because Galileo and Newton revolutionized the conception of the universe, thus opening the way to scientific discoveries and laying the groundwork for the rise of industrial civilization, because the French Revolution occurred and the ideas of freedom, democracy, and social justice shook the Western world to its foundations after the Napoleonic wars—and so on.

... But he would at once have to add: events that took place *in mythical times* and therefore make up a *sacred history* because the actors in the drama are not men but Supernatural Beings. In addition, while a modern man, though regarding himself as the result of the course of Universal History, does not feel obligated to know the whole of it, the man of the archaic societies is not only obliged to remember mythical history but also to *re-enact* a large part of it periodically.[10]

The esoteric knowledge contained in myth is something in which a believer participates, and in that knowledge of the origin of a thing, acquires "a magical power over them by which they can be controlled, multiplied or reproduced at will."[11] Thus, "In most cases it is not enough to *know* the origin myth, one must *recite* it; this, in a sense, is a proclamation of one's knowledge, *displays* it. But this is not all. He who recites or performs the origin myth

10   ibid., p. 12–13.
11   ibid., p. 15.

is thereby steeped in the sacred atmosphere in which these miraculous events took place."[12]

Operating from such an understanding of myth, one understands that for the adherent of a myth, the alienation from the past which Ortega so dreaded is eliminated. But whereas Ortega's concern was for that alienation which is rooted in the inability of modern man to reshape the dead into one's own likeness, the adherent of a myth lives in the expectation that the mythical past reshapes him. Whether for good or for ill, the myth plays a fundamentally conservative role in the culture—and *cultus*—which it shapes or influences. If Ortega is right—that man is continually endeavoring to recast the past to shape present needs—myth applies pressure in the opposite direction: reshaping the present to bring it into conformity with the past.

In an brief essay entitled "Myth Became Fact,"[13] C.S. Lewis maintains that "It is the myth that gives life."[14] For Lewis, the myth delivers its adherents from battle between the burden of concrete events and the disconnection from such events by means of an abstraction. Myth provides a deeper understanding of the concrete than could ever be rendered by a cold analysis of various facts:

> What flows into you from the myth is not truth but reality (truth is always *about* something, but reality is that *about which* truth is), and, therefore, every myth becomes the father of innumerable truths on the abstract level. Myth is the mountain whence all the different streams arise which become truths down here in the valley; *in hac valle abstractionis*. Or, if you prefer, myth is the isthmus which connects the peninsular world of thought with that

---

12   ibid., p. 17–18.
13   in *The Grand Miracle,* (New York: Ballantine Books, 1983) p. 38–42.
14   ibid., p. 40.

22

vast continent we really belong to. It is not, like truth, abstract; nor is it, like direct experience, bound to the particular.[15]

One must recognize that there is a danger in such a view of myth which runs near to a form of universalism, drawing an equivalence between various mythic structures which offer their various 'realities.' The temptation is to see various mythologies after the fashion in which pagans once viewed their religions— as equally true and salvific. But this, at the least, is not Lewis' intention, for he upholds the notion that there is only one myth with is also a *fact* of history—both sacred and secular:

> Now as myth transcends thought, incarnation transcends myth. The heart of Christianity is a myth which is also a fact. The old myth of the dying god, *without ceasing to be myth*, comes down from the heaven of legend and imagination to the earth of history. It *happens*—at a particular date, in a particular place, followed by definable historical consequences. We pass from a Balder or an Osiris, dying nobody knows when or where, to a historical person crucified (it is all in order) *under Pontius Pilate*. By becoming fact it does not cease to be myth: that is the miracle. I suspect that men have sometimes derived more spiritual sustenance from myths they did not believe than from the religion they professed. To be truly Christian we must both assent to the historical fact and also receive the myth (fact though it has become) with the same imaginative embrace which we accord to all myths. The one is hardly more necessary than the other.[16]

This understanding that Christianity is thus the intersection of

---

15   ibid., p. 41.
16   ibid., p. 41–42.

all three conceptions of history—mythological, sacred and secular—is what brings us to the next aspect of our exploration of a Christian understanding of history. It is the 'historicity' of sacred history which must be understood. It is not that we shall seek to 'prove' the secular validity of the Scriptural record of events; Holy Scripture is of a higher order of authority than the feeble testimony offered by men. Rather, our concern is to demonstrate the express understanding of the incarnate Son of God that sacred and secular history are one in anticipating His incarnation, and that the events of the world from Adam until the reign of Caesar Augustus—as those events are contained in Holy Writ—are a faithful record of the history of man.

24

CHAPTER 2.
CHRISTOLOGY AND HISTORICITY.

n the Christian verity, we encounter the intersection of secular and sacred history. This is to say, the events which are at the heart of the faith did actually transpire *in time*. However, it has become increasingly common in this age of "demythologization" in religion to view the events recorded in Sacred Scripture as if they were fictitious—and thus labelled (according to the common use of the term) "mythical." For example, in a recent book, John Gray, professor emeritus of European Thought at the London School of Economics, offered a rather typical example of the confusion of "mythical" and "sacred" history:

> The heart of all religions is practice—ritual and meditation. Practice comes with myths, but myths are not theories in need of rational development. The story of Icarus has not been rendered redundant by progress in psychology. The Genesis story is not obsolete because there have been advances in palaeontology. Myths like these will endure for as long as humans remain human. Myths are narratives that deal with unchanging features of human experience. It is the story of Jesus dying on the cross and his miraculous resurrection that gives meaning to the lives of Christians. Atheists who question whether this story is based on fact are making the same mistake as believers who insist that it is literally true. Here, as is often the case, rationalism and fundamentalism go together.[1]

An utter confusion of the concepts of 'sacred history' and 'mythology' is readily in evidence. The attempt to 'save' some ahis-

---

1   John Gray, *The Immortalization Commission*, (New York: Farrar, Straus and Giroux, 2011), p. 226.

torical significance for the doctrine of the resurrection is refuted from the clear, intended sense of the scriptural text. Any attempt to 'demythologize' the Christian faith by interpreting the resurrection in anything other than the most literal sense imaginable not only does violence to the text—it overturns the entire Christian faith. The numerous examples offered in the Gospel text to the historical reality of the resurrection—including Jesus' words to St. Thomas[2] and His eating in the presence of His disciples[3]—make it abundantly clear that the Evangelists did not intend to record some sort of 'mythological' or even a 'spiritual' resurrection. And St. Paul's declaration in 1 Corinthians 15:12–20 precludes any compromise on the historical reality of Jesus' bodily resurrection:

> Now if Christ is preached that He has been raised from the dead, how do some among you say that there is no resurrection of the dead? But if there is no resurrection of the dead, then Christ is not risen. And if Christ is not risen, then our preaching is empty and your faith is also empty. Yes, and we are found false witnesses of God, because we have testified of God that He raised up Christ, whom He did not raise up—if in fact the dead do not rise. For if the dead do not rise, then Christ is not risen. And if Christ is not risen, your faith is futile; you are still in your sins! Then also those who have fallen asleep in Christ have perished. If in this life only we have hope in Christ, we are of all men the most pitiable. But

---

2   "Then He said to Thomas, 'Reach your finger here, and look at My hands; and reach your hand here, and put it into My side. Do not be unbelieving but believing.'" (John 20:27)

3   "And He said to them, 'Why are you troubled? And why do doubts arise in your hearts? Behold My hands and My feet, that it is I Myself. Handle Me and see, for a spirit does not have flesh and bones as you see I have.' But while they still did not believe for joy, and marveled, He said to them, 'Have you any food here?' So they gave Him a piece of broiled fish and some honeycomb. And He took it and ate in their presence." (Luke 24:38–43)

now Christ is risen from the dead, and has become the firstfruits of those who have fallen asleep.

The historicity of the bodily resurrection of the Christ is not some sort of metaphysical football to be punted around by atheists and 'fundamentalists'—it is the very heart of the faith. It is also inextricably linked to the most difficult historical fact in all of Holy Scripture for sin-darkened human reason to accept. Other historical events (including the Creation and the Flood) are historically remote and unrepeatable events. The fact of the resurrection is indivisible from the hope which each Christian shares—a point which St. Paul makes the very heart of his argument in 1 Corinthians 15. If one believes what Scripture teaches concerning the resurrection of the Son of God, are other events such as pertain to Jonah or the burning bush more 'difficult' to believe, by comparison?

It is therefore troubling when even Christian philosophers are inclined to dismiss the historical character of events in salvation history. Thus, for instance, Russell Kirk wrote as follows:

> Therefore the Old Testament, a sacred history, ought not to be read as if it were simply an account of everyday events. Often it is symbolic and poetical, for many truths are most accurately expressed in symbol. The story of Jonah, for instance, really is a kind of parable: it teaches how a people, through their religious faith, may preserve their identity even though conquered and enslaved by some immense power—as if a man were to be swallowed by a sea monster. Just so the Jews, through faith in Jehovah, survived their Babylonian Captivity.
>
> Similarly, it is not a conceivable "historical Moses"—unknown to us, because no documents or even artifacts or bones survive from that remote time and

that obscure people—who really matters. The important Moses is the figure portrayed by the scribes—the man who experienced a "leap in being," who was granted moments of transcendence perhaps comparable to Pascal's, who through that experience was enabled to describe the Law for the Hebrews. One might as well search for "the historical Don Quixote de la Mancha."[4]

Of course, no one would claim that sacred history should be read "as if it were simply an account of everyday events"—that would make it *secular* history. But sacred history is not fictive; rather, it is history with the sacred meaning set forth for those who have ears to hear it. For the secular reading of history, Caesar Augustus belongs to the rank of dead emperors, largely forgotten. For the faithful, the fact that "...it came to pass in those days that a decree went out from Caesar Augustus that all the world should be registered" (Luke 2:1) is inextricably bound up with the salvation of mankind.

The targeting of the historicity of Jonah (a not-uncommon phenomena) is not a minor matter for the veracity of Holy Scripture. The wisdom of men might be inclined to distance itself from the account of a prophet spending three days in the belly of a great fish. However, the incarnate Son of God did not treat the history of Jonah as an edifying fairy tale: Jesus set forth on several occasions the declaration that a type-antitype relationship exists between Jonah's three days in the great fish and His own three days in the earth. Thus, for example, we read in Matthew 12:

> Then some of the scribes and Pharisees answered, saying, "Teacher, we want to see a sign from You."
> But He answered and said to them, "An evil and

---

4   Russell Kirk, *The Roots of American Order,* 3rd ed. (Washington, D.C.: Regnery Gateway, 1991) p. 40.

adulterous generation seeks after a sign, and no sign will be given to it except the sign of the prophet Jonah. For as Jonah was three days and three nights in the belly of the great fish, so will the Son of Man be three days and three nights in the heart of the earth. The men of Nineveh will rise up in the judgment with this generation and condemn it, because they repented at the preaching of Jonah; and indeed a greater than Jonah is here." (v. 38–41)

With these words, Jesus sets forth the sign of Jonah as from the lesser burial of Jonah in the belly of the fish to His own greater burial in the tomb. The emergence of Jonah from the fish—the sign of Jonah—has its greater fulfillment in Christ's resurrection from the grave.[5]

Jesus also did not make some sort of distinction between the "historical Moses" and the Moses recorded in Scripture. In point of fact, when discussing with the Pharisees the teaching of God's Word regarding marriage and divorce, Jesus was asked, "Why then did Moses command to give a certificate of divorce, and to put her away?" Jesus did not reply with distinction between what the "historical Moses" might, or might not, have done: "He said to them, 'Moses, because of the hardness of your hearts, permitted you to divorce your wives, but from the beginning it was not so.'" (Mat. 19:7–8)

Actually, Jesus consistently spoke of the figures of the Old Testament as historical figures. Speaking woe to the scribes and Pharisees, He declared, "Therefore, indeed, I send you prophets, wise men, and scribes: some of them you will kill and crucify, and some of them you will scourge in your synagogues and persecute from city to city, that on you may come all the

---

5   Jesus reiterated the teaching of the "sign of the prophet Jonah" in Mat. 16:2–4 and Luke 11:29–32.

righteous blood shed on the earth, from the blood of righteous Abel to the blood of Zechariah, son of Berechiah, whom you murdered between the temple and the altar." (Mat. 23:34–36) These words also affirm the historicity of the prophets from the first generation born of Adam. Of course, affirming the existence of Abel brings in the thorny fact that Jesus also treats the Flood as a historical event, making an explicit connection between the state of the world in the time of Noah and its state when He returns in glory:

> But as the days of Noah were, so also will the coming of the Son of Man be. For as in the days before the flood, they were eating and drinking, marrying and giving in marriage, until the day that Noah entered the ark, and did not know until the flood came and took them all away, so also will the coming of the Son of Man be. (Mat. 24:37–39)

These few cases which have been cited are but a few of the concrete linkages which Jesus made between historical events of the Old Testament, and their fulfillment in the New Testament era. While such examples could easily be multiplied, for our purposes it is sufficient to have made the point that Jesus affirmed the existence of men such as Abel, Noah, Moses and Jonah, and testified to the historical accuracy of the biblical record of their lives. Thus, to challenge the Old Testament account requires a direct assault on the omniscience of the Christ; if one maintains that Jesus was somehow ignorant of the actual events of the Old Testament era, or accommodated His message to the ignorance of His hearers, then one might as well admit that one is abandoning Christianity altogether, because His intent for all of His teaching will be undermined, and—in point of fact—one may well wonder whether *any* of His teaching may be relied upon.

Jesus taught His disciples to rely on the faithfulness of the entirety of the Old Testament record when He chastised them on the road to Emmaus with the words, "O foolish ones, and slow of heart to believe in all that the prophets have spoken!" (Luke 24:25) He did not tell them to heed the 'edifying' parts and pay no attention to that which treats of historical events.

From the perspective of Pharisees ancient and modern, the most grievous point is that Jesus proclaims Himself to have first hand knowledge of the historicity and factual character of all that the prophets have spoken, for He declared to the Jews, "Your father Abraham rejoiced to see My day, and he saw it and was glad," and when they countered, "You are not yet fifty years old, and have You seen Abraham," He delivered the *coup de grâce* to all of their arguments: "Most assuredly, I say to you, before Abraham was, I AM." (John 8:56–58) Christ's claim is that He is the One who spoke to Moses from the burning bush, and led the people through the wilderness. At that point, the enemy of the Gospel is left with no alternative but to either repent of one's doubt and denial, or to take up stones.

As we shall explore in the next section, some of the most brutal wielders of stones in the modern era have been those who have sought to 'save' the faith by 'demythologizing' it. There are few people more inherently dangerous than those who are willing to destroy something in order to save it. The demythologizers have been willing to dismiss all of Christ's words, and His miracles, and the "sign of Prophet Jonah," if that is what it takes to make the faith palatable in the assessment of a rationalist and naturalist.

CHAPTER 3.
EUHEMERISM AND THE ORIGIN OF MYTH.

*Modern man is free to despise mythologies and theolo-
gies, but that will not prevent his continuing to feed upon
decayed myths and degraded images.*[1]

eeking the origins of the myths of men—the various tales
of gods and their works—one is torn between that which is
born of the imagination of men, that which is of demonic inspiration, and that which is in conformity with C.S. Lewis' assessment of myth:

> In the enjoyment of a great myth we come nearest to
> experiencing as a concrete what can otherwise be under-
> stood only as an abstraction. ...
>
> ... What flows into you from the myth is not truth
> but reality (truth is always *about* something, but real-
> ity is that *about which* truth is), and, therefore, every
> myth becomes the father of innumerable truths on the
> abstract level. Myth is the mountain whence all the dif-
> ferent streams arise which become truths down here in
> the valley; *in hac valle abstractionis.* Or, if you prefer,
> myth is the isthmus which connects the peninsular world
> of though with that vast continent we really belong to. It
> is not, like truth, abstract; nor is it, like direct experience,
> bound to the particular.[2]

Perhaps it may seem an idle curiosity to attempt to determine

1   Mircea Eliade, *Images and Symbols*, (Princeton: Princeton University Press, 1991) p. 19
2   C.S. Lewis, "Myth Became Fact," in *The Grand Miracle,* (New
York: Ballantine Books, 1983) p. 40–41.

what is born of human corruption, and that which is entirely of the lie of the enemy, but there is a reason for such exploration. As was explored in the first chapter, there are some scholars who attempt to collapse sacred history into the realm of the mytho-logical: the 'events' of sacred history are treated as if they are fic-tion, and if they are 'true,' it is not in the sense of factual events observed by human beings. Such an effort to collapse sacred history into mythology does violence to the Christian verity—a point which was documented at length in the second chapter.

However, there has also been a significant temptation throughout the generations to collapse mythology into sacred and secular history; that is, men have sought a basis for a myth in a poorly remembered historical event, which gained a theo-logical significance only over time, as those who related the myth were no longer conscious of the historical events which are its foundation. This school of thought is known as Euhemerism, which takes its name from Euhemerus, a 4th century B.C. citizen of Macedon who served in the court of King Cassander.

It was Euhemerus' belief that the myths of the gods and their labors were a corruption of the memory of the works of great men from the dimly remembered mists of antiquity. Ironi-cally, Euhemerus' actual writings are now lost, but fragments are often quoted in other ancient sources, and it seems apparent that his theory resonated with early Christian apologists who were likely influenced by a similar argument in the *Wisdom of Solo-mon*, which is among the Apocryphal books. We read in Wisdom 14:12–21:

> For the devising of idols was the beginning of spiritual fornication, and the invention of them the corruption of life. *(13)* For neither were they from the beginning, nei-ther shall they be for ever. *(14)* For by the vain glory of men they entered into the world, and therefore shall

they come shortly to an end. *(15)* For a father afflicted with untimely mourning, when he hath made an image of his child soon taken away, now honoured him as a god, which was then a dead man, and delivered to those that were under him ceremonies and sacrifices. *(16)* Thus in process of time an ungodly custom grown strong was kept as a law, and graven images were worshipped by the commandments of kings. *(17)* Whom men could not honour in presence, because they dwelt far off, they took the counterfeit of his visage from far, and made an express image of a king whom they honoured, to the end that by this their forwardness they might flatter him that was absent, as if he were present. *(18)* Also the singular diligence of the artificer did help to set forward the ignorant to more superstition. *(19)* For he, peradventure willing to please one in authority, forced all his skill to make the resemblance of the best fashion. *(20)* And so the multitude, allured by the grace of the work, took him now for a god, which a little before was but honoured. *(21)* And this was an occasion to deceive the world: for men, serving either calamity or tyranny, did ascribe unto stones and stocks the incommunicable name.

For purposes of our discussion, the explanation set forth in Wisdom 14 is a classic statement of Euhemerism, which allows for a gradual development of idolatry arising from a misplaced veneration of the dead—a development, one might add, which does not seem far removed from the development of the cult of the saints in Roman Catholic theology.

Turning to the canonical Scriptures, one finds a different emphasis in the explanation of the rise of idolatry. Thus, for example, St. Paul wrote in Romans 1:18–25:

For the wrath of God is revealed from heaven against all ungodliness and unrighteousness of men, who hold the truth in unrighteousness; because that which may be known of God is manifest in them; for God hath shewed it unto them. For the invisible things of him from the creation of the world are clearly seen, being understood by the things that are made, even his eternal power and Godhead; so that they are without excuse: Because that, when they knew God, they glorified him not as God, neither were thankful; but became vain in their imaginations, and their foolish heart was darkened. Professing themselves to be wise, they became fools, and changed the glory of the uncorruptible God into an image made like to corruptible man, and to birds, and fourfooted beasts, and creeping things. Wherefore God also gave them up to uncleanness through the lusts of their own hearts, to dishonour their own bodies between themselves: who changed the truth of God into a lie, and worshipped and served the creature more than the Creator, who is blessed for ever. Amen.

Paul's inspired explanation in Romans 1 does not exclude the possibility of Euhemerism explaining the process of *which* men were thus venerated as gods, but it certainly clarifies the degree to which the development of idolatry was a perverse attempt to arrive at an explanation of the natural knowledge of God. That is, men could see a testimony to the reality, and some attributes, of God through the testimony of their senses and powers of their reason, but their sin blinded them to the truth, and thus they turned to the lie of idolatry.

Whether most immediately influenced by Euhemerus or the Wisdom of Solomon, the church fathers picked up on the Euhemerist argumentation in their disputes with the adherents of the pagan religions. Thus, for example, Cyprian of Carthage († AD 258) applied the Euhemeristic interpretation of the pagan deities in his treatise, *On the Vanity of Idols*[3]:

> That those are no gods whom the common people worship, is known from this. They were formerly kings, who on account of their royal memory subsequently began to be adored by their people even in death. Thence temples were founded to them; thence images were sculptured to retain the countenances of the deceased by the likeness; and men sacrificed victims, and celebrated festal days, by way of giving them honour. Thence to posterity those rites became sacred which at first had been adopted as a consolation. And now let us see whether this truth is confirmed in individual instances. ...
>
> 3. From this the religion of the gods is variously changed among individual nations and provinces, inasmuch as no one god is worshipped by all, but by each one the worship of its own ancestors is kept peculiar. Proving that this is so, Alexander the Great writes in the remarkable volume addressed to his mother, that through fear of his power the doctrine of the gods being men, which was kept secret, had been disclosed to him by a priest, that it was the memory of ancestors and kings that was (really) kept up, and that from this the rites of worship and sacrifice have grown up. But if gods were born at any time, why are they not born in these days also?—unless, indeed, Jupiter possibly has grown too old, or the faculty of bearing has failed Juno.
>
> 4. But why do you think that the gods can avail on behalf of the Romans, when you see that they can do nothing for their own worshipers in opposition to the Roman arms? For we know that the gods of the Romans are in-

---

3   Accessed online at http://www.ccel.org/ccel/schaff/anf05.iv.v.vi.html on 5 May 2012.

digenous. Romulus was made a god by the perjury of Proculus, and Picus, and Tiberinus, and Pilumnus, and Consus, whom as a god of treachery, Romulus would have to be worshipped, just as if he had been a god of counsels, when his perfidy resulted in the rape of the Sabines. Tatius also both invented and worshipped the goddess Cloacina; Hostilius, Fear and Paleness. By and by, I know not by whom, Fever was dedicated, and Acca and Flora the harlots. These are the Roman gods. But Mars is a Thracian, and Jupiter a Cretan, and Juno either Argive or Samian or Carthaginian, and Diana of Taurus, and the mother of the gods of Ida; and there are Egyptian monsters, not deities, who assuredly, if they had had any power, would have preserved their own and their people's kingdoms. Certainly there are also among the Romans the conquered Penates whom the fugitive Æneas introduced thither. There is also Venus the bald,—far more dishonoured by the fact of her baldness in Rome than by her having been wounded in Homer.

But Cyprian did not neglect the demonic aspect of the rise of the worship of idols, and understood that the supposedly miraculous works attributed to the idols were in fact the work of demons:

7. These spirits, therefore, are lurking under the statues and consecrated images: these inspire the breasts of their prophets with their afflatus, animate the fibres of the entrails, direct the flights of birds, rule the lots, give efficiency to oracles, are always mixing up falsehood with truth, for they are both deceived and they deceive; they disturb their life, they disquiet their slumbers; their spirits creeping also into their bodies, secretly terrify their minds, distort their limbs, break their health, excite diseases to force them to worship of themselves, so that when glutted with the steam of the altars and the piles

of cattle, they may unloose what they had bound, and so appear to have effected a cure. The only remedy from them is when their own mischief ceases; nor have they any other desire than to call men away from God, and to turn them from the understanding of the true religion, to superstition with respect to themselves; and since they themselves are under punishment, (they wish) to seek for themselves companions in punishment whom they may by their misguidance make sharers in their crime. These, however, when adjured by us through the true God, at once yield and confess, and are constrained to go out from the bodies possessed. You may see them at our voice, and by the operation of the hidden majesty, smitten with stripes, burnt with fire, stretched out with the increase of a growing punishment, howling, groaning, entreating, confessing whence they came and when depart, even in the hearing of those very persons who worship them, and either springing forth at once or vanishing gradually, even as the faith of the sufferer comes in aid, or the grace of the healer effects. Hence they urge the common people to detest our name, so that men begin to hate us before they know us, lest they should either imitate us if known, or not be able to condemn us.

A case in point in Scripture which demonstrates Cyprian's point quite well is in Acts 16:16–19, when St. Paul casts the spirit of divination out of the slave:

Now it happened, as we went to prayer, that a certain slave girl possessed with a spirit of divination [πνεῦμα πύθωνα] met us, who brought her masters much profit by fortune-telling. This girl followed Paul and us, and cried out, saying, "These men are the servants of the Most High God, who proclaim to us the way of salvation." And this she did for many days. But Paul, greatly annoyed, turned and said to the spirit, "I command you in the name of Jesus Christ to come out of her." And he came out that very hour. But when her masters saw that their hope of profit was gone, they seized Paul and Silas and dragged *them* into the marketplace to the authorities.

The "spirit of divination" is literally a "spirit of a python"—πύθωνα is a *hapax legomenon* of the Greek New Testament, and the usage is extremely significant because of its connection with Greek mythology. Apollo was the purported protector of the Oracles of Delphi, and was revered as Pythian Apollo because of the origin of the divinatory powers which he supposedly conveyed on the oracles. The text of a Homeric hymn credits Apollo with having slain a monstrous dragon (the aforementioned πύθωνα) and taking its divinatory powers to himself. Greek mythology and demonic influence were confronted by Paul in the streets of Philippi.

Cyprian was not the only writer of the early church to take up the Euhemerist theme. Lactantius (ca. AD 240–ca. 320), who became an advisor to Constantine, left behind several apologetic works written in the context of the struggle against paganism. One of particular concern for our understanding of the early Christian endeavor to approach pagan mythology is Lactantius' *The Divine Institutes* (*Divinarum Institutionum Libri VII*), which was written between 303 and 311. In the first book of *The Divine Institutes*, as Lactantius sought to distinguish the one true God from the idols of the nations, he embraced Euhemerus' theory as the means for understanding the rise of the Greek and Roman pantheons. Having specifically cited "Ennius ... in his (translation of) Euhemerus" in Chapter XIII, Lactantius declared in Chapter XV:

Now, since it is evident from these things that they were men, it is not difficult to see in what manner they began to be called gods. For if there were no kings before Saturn or Uranus, on account of the small number of men who lived a rustic life without any ruler, there is no doubt but in those times men began to exalt the king himself, and his whole family, with the highest praises and with new honours, so that they even called them gods; whether on account of their wonderful excellence, men as yet rude and simple really entertained this opinion, or, as is commonly the case, in flattery of present power, or on account of the benefits by which they were set in order and reduced to a civilised state. Afterwards the kings themselves, since they were beloved by those whose life they had civilised, after their death left regret of themselves. Therefore men formed images of them, that they might derive some consolation from the contemplation of their likenesses; and proceeding further through love of their worth, they began to reverence the memory of the deceased, that they might appear to be grateful for their services, and might attract their successors to a desire of ruling well. ... Thus by degrees religious honours began to be paid to them; while those who had known them, first instructed their own children and grandchildren, and afterwards all their posterity, in the practice of this rite. And yet these great kings, on account of the celebrity of their name, were honoured in all provinces.

But separate people privately honoured the founders of their nation or city with the highest veneration, whether they were men distinguished for bravery, or women admirable for chastity; as the Egyptians honored Isis, the Moors Juba, the Macedonians Cabirus, the Carthaginians Uranus, the Latins Faunus, the Sabines Sancus, the Romans Quirinus. In the same manner truly Athens worshipped Minerva, Samos Juno, Paphos

Venus, Lemnos Vulcan, Naxos Liber, and Delos Apollo. And thus various sacred rites have been undertaken among different peoples and countries, inasmuch as men desire to show gratitude to their princes, and cannot find out other honours which they may confer upon the dead. Moreover, the piety of their successors contributed in a great degree to their error; for, in order that they might appear to be born from a divine origin, they paid divine honour to their parents, and ordered that they should be paid by others.[4]

One may readily notice that there is a great deal of parallel between Lactantius' writing and that of Cyprian, and yet without the sense of a deliberate copying. Certainly both men saw the Euhemerist means of interpretation as one which accounted for the various 'national' origins of the gods, and it provided a means of interpreting the rise of such idolatry by means of a perversion of the virtue of honoring one's fathers—fathers of blood and office.

It is not our intention to create a complete catalog of the instances of Euhemerism throughout the history of the Christian Church. Two more examples will be sufficient for our purposes. First, we turn to Eusebius of Caesarea's *Preparation for the Gospel*.[5] Eusebius is the first writer under our consideration to have written after the legalization of the Christian religion. Like Lactantius, Eusebius attributes his interpretation to Euhemerus, taking his excerpts from the writings of Diodorus, which date to the first century before Christ. Eusebius takes up the theme of Euhemerism in Book II, Chapter II, which largely repeats many

---

4   *Ante-Nicene Christian Library,* (Edinburgh: T&T Clark, 1871) vol. xxi, p. 40–41.

5   trans. by Edwin Hamilton Gifford, 2 vols., (Eugene, Oregon: Wipf and Stock, 2002).

of the points already noted by Clement and Lactantius. Eusebius does offer a few more details regarding Euhemerus and his work, quoting directly from Diodorus:

> With regard then to gods the men of old have handed down to their posterity two sets of notions. For some, say they, are eternal and imperishable, as the Sun and Moon and the other heavenly bodies, and besides these the winds, and the rest who partake of the like nature with them; for each of these has an eternal origin and eternal continuance. Other deities they say were of the earth; but, because of the benefits which they conferred on mankind, they have received immortal honour and glory, as Heracles, Dionysus, Aristaeus, and the others like them.
>
> Concerning the terrestrial gods many various tales have been handed down in the historical and mythological writers. Among the historians Euemerus [sic], the author of the *Sacred Record*, has written a special history; and of the mythologists Homer, Hesiod, Orpheus, and such others as these, have invented very marvelous myths concerning the gods: and we shall endeavor to run over what both classes have recorded concisely and with a view to due proportion.[6]

Eusebius' view is probably the most carefully nuanced, recognizing that while the Euhemerist theory is explanatory, it is not a comprehensive explanation. There is a recognition that there is more than simply 'corrupted history' at work; understanding how that which has "an eternal origin and eternal continuance" came to be connected to the mortal and terrestrial is more complicated than a shallow Euhemerism is likely to comprehend.

---

6   ibid., 59b

Lastly, we briefly consider the writings of Snorri Sturluson (1179–1241), who was responsible for recording much of what is now known of Norse mythology. It seems highly likely that Snorri took his inspiration from the explanation of classical mythology rendered by the early fathers. His *Heimskringla* begins from the assumption that Odin was mortal king of a kingdom known as Asgarth, and that his people—the Aesir—waged war with another tribe called the Vanir. At the conclusion of their hostilities, Freya and Freyr were given to the Aesir as part of an exchange of hostages, with the intention of guaranteeing the peace. Thus, several of the Vanir entered into the mythology of the Aesir.[7]

This rather cursory survey of Euhemerist interpretation testifies to an ongoing use of this means of interpretation over the course of at least 1,000 years of Christian history. Thus, one may safely affirm that Euhemerism has been deemed a generally acceptable means of tracing at least a portion of the origins of ancient myths, and that the influential Wisdom of Solomon provided nearly-biblical support to such a line of interpretation.

However, some modern students of mythology are strongly disinclined to accept the Euhemerist analysis. Thus, for example, the authors of *Hamlet's Mill* are, in fact, quite dismissive of such a means of interpreting the origins of mythology:

> To recapitulate for clarity, whatever is true myth has no historical basis, however tempting the reduction, however massive and well armed the impact of a good deal of modern criticism on that belief. The attempt to reduce myth to history is the so-called "euhemerist" trend, from the name of Euhemeros, the first debunker. It was a wave of fashion which is now receding, for it was

---

7   for a modern edition, see *Heimskringla—History of the Kings of Norway*, trans. by Lee M. Hollander, (Austin: University of Texas, 1991) 6–8.

too simpleminded to last. Myth is essentially cosmological. As heaven in the cosmos is so vastly more important than our earth, it should not be surprising to find the main functions deriving from heaven.[8]

Given that Euhemerus lived in the fourth century B.C. and that his interpretation of mythology has endured across the centuries and civilizations which have passed in the interim, it is hard to dismiss it as "too simpleminded to last"—in fact, such a dismissal feels more like a desperate move to remove a theory without having to answer it. At the same time, however, it is apparent that Euhemerism might afford a certain degree of insight into the genesis of particular mythic figures *if* one could arrive at a more certain historical knowledge regarding those mythic figures. And this is where Euhemerism goes awry. Euhemerism does not substitute *fact* for *fiction*; instead, it substitutes *supposition* for *tradition*.

It is the skepticism of Euhemerism which undergirds the demythologizing agenda of Rudolf Bultmann's (1884–1976) form criticism. Attempts to strip away the "mythology" of the Scriptural account in order to arrive at the 'actual' sayings of Jesus in a search for the 'historical Jesus' presupposes that those elements of sacred history which cannot be attributed to non-divine, non-miraculous causation must be purged as "mythology." For Bultmann:

> "It is impossible to repristinate a past world picture by sheer resolve, especially a *mythical* world picture, now that all of our thinking is irrevocably formed by science. A blind acceptance of New Testament mythology would be simply arbitrariness; to make such acceptance a de-

---

8   Giorgio de Santilla and Hertha von Dechend, *Hamlet's Mill—An Essay Investigating the Origins of Human Knowledge and its Transmission through Myth,* (Jaffrey, New Hampshire: Nonpareil Books, 1977) p. 50.

mand of faith would be to reduce faith to a work"[9]

What Bultmann and his ilk endeavor to do to the life and ministry of Jesus is akin to similar acts in ages past by pagans. As Eliade declares in *Myth and Reality*:

> The great mythologies—those consecrated by such poets as Homer and Hesiod and the anonymous bards of the Mahābhārata, or elaborated by ritualists and theologians (as in Egypt, India, and Mesopotamia)— are more and more inclined to narrate the *gesta* of the Gods. And at a certain moment in History—especially in Greece and India but also in Egypt—an elite begins to lose interest in this *divine history* and arrives (as in Greece) at the point of no longer believing in the *myths* while claiming still to believe in the *Gods*.[10]

As among the Greeks, so we find in our own age that the demythologizers arise from a self-professed elite who want to retain the faith in the absence of that which *upholds* the faith. For example, that Bultmann attempted to uphold "justification by faith" in the absence of the object of that faith—belief in the atoning death of the Son of God, who then bodily rose from the grave— was a point of great consternation to philosopher Karl Jaspers, who had the audacity to examine the foundations of Bultmann's demythologizing agenda.[11] And, by examining the roots of the demythologization which took place among the Greeks, Indians and Egyptians, Eliade touches on the heart of the problem for the moderns who follow in their steps:

> To be sure, even in the archaic cultures a myth

9   Bultmann, Rudolf. *New Testament and Mythology and Other Basic Writings*. ed. Schubert M. Ogden, (Philadelphia: Fortress, 1984) p. 3.

10   Mircea Eliade, *Myth and Reality,* trans. by Willard R. Trask, (Long Grove, Illinois: Waveland Press, Inc., 1998) p. 111.

11   Karl Jaspers and Rudolf Bultmann, *Myth and Christianity,* (Amherst, New York: Prometheus Books, 2005) p. 35.

would sometimes be emptied of religious meaning and become a legend or a nursery tale; but other myths remained in force. In any case, there was no question here, as there was in Pre-Socratic Greece and Upanishadic India, of a cultural phenomenon of the first importance, whose consequences have proved to be incalculable. For after this "demythicization" process, the Greek and Brahmanic mythologies could no longer represent for the respective elites of those countries what they had represented for their forefathers.

For these elites the "essential" was no longer to be sought in the history of the Gods but in a "primordial situation" preceding that history. We witness an attempt to go beyond mythology as divine history and to reach a primal source from which the real had flowed, to identify the womb of Being. It was in seeking the source, the principle, the *arche*, that philosophical speculation for a short time coincided with cosmogony; but it was no longer the cosmogonic myth, it was an ontological problem.[12]

The problem for the demythologizers is that in seeking to strip sacred history of all that which does not conform to their rationalism, they have not actually demythologized the text, they have simply eliminated the ground upon which they stood. The entirety of the civilization in which the demythologizers have arisen is axiomatically predicated on the Christian verity. Thus, for example, the much vaunted Western science—to which Bultmann offered his votives—requires a belief in the fundamental rationality and intelligibility of the universe, with man having been made in the image of his Creator. There is no inherent need for the universe to be rational, or comprehensible to human reason. As Gonzales and Richards observed in their book, *The Privileged Planet*:

12   Eliade, p. 111.

We've seen that scientific progress and discovery depend on nature being more than meaningless matter in motion, even motion that can be generalized with natural laws. It's an exquisite structure that preserves vast stores of information about itself and its past. Our habitable environment provides access to an exceptional and highly sensitive collection of information-recording "devices," accurately embedding information about the natural world. We, in turn, possess the materials, and the physical and intellectual capacities, to create technologies to decode these devices. ...

... And yet as we stand gazing at the heavens beyond our little oasis, we gaze not into a meaningless abyss but into a wondrous arena commensurate with our capacity for discovery. Perhaps we have also been staring past a cosmic signal far more significant than any sequence of numbers, a signal revealing a universe so skillfully crafted for life and discovery that it seems to whisper of an extra-terrestrial intelligence immeasurably more vast, more ancient, and more magnificent than anything we've been willing to expect or imagine.[13]

The demythologizers have not purified the faith, they have destroyed themselves, rendering the universe unintelligible and their lives ultimately meaningless—and they have done so on the basis of false premises. For example, Jaspers notes that Bultmann's "demand for demythologizing of religion" rests on two premises: "The first is his conception of modern science and of the modern view of the world, which leads him to negate many articles of the Christian faith. The second is his conception of philosophy, which enables him to give an existentialist interpretation to certain contents of the faith, that, in his opinion, are still

---

13   Guillermo Gonzalez and Jay W. Richards, *The Privileged Planet,* (Washington, D.C.: Regnery Publishing, 2004) p. 334–335.

true."[14] The demythologizers thus rest once again on axioms; for man is no more compulsively credulous now than he was in the first century *anno domini*. And doctrine which is predicated on the historical veracity of the Gospel (consider again St. Paul's affirmation in 1 Corinthian 15 of Christ's quite literal resurrection) cannot survive abstracted from those historical events, for the Christian verity is not a Gnostic thought experiment.

The petulant demand of Bultmann and his ilk to demythologize the Christian faith of those details which are unacceptable to modern rationalism is particularly worthy of scorn, since it simply exposes the historical ignorance of the demythologizers. Jaspers' caustic wit captures the point quite well:

> Thus materialism and a naturalistic realism have always been with us; similarly, man's disposition to believe in the absurd is as unchanged as ever, no less strong today than it was then. It is only the contents of this faith in the absurd that arc partly new: for example, belief in the advent of a definitive happiness for all in a classless society magically brought to birth through violence. ... The absurd faiths of the modern era, ranging from astrology to theosophy, and from National Socialism to Bolshevism, suggest that superstition has no less power over the human mind today than it had formerly. Such permanent elements of human nature are universal, and have nothing to do with modern science no more than with similar permanent elements of rationality. Absurd modern faiths may very well make occasional use of scientific results, without grasping their origin or meaning.[15]

Implicit in this point is a critical fact: myth is most certainly still with us, and it animates every creed and ideology. The myth

---

14   Jaspers and Bultmann, p. 22.
15   ibid., p. 23.

gives its adherent at least the sense of participating in sacred history and to actualize in one's own experience the central events of that history. The National Socialist seeking to bring about the *tausendjährige Reich*, or the Bolshevik who dreams of the transition from the dictatorship of the proletariat to stateless communism is certainly seeking such participation no less than the astrologer who 'reads the heavens' to perceive the destinies of men.

Against the demythologizers, Jaspers insists that "Mythical thinking is not a thing of the past, but characterizes man in any epoch." He then sets forth three elements which "myth" must contain:

(1) The myth tells a story and expresses intuitive insights, rather than universal concepts. The myth is historical, both in the form of its thinking and in its content. It is not a cloak or disguise put over a general idea, which can be better and more directly grasped intellectually. It explains in terms of historical origins rather than in terms of a necessity conceived as universal law.

(2) The myth deals with sacred stories and visions, with stories about gods rather than with empirical realities.

(3) The myth is a carrier of meanings which can be expressed only in the language of myth. The mythical figures are symbols which, by their very nature, are untranslatable into another language. They are accessible only in the mythical element, they are irreplaceable, unique. They cannot be interpreted rationally; they are interpreted only by new myths, by being transformed. Myths interpret each other.[16]

Jaspers' points certainly continue to build on aspects of myth which have been discussed previously. However, there is a demythologizing tendency within his own points when Jaspers

16   ibid., p. 31.

distinguishes between "stories about gods" and "empirical realities." It is, for example, an "empirical reality" that the incarnate Son of God was born of the Virgin Mary in Bethlehem. Jaspers, however, would exclude from "empirical reality" the assertions that Jesus is the incarnate Son of God, and that he was born of the *Virgin* Mary. Actually, Jaspers excludes from the realm of "empirical reality" the most important historical details in the entire Scriptural record of the life of Jesus:

> A corpse cannot come to life and rise from the grave. Stories based on the reports of contradictory witnesses and containing scanty data cannot be regarded as historical facts. Because materialism is a common way of thinking, the cipher language of myth will always be degraded into a language of the tangible, which is guaranteed and provides guarantees; this took place among the earliest Christians, and has taken place everywhere in the world.[17]

Thus we see that Jaspers quickly takes with the one hand what he has given with the other, in that he has no more belief in the historical reality of the Scriptural record than Bultmann does; their dispute is not over whether the myths are actually historically true, but whether Christianity can survive without them. Both would claim to desire the survival of Christianity, but one (Jaspers) would require belief in what one acknowledges to be unreal in any tangible way, while the other (Bultmann) would require faith to hang in mid-air, supported by nothing in the world whatsoever.

The Christian must break free of both Bultmann and Jaspers, and affirm the empirical reality of the events of sacred history and myth—as these terms may pertain to the Christian verity. As C.S. Lewis affirmed:

---

17   ibid., p. 32.

Now as myth transcends thought, incarnation transcends myth. The heart of Christianity is a myth which is also a fact. The old myth of the dying god, *without ceasing to be myth,* comes down from the heaven of legend and imagination to the earth of history. It *happens*—at a particular date, in a particular place, followed by definable historical consequences. We pass from a Balder or an Osiris, dying nobody knows when or where, to a historical person crucified (it is all in order) *under Pontius Pilate.* By becoming fact, it does not cease to be myth: that is the miracle. ...

Those who do not know that this great myth became fact when the Virgin conceived are, indeed, to be pitied. But Christians also need to be reminded ... that what became fact was a myth, that it carries with it into the world of fact all the properties of a myth. God is more than a god, not less; Christ is more than Balder, not less. We must not be nervous about "parallels" and "pagan Christs": they *ought* to be there—it would be a stumbling block if they weren't.[18]

And there is the fact that as Christians, we participate in that sacred history, being justified by grace through faith in the Christ who died and rose for us. Though the historical events are nearly 2,000 years removed from us, we still partake of them when we are baptized into Christ's death and resurrection (Rom. 6:3–4).

There is undeniably an element of truth to the Euhemerist argument, when applied to the idolatry of the nations—a point which is made clear in Wisdom 14 and the writings of the ancient fathers. But Euhemerism is not the entire answer, and the existence of the "parallels" to which Lewis referred are not exhausted by Euhemerism—indeed, they are not even addressed.

---

18   Lewis, p. 42.

CHAPTER 4.
THE GOLDEN AGE *VERSUS* PARADISE—
CYCLICAL AND LINEAR CONCEPTIONS OF TIME.

That which has been is what will be,
That which is done is what will be done,
And there is nothing new under the sun.
Is there anything of which it may be said,
"See, this is new"?
It has already been in ancient times before us.
There is no remembrance of former things,
Nor will there be any remembrance of things that are to come
By those who will come after. (Ecc. 1:9–11 NKJV)

he wisdom of the Preacher, the son of David and king of Jerusalem (Ecc. 1:1) is rarely seen as a cheerful book, for it paints the reality of man's life and labor in the stark terms of life in a fallen world. The Preacher declares, "I have seen all the works that are done under the sun; and indeed, all is vanity and grasping for the wind." (Ecc. 1:14) Men tend to imagine their labors in quite grandiose terms, leaving a legacy for their family, improving their society, and so forth. But all that they build may fall away quite suddenly, and the heritage which they imagined to pass along may be turned to the absolute opposite ends from that which they had purposed for it. Indeed,

> What profit has the worker from that in which he labors? I have seen the God-given task with which the sons of men are to be occupied. He has made everything beautiful in its time. Also He has put eternity in their hearts, except that no one can find out the work that God does from the

> beginning to end. I know that nothing is better for them than to rejoice, and to do good in their lives, and also that every man should eat and drink and enjoy the good of all his labor—it is the gift of God. (3:9–13)

Again,

> Here is what I have seen: It is good and fitting for one to eat and drink, and to enjoy the good of all his labor in which he toils under the sun all the days of his life which God gives him; for it is his heritage. As for every man to whom God has given riches and wealth, and given him power to eat of it, to receive his heritage and rejoice in his labor—this is the gift of God. For he will not dwell unduly on the days of his life, because God keeps him busy with the joy of his heart. (5:18–20)

Essentially, a man is blessed if he has sufficient fruit of his labor, and recognizes that blessing, and enjoys it. But the overall context of the life of man is that it is dominated by futility—vanity. Man is born into the world and labors, accomplishes little, and then dies, because sin has rendered life to be virtually meaningless in a man's own eyes.

Understanding the vanity of the lives of men, the wisdom of the Preacher sets forth the life of all men within the broader scope of the flow of time. He does not offer the "bookends" of Time—the Creation described in Genesis and the New Creation in Revelation—but instead describes man in the time in between. Thus, although the overall flow of history in the Holy Scriptures is *linear*—from creation to fall to redemption to the gates of the new Jerusalem—the time in Ecclesiastes is primarily *cyclical*.

> What profit has a man from all his labor in which he toils under the sun? One generation passes away, and another

generation comes; but the earth abides forever. The sun also rises and the sun goes down, and hastens to the place where it arose. The wind goes toward the south, and turns around to the north; the wind whirls about continually, and comes again on its circuit. All the rivers run into the sea, yet the sea is not full; to the place from which the rivers come, there they return again. All things are full of labor; men cannot express it. The eye is not satisfied with seeing, nor the ear filled with hearing. (1:3–8)

The life of man is vanishingly brief, and although linear of itself, is lived out within the cyclical flow of the abiding earth around him. The generations are transient; "but the earth abides forever."

That which has been is what will be, that which is done is what will be done, and there is nothing new under the sun. Is there anything of which it may be said, "See, this is new"? It has already been in ancient times before us. There is no remembrance of former things, nor will there be any remembrance of things that are to come by those who will come after. (1:9–11)

The humorous irony is that when such a passage is read, the modern man—being a slave to the ideology of Progress—immediately protests, and endeavors to invoke some technological innovation as the 'proof' that something new has emerged. Being unable to comprehend the central point—that man has forgotten those things which once were—the modern man invokes his imagined comprehensive knowledge of man's history as the proof that something 'new' has emerged. The vanity of man's labors is manifested in the midst of his ignorance, committing him to repeat the mistakes of the past. And thus the tragic cycle of his futile labors continues across the ages. Even wisdom offers no deliverance from the cycle of vanity:

The wise man's eyes are in his head, but the fool walks in darkness. Yet I myself perceived that the same event happens to them all. So I said in my heart, "As it happens to the fool, it also happens to me, and why was I then more wise?" Then I said in my heart, "This also is vanity." For there is no more remembrance of the wise than of the fool forever, since all that now is will be forgotten in the days to come. And how does the wise man die? As the fool! (2:14–16)

The flow of biblical history is one which is *linear* when one considers the entire flow of time from Creation to New Creation, and *linear* within the life of each man, from his conception through endless ages. It is *cyclical* in those matters attending to the abiding earth within the flow of seasons, movement of the heavens, etc., in the span from the fall to the return of the Christ in glory and it is *cyclical* in the rise and fall of nations, and all aspects of the vanity of our existence in this fallen world.

The divinely-given understanding of history—both in its cycles and its fundamentally linear flow—is markedly different from the understanding of history common among the nations. Certainly, it is quite different from the common, cyclical view of ancient man, in which inevitably and inexorably, the cycle of the ages come and go, with man's fate rising and falling with each passing age. As Mircea Eliade wrote in *The Myth of the Eternal Return*:

> Almost all these theories of the "Great Time" are found in conjunction with the myth of successive ages, the "age of gold" always occurring at the beginning of the cycle, close to the paradigmatic *illud tempus*. In the two doctrines—that of cyclical time, and that of limited cyclical time—this age of gold is recoverable; in other words, it is repeatable, an infinite number of times in the

former doctrine, once only in the latter.[1]

As Eliade observed, Indian speculation "amplifies and orchestrates the rhythms that govern the periodicity of cosmic creations and destructions" into a series of *yugas*, or "ages"— but the presence of similar myths in "the Germanic tradition" of Ragnarok does not "destroy the authenticity and autochthonous character of the Ragnarok myth."[2] This is to say, in Eliade's assessment, the similarity of such cyclical understandings of the sweep of history is not diffusionist in origin; rather, men have come to this notion independently (or at least, partially so) time and again.

One effect of such a cyclical view of history is a fundamental pessimism regarding one's place in that history. Eliade acknowledged that the Indian assessment was that "we are now living in the Kali Yuga, hence in an 'age of darkness,' which progresses under the sign of disaggregation and must end by a catastrophe, [thus] it is our fate to suffer more than the men of preceding ages."[3] History is only repetition, without redemption, and the Indian seeks only to escape from time altogether, while the Greek looks for an endless cycle of ages to come. As Bury wrote in his 1920 book, *The Idea of Progress*:

> The theory of world-cycles was so widely current that it may almost be described as the orthodox theory of cosmic time among the Greeks, and it passed from them to the Romans. According to some of the Pythagoreans, each cycle repeated to the minutest particular the course and events of the preceding. If the universe dissolves into the original chaos, there appeared to them

1   trans. by Willard R. Trask, (Princeton and Oxford: Princeton University Press, 1965) p. 112.
2   ibid., p. 113.
3   ibid., p. 118.

to be no reason why the second chaos should produce a world differing in the least respect from its predecessor. The nth cycle would be indeed numerically distinct from the first, but otherwise would be identical with it, and no man could possibly discover the number of the cycle in which he was living. As no end seems to have been assigned to the whole process, the course of the world's history would contain an endless number of Trojan Wars, for instance; an endless number of Platos would write an endless number of *Republics*. Virgil uses this idea in his Fourth Eclogue, where he meditates a return to the Golden Age:

> *Alter erit tum Tiphys, et altera quae uehat Argo*
> *Delectos heroas, erunt etiam altera bella,*
> *Atque iterum ad Troiam magnus mittetur Achilles.*[4]

The periodic theory might be held in forms in which this uncanny doctrine of absolute identity was avoided; but at the best it meant an endless monotonous iteration, which was singularly unlikely to stimulate speculative interest in the future.[5]

There is an inherent bleakness to the cyclical view; although Golden Ages of wisdom, innocence, and prosperity will purportedly come again, so will new Iron Ages of death and violence. With a cyclical view of history, mankind is not "going" anywhere, because all of this has happened before, and all of it will happen again, throughout endless ages to come. And whatever wonders would be witnessed—again—in a new age, it would

---

4   "Then behold/Another Tiphys take the helm and steer/Another Argo, manned by chosen souls/Seeking the golden, undiscovered East./New wars shall rise, and Troy renewed shall see/Another great Achilles leap to land." (From the translation of R. S. Conway included in *Virgil's Messianic Eclogue—Its Meaning, Occasion, and Sources*, [London: John Murray, 1907].)

5   J. B. Bury, *The Idea of Progress—An Inquiry into its Origin and Growth,* (London: MacMillan and Co., 1920) p. 12.

only come after fire has destroyed this age. In Eliade's words:

> Drawing from Heraclitus, or directly from Oriental gnosticism, Stoicism propagates all these ideas in regard to the Great Year and to the cosmic fire (*ekpyrosis*) that periodically puts an end to the universe in order to renew it. In time, these motifs of eternal return and of the end of the world come to dominate the entire Greco-Roman culture. The periodic renewal of the world (*metacosmesis*) was, furthermore, a favorite doctrine of Neo-Pythagoreanism, the philosophy that ... together with Stoicism, divided the allegiance of Roman society in the second and first centuries B.C.[6]

Nevertheless, the notion of the "Golden Age" has often held an appeal in recent centuries which has divorced it from its setting within an endless succession of rising and falling ages. The appeal of the Paradise which man lost in his fall into sin continues to draw men to lust for a world now irretrievably past. Man was cast out of the Garden to preserve him from an eternal 'living death'; thus we read in Genesis 3:

> Then the LORD God said, "Behold, the man has become like one of Us, to know good and evil. And now, lest he put out his hand and take also of the tree of life, and eat, and live forever"—therefore the LORD God sent him out of the garden of Eden to till the ground from which he was taken. So He drove out the man; and He placed cherubim at the east of the garden of Eden, and a flaming sword which turned every way, to guard the way to the tree of life. (v. 22–24)

The time of the Garden of Eden is concluded for mankind; what awaits the elect is now the hope of the new heavens and the new earth. But in the modern era, men have desired more the world

6   Eliade, *The Myth of the Eternal Return*, p. 122–123.

60

that they have lost, and than that which the Son of God attained for us through His suffering and death.

The "high point" (both figuratively and literally) in the notion of the cycle of history has been the "Golden Age." In his thorough study of the concept, *The Myth of the Golden Age in the Renaissance*, Harry Levin observed (in keeping with the assessment of Eliade and Bury) that the notion of such an age was widespread in antiquity:

> Something like a golden age had been presupposed by a number of ancient civilizations as a mythological prelude to their recorded histories. Some sort of halcyon stage, when men lived on intimate terms with their gods, usually heralded a regression into a more troublesome and more recognizable era. Such a myth of the fore-world, sometimes involving a more or less parallel sequence of four or five stages, is to be found among the Egyptians, the Hindus, the Buddhists, the Zoroastrians, the Aztecs, and other adherences of the most venerable creeds. As a motif of folklore, to be caught in the wide net cast by Stith Thompson, it has turned up in versions from the Irish, the Icelandic, the Lappish, the Chinese, the American Indian, and numerous other sources. The analogy of the *Völuspâ*, the prophecy in the Norse Eddas, may not quite be an independent parallel, since it might have been influenced by classical mythology. But a plentitude of examples, as abundant as the golden age itself, exists to prove its universality.[7]

The gradual degradation of society—the succession of ages—is linked with a succession of metals: gold, silver, brass and then iron, wryly observing that, "The bronze age and the iron age, of course, are recognized by archaeological science; the golden age

7   (Bloomington and London: Indiana University Press, 1969) p. 10.

and the silver age, alas, have a purely mythical significance, and
the metals themselves have no place in those myths, except as
chronological metaphors."[8] (But by now, of course, one should
understand that nothing is 'merely' mythological.) Levin cites a
biblical precedence for such a sequence:

> The sequence of four metals has the ethical sanction of
> the Old Testament, as well as of the Classics. ... The
> monstrous statue in Nebuchadnezzar's dream, with its
> head of gold, its breast of silver, belly of brass, legs of
> iron, and feet of clay, has portended a declining succes-
> sion of kingdoms for a long line of prophets extending
> from Daniel.[9]

It is perhaps worth considering whether the sixth century B.C.
imagery of Nebuchadnezzar's dream could either be the source
of such imagery, or at least helped to shape and define it. Giv-
en the scope and might of his empire, it is not hard to believe
that such a significant dream given to Nebuchadnezzar would
work its way throughout the world. However, Hesiod (ca. B.C.
750–650) lived at least several generations before Nebuchadnezzar, and his *Works and Days* contained the *locus classicus* (in
Levin's estimation) of the notion of the various "ages" of man:

> He [Hesiod] sings of five generations, the first of
> them a golden race (χρύσεον γένος), mortal men living
> like gods and loved by the gods while Kronos was reign-
> ing in heaven. Free from care, they dwelt in ease and
> peace among their flocks and on land which yielded its
> fruits without being forced. After long lives and pain-
> less deaths, they became benevolent spirits, and were
> replaced by a silver race which was weaker, inconsider-
> ate toward fellow men and neglectful of the immortals.
> Meanwhile, the reign of the Titans had been overthrown

---

8   ibid., p. 13.
9   ibid.

by the Olympians; it was Zeus who put an end to the silver generation, creating a brazen race which was stronger and more warlike, and which ended by destroying itself. ... At this point, the deteriorating trend is interrupted by a nobler interlude. Zeus creates the famous race of heroes who become demigods, performing the great exploits of Thebes and Troy, and surviving to abide forever in the far-flung islands of the blest, where Kronos is reestablished as their ruler. ... Significantly, his fourth race has no metallic ascription, and it is omitted by most of those who retell the tale.

The fifth generation, which would normally be considered the fourth, is the worst of all, the iron race. It is still going strong, and this is where we came in.[10]

This is hardly the occasion for an attempt at retelling the various interpretations of the kingdoms of Nebuchadnezzar's dream in Daniel 2. It is sufficient to observe it does not carry the sense of Eliade's *illud tempus*—"that time," in the sense of a primordial 'first time' when gods and men lived together in peace—for Daniel interprets the golden head of the statue to be Nebuchadnezzar himself:

You, O king, are a king of kings. For the God of heaven has given you a kingdom, power, strength, and glory; and wherever the children of men dwell, or the beast of the field and the birds of the heaven, He has given them into your hand, and has made you ruler over them all—you are this head of gold. But after you shall arise another kingdom inferior to yours; then another, a third kingdom of bronze, which shall rule over all the earth. And the fourth kingdom shall be as strong as iron, inasmuch as iron breaks in pieces and shatters everything; and like iron that crushes, that kingdom will break in

_____

10   ibid., p. 14–15.

pieces and crush all the others. Whereas you saw the feet and toes, partly of potter's clay and partly of iron, the kingdom shall be divided; yet the strength of iron shall be in it, just as you saw the iron mixed with ceramic clay. (Dan. 2:38–41)

Certainly the dream sets forth a pattern of degradation and decline in future kingdoms—the kingdom of iron is one of brute force, after all. But the manifest interpretation is that each kingdom is one which is far from mythological; instead, beginning with Nebuchadnezzar's golden kingdom, a series of historical kingdoms is what is indicated by the dream. Hesiod's earlier succession, then, is not to be confused with the sequence of Daniel, for the first four out of the five races are those which lived in direct association with the gods.

However, at the beginning of the modern era, the language of the Golden and Iron Ages was co-opted during the Renaissance to serve a very different agenda from that of Hesiod and the ancients. While the ancient pagans saw the ages as a cyclical succession, many of the men of the Renaissance became obsessed with the notion of a restoration of an Edenic existence by means of establishing a new "Golden Age." In Levin's words:

> The golden age, as its temporal counterpart, was charged with the sort of kinetic energies that would burst forth in the Renaissance. Boethius, that belated Roman, imprisoned and condemned to death by the Goths in 522 A.D., had sought appropriate consolation by recalling the *prior aetas*. Jean de Meun reanimated the topos in the late thirteenth century, with his revival, completion, and transformation of the conventional allegory by Guillaume de Lorris, *The Romance of the Rose*. During the seven hundred and fifty years between the memory-haunted Boethius and the forward-looking Jean de Meun, the golden

64

age might be said to have gone underground.[11]

This restored interest in the "Golden Age" coincided with a significant change in the aspirations of Western man in the midst of this fallen world. As David Noble wrote in *The Religion of Technology*, "… beginning in the middle of the twelfth century, there emerged from within the monastic world a radically renewed millenarian conception of Christian history, a dynamic and teleological sense of time which would profoundly excite Christian expectation and accelerate the technological development that was now bound up with it."[12] The notion of restoring a Golden Age to mankind was viewed as a technical feat to be accomplished—"Technology now became at the same time eschatology."[13]

At the very moment when technology began to be employed in man's quest for spiritual improvement, the search for an earthly paradise began. As Levin wrote: "The Middle Ages had buried the golden age under the conception of Eden; the Renaissance not only revived the original conception, but ventured forth on a quest to objectify it. When its locus shifted from the temporal to the spatial, it became an attainable goal and a challenge to the explorers."[14] Perhaps one might say that, to an extent, the Middle Ages had not so much *buried* the "Golden Age" as endeavored to *redeem* it; attributing the notion of such an age to a dim remembrance of the perfection of creation at the beginning, the theologians were more willing to attribute pagan utterances concerning the "Golden Age" to that time when the first man could hear the Lord God walking in the garden in the cool of the day (Gen. 3:8). Renaissance man—for reasons we

11   ibid., p. 34.
12   David Noble, *The Religion of Technology*, (New York: Penguin, 1999) p. 21.
13   ibid., p. 22.
14   Levin, p. 59.

will explore more fully later—sought both to locate paradise in the midst of this world as a place attainable, and to recreate paradise by means of man's labors. As men were unwilling to be sent forth into the world in the days following the flood, and instead sought to make a name for themselves by means of the Tower of Babel (Gen. 11:5), so men sought once again by means of technological achievement to build a paradise upon the Earth.

Christopher Columbus was the man who was most prominent among those who sought to regain paradise for man by means of exploration. As David Noble observes:

> Columbus saw himself as a "divinely inspired fulfiller of prophecy." He was firmly convinced that the world would end in about a century and a half, based on the calculations by d'Ailly, and that in the meantime, all prophecies had to be fulfilled, including the conversion of all peoples and the recovery of Mount Zion (Jerusalem). ...
> ... To his eyes, the discovery of the New World signaled the imminent End of the World, and hence the promised recovery of perfection. Identifying the Orinoco as one of the four rivers of the Garden of Eden, Columbus repeatedly insisted that he had indeed recovered the earthly paradise. "I am completely persuaded in my own mind," he wrote, "that the Terrestrial Paradise is the place I have said." And in the manner of a new Adam, he obsessively named all that he surveyed, confident in his expectation that mankind's original dominion might soon be restored.[15]

The pretensions of establishing a "Golden Age" of mankind were not limited to enthusiastic explorers; those who contended they were the very pillars of society saw themselves in

15   Noble, p. 33–34.

such a light. For circles associated quite closely with Renaissance papal power, the imagery of the "Golden Age," and the effort to bring about a new paradise on earth, was an agenda which was actively pursued. Again, in Noble's words:

> The new spiritual man of the fifteenth and sixteenth centuries, heirs of medieval millenarianism and precursors of the Reformation, sought in the study of nature and the recovery of ancient lore about the natural world the means of rekindling the true light of early Christianity. Thus the great humanist scholars Marsilio Ficino and Pico della Mirandola labored to unearth the lost secrets of hermetic natural philosophy and the occult arts, and in the view of the Joachimite Augustinian abbot Egidio of Viterbo, as "messenger[s] of divine providence who had been sent to show that mystical theology everywhere concurred with our holy institutions and was their forerunner."[16]

The Florentine branch of the Renaissance was obsessed with the notion of the "Golden Age," and that which Marsilio Ficino (1433–1499) defended with words, the dominant family of that famous city—the Medicis—sought to put into practice:

> Ficino, ardent Platonist that he was, associated Hesiod's four ages with Plato's four talents, and had no hesitation in evaluating the talent of his own age: "For this golden century, as it were, has brought back to light the liberal arts, which were all but extinguished: grammar, poetry, oratory, painting, sculpture, architecture, music, the ancient chanting of songs to the Orphic Lyre, and all this in Florence." …
>
> When [Lorenzo de' Medici's] second son was elected to the papacy, through which—as Leo X—he would extend the bounties of the renewed golden age to Rome, the new pope's native town outdid itself in spec-

---

16   ibid., p. 35.

tacular celebration. The climax of the carnival was a procession designed by a local humanist, Jacopo Nardi, and executed by the artist Pontormo. Its triumph was conveyed by no less than seven chariots. The first carried figures personifying Saturn and Janus with their condign attributes, attended by elaborately undressed shepherds on horseback; the next five cars gave majestic representation to other episodes from ancient legend. The seventh and climactic episode is thus depicted by Vasari in his life of Pontormo:

> After these six came the car, or rather, the triumphal chariot, of the age or epoch of gold, wrought with the richest and most beautiful artistry, with any figures in relief executed by Baccio Bandinelli, and with very beautiful paintings by the hand of Pontormo among which those of the four cardinal virtues were highly praised. From the center of the car rose a great globe in the form of the world, upon which a man lay prostrate on his face as if dead, his armor all rusted, and from the open fissure of whose sundered back emerged a small boy all naked and gilded, representing the revival of the golden age and the end of the iron age, which expired and was reborn through the election of the pope … I should not omit the fact that the gilded infant, who was the child of a baker, died shortly afterwards through the suffering that he endured in order to gain ten crowns.[17]

When one recognizes that Leo X—the man who made it his mission to extirpate the Lutheran 'heresy'—viewed himself in such terms—as the initiator of a new "Golden Age"—the true state of the papacy at the time of the Reformation can begin to

17   Levin, p. 39–40.

be more clearly discerned. The debauch which was the papacy of Leo X was not enough to dissuade belief in the coming of a new "Golden Age," the establishment of an earthly paradise. In the words of Noble:

> In the sixteenth century, inventors and mechanics had increasingly invoked the image of God as craftsman and architect in order, by analogy, to lend prestige to their own activities: in their humble arts, they were imitating God and hence reflecting his glory. In the seventeenth century, the scientists began to carry this artisanal analogy between the works of man and God somewhat further, toward a real identity between them. Again, as Milton had written, they strove to know God not just in order to love and imitate him, but also "to be like him."
>
> …
>
> Increasingly, in the inspired imagination of the time, man's contribution to creation loomed ever larger in the scheme of things. Despite their caveats about the necessity of humility, and despite their devout acknowledgement of divine purpose in their work, the scientists subtly but steadily began to assume the mantle of creator in their own right, as gods themselves. Francis Bacon, for example, had insisted that man's mission to remake the world was in reality but "the footsteps of the Creator imprinted on his creatures." "God forbid that we should give out a dream of our own imagination for a pattern of the world," he declared. Yet, at the end of his life, in his *New Atlantis*, he predicted that men would one day create new species and become as gods—"the undeclared ultimate goal" of modern science, as Lewis Mumford put it.[18]

Turning away from perceiving the vanity of man's labors in this

18   Noble, p. 65–66, 67.

fallen world, men dreamed of becoming gods, and establishing their works as the proof of their divinity. They had forgotten the warning of the Preacher: "There is no remembrance of former things, nor will there be any remembrance of things that are to come by those who will come after." (1:11)

It was Cain and his sons who excelled in worldly pursuits: Cain established the first known city (Gen. 4:17), and his descendants included "the father of those who dwell in tents and have livestock," (4:20) "the father of all those who play the harp and flute," (4:21) and "an instructor of every craftsman in bronze and iron." (v. 22) It was not, of course, that the pursuit of such abilities and technologies were evil; but it is remarkable that such pursuits defined the heritage of the sons of Cain.

At the end of the age, it will be a confusion regarding the cyclical and linear aspects of history which will catch the world unprepared for the Christ's return in glory. As Jesus declares in Luke 17: "And as it was in the days of Noah, so it will be also in the days of the Son of Man: They ate, they drank, they married wives, they were given in marriage, until the day that Noah entered the ark, and the flood came and destroyed them all." (v. 26–27) And St. Peter records the thoughts of the men of those days:

...that scoffers will come in the last days, walking according to their own lusts, and saying, "Where is the promise of His coming? For since the fathers fell asleep, all things continue as they were from the beginning of creation." For this they willfully forget: that by the word of God the heavens were of old, and the earth standing out of water and in the water, by which the world that then existed perished, being flooded with water. But the heavens and the earth which now exist are kept in store by the same word, reserved for fire until the day of judgment and perdition of ungodly men. (2 Pet. 3:3–7)

In the cyclical time of the generations of men, earth abides, and the works of men perish even as their generations pass away. But in the fullness of time, that cycle of the earth will cease, and the last days will come.

CHAPTER 5.
JOACHIMISM AND THE NOTION OF THE THIRD AGE OF MAN.

In the parlance of discussions of all matters historical, the standard practice is to refer to our age as one which is the "modern" or "post-modern" age. The designation of a *period* of time being "modern" is somewhat problematic, particularly since it is generally intended to cover a time of roughly five centuries and covering the cultures of several continents. The conception of a "post-modern" age clearly has meaningful content only if one understands "modern" in an ideological rather than a temporal sense. The designation of a "modern age" is not merely a designation of *when* one is; it is a declaration of what one believes regarding a greater significance of the period within the context of human history, while the declaration that one is in a "post-modern" era carries within it the declaration that the ideological content of modernism has, to one degree or another, failed or has been supplanted.

It is rarely appreciated just how novel—and polemical—the notion of a "modern age" truly is, and yet modernism can only exist in contradistinction to a definable, discernible "Middle Ages" and "Antiquity." In the conception of those who created the notion of a "Middle Ages" which was distinct from modernity, the era of Christendom—the aforementioned Middle Ages—was an age of degradation in human thought and culture. For the man of the *Renaissance* (literally, *rebirth*[1]), the Middle Ages were conceived of as an interim between the high culture of antiquity and the rebirth of that culture in the modern era. Thus, as Gillespie observes in *The Theological Origins of Modernity*:

---
1   The term comes, somewhat ironically, from the Vulgar Latin, *renāscere*.

The term *modernitas* was used in the twelfth century to distinguish contemporary times from those of the past. Shortly thereafter, the term began to appear in the vernacular. Dante used the Italian *moderno* around 1300, and in 1361 Nicholas or Oresme used the French *moderne*. However, the term was not used to distinguish 'ancient' and 'modern' until 1460 and was not used in its contemporary sense to distinguish a particular historical period until the sixteenth century. The English term 'modern' referring to modern times first appeared in 1585, and the term 'modernity' was not used until 1627. The concept of modernity as a historical epoch was originally and often since understood in opposition to antiquity. The term 'middle ages' does not appear in English until 1753, although the term 'Gothic' was used in the same sense in the sixteenth century and Latin equivalents even earlier.

While the distinction of old and new was already present in antiquity, it was never used in its modern sense, in large measure because the terms were deployed in the context of a cyclical view of time that was present in ancient mythological accounts of the nature and origin of the cosmos, which were later adopted by ancient philosophers and historians as well. "New" in this context was almost invariably equated with degeneration and decline, as in Aristophanes' *Clouds*, where the newfangled ways of the Athenians are contrasted with the superior mores of the generation that fought at Marathon.[2]

The Renaissance formulation of "modern" and "postmodern" ages thus presumes a radical break in the understanding of the period following the Ascension of the Christ from that which had previously been predominant. Through the period now known as the Middle Ages, the common understanding of

2   (Chicago and London: The University of Chicago Press, 2008) p. 3.

the current age was defined by St. Augustine as the senescence of the world. In the words of Eric Voegelin, "According to the Augustinian construction, the phase of history since Christ was the sixth, the last earthly age—the *sæculum senescens*, the time of the senility of mankind. The present had no earthly future; its meaning was exhausted in a waiting for the end of history through eschatological events."[3] The world is now marking time between the Ascension of the Christ and His return in glory at the end of the age. It was understood that the return of the Christ would bring about a fundamental reordering of man's relationship to time, and thus this period from the Ascension onward was, in a very significant way, a transitional time. After Jesus ascended, the angels asked of the apostles: "Men of Galilee, why do you stand gazing up into heaven? This *same* Jesus, who was taken up from you into heaven, will so come in like manner as you saw Him go into heaven." (Acts 1:11) There is an inherent sense of such upward gazing throughout the age of Christendom   throughout the generations of persecutions, conversions and the rise and fall of kingdoms, there was an enduring anticipation of the imminent arrival of the Christ in glory. Apart from that last event, the major events of salvation history would seem to be concluded—especially when the last of the apostles had been laid to rest.

Such an understanding of this age of mankind has profound implications for one's assessment of the meaning of worldly events. Thus Karl Löwith declares that for St. Augustine, "the history of the world has for him no intrinsic interest or meaning."[4] The purpose of the various nations and empires which rise and fall is simply to provide worldly peace in which

3   Eric Voegelin, *Science, Politics and Gnosticism,* (Wilmington, Delaware: ISI Books, 2004) p. 69.
4   Karl Löwith, *Meaning in History,* (Chicago and London: The University of Chicago Press, 1949) p. 166.

the Gospel might have free course. As St. Paul wrote to St. Timothy:

> Therefore I exhort first of all that supplications, prayers,
> intercessions, *and* giving of thanks be made for all men,
> for kings and all who are in authority, that we may lead
> a quiet and peaceable life in all godliness and reverence.
> For this *is* good and acceptable in the sight of God our
> Savior, who desires all men to be saved and to come to
> the knowledge of the truth. (1 Tim. 2:1–4 NKJV)

The governing authorities may serve instrumentally to provide worldly peace, but this is of no direct significance to the Christian; "For Augustine the historical task of the church is not to develop the Christian truth through successive stages but simply to spread it, for the truth as such is established. … That everything in this *sæculum* is subject to change goes for Augustine without saying; for this very reason profane history has no immediate relevance for faith in things everlasting."[5] What matters is the proclamation of the Gospel, and the means of grace do not change: the Lord continues to be at work through the Word and Sacrament which He has given to accomplish the salvation of men. The relative brevity of the Sacred Scriptures speaks to the fact that they are not intended to serve as a comprehensive history of all events of the ages in which they were written; indeed, not even the Gospels contain a complete record of all things that Jesus did. It is as St. John wrote: "And truly Jesus did many other signs in the presence of His disciples, which are not written in this book; but these are written that you may believe that Jesus is the Christ, the Son of God, and that believing you may have life in His name." (John 20:30–31 NKJV) In all his various vocations, the Christian has an active concern for the things of this world, as he lives out his various vocations in Church, State and Home, so that he might serve God and his neighbor in his daily walk. But the Christian, *coram Deo,* has little abiding concern for the

5   ibid., p. 166.

changing circumstances of this world; he is a stranger in its midst, one who is passing through and confessing Christ as he walks the path of salvation. "Profane events and transcendent goal are, in this view, separated in principle and yet related through the *peregrinatio* or 'pilgrimage' *in hoc sæculo* of the faithful toward the ultimate *telos*."[6]

The Christian, being in the midst of an earthly 'pilgrimage,' is therefore one who is simply 'passing through.' In his essay, "Configurations of History,"[7] Voegelin describes such a category of historical understanding as being one of "exodus":

> According to St. Augustine, in man, in the soul, there are organizing centers. The two principal centers are the love of self and the love of God; these are the emotional orienting centers in the soul. Between these two centers there is continual tension: man is always inclined to fall into the love of self and away from the love of God. On the other hand, he is always conscious that he should orient himself by the love of God, and he tries to do so in many instances. Exodus is defined by St. Augustine as the tendency to abandon one's entanglements with the world, to abandon the love of self, and to turn toward the love of God. …
>
> This tension, I should say, is central to the interpretation of history. Wherever changes in the existent order occur, they are changes in the direction of the exodus mentioned. Wherever this tension is understood, new insights into order occur, and there the actual pattern of an exodus appears.[8]

---

6   ibid., p. 167.

7   included in *Published Essays 1966–1985*, vol. 12 of *The Collected Works of Eric Voegelin,* ed. by Ellis Sandoz, (Baton Rouge and London: Louisiana State University Press, 1990) p. 95–114.

8   ibid., p. 105–106.

Voegelin noted that this *exodus* is not figurative, but is literal, whether one is speaking of an individual, or of a group (the flight of the Pilgrims to New England is one such exodus), in which worldly history is driven by the theological consideration of withdrawal from the self-serving corruption to rededicate one's self to the Triune God. However, for the Christian, such acts of exodus are always a 'stop-gap' measure, because of the corrupting power of original sin to eventually undermine each such exodus—the withdrawal from the corruption is spiritually necessary, but until the Last Day or one's own death, it is a withdrawal which is, at most, a temporary victory. Voegelin explains that pursuit of such an exodus opens up two fundamental possibilities for engagement with history:

> One is to project the kingdom of God into the future, that is, to assume that somehow the structure of history, in which we are living and in which we experience this tension toward God, will actually be replaced, in history, by a perfected kingdom of God. This is the escape by objectification, which is usually called apocalyptic, as in the Apocalypse of Daniel, telling of that which is to come with the fifth monarchy, or as in the Apocalypse of St. John, telling of a millennium, or as in the modern apocalyptic visions of the perfect realm of reason, the perfect real of positivist science in the Comtian sense, or the perfect realm of Marxist Communism. ...
>
> There is also another type of objectifying escape, which is not into a future time, but rather into the beyond, into perfection in a spiritually understood eternity beyond this world. This escape into the beyond, with various means of escaping the structure of this world of society and history, is what was called in antiquity gnosis.[9]

The attempts to historically realize a future kingdom became

---

9   ibid., p. 106–107.

dangerous when men began to look for a fundamental improvement in the state of man in this world, by means of the initiation of a new age. When the Augustinian conception of history prevailed, men understood the world to be coming to an end in which the kingdom of God would be realized by direct divine intervention: the world would be remade, and elect men would live at peace with God in the New Jerusalem. However, when men began to imagine that another age in human history stood between the Ascension and Christ's *parousia*, a corruption entered into the historical anticipation of the coming kingdom. And the prospect of such a new age in human history entered the Western mind through the speculations of Joachim of Fiore (A.D. 1135–1202). Suddenly man was no longer simply 'passing through'; now he was building something new for a coming new age of man.

Marjorie Reeves explains in *Joachim of Fiore and the Prophetic Future* that Joachim fundamentally reconceptualized the flow of all of human history:

The third *status* could quickly become a third age, with a new 'testament', a new authority and new institutions. There was concealed dynamite here.

Joachim's imagination had a kaleidoscopic quality: the pieces of his mind were always forming new patterns. Besides twos and threes, sevens occupied his mind much. Here he could start with the well-known pattern inherited from St Augustine of seven ages (*etates*) corresponding to the Seven Days of Creation: five before the Incarnation, the sixth from the Incarnation to his own time, and the seventh, the Sabbath Age of rest and beatitude—but when? For St Augustine and those who used this idea prior to Joachim it would seem that the Seventh Age lay beyond history, but for Joachim this Sabbath clearly coincided with and added to the understanding of the third *status*.[10]   ❦

Joachim's concept of history broke all of time into three distinct ages, with one age for each Person of the Holy Trinity. With the incarnation, mankind entered the second age; but Joachim predicted that a new, third age would soon begin, which would be an Age of the Spirit:

> The general scheme of Joachim's discriminating interpretation is based on the trinitarian doctrine. Three different dispensations come to pass in three different epochs in which the three persons of the Trinity are successively manifested. The first is the dispensation of the Father, the second that of the Son, the third that of the Holy Spirit. The latter is beginning just now (i.e., toward the end of the twelfth century) and is progressing toward the complete "freedom" of the "spirit."[11]

However, such a period of human history would not begin without the emergence of a leader for the new age; "As the first age began with Abraham and the second with Christ, so the third was to begin in the year 1260 with the appearance of a *dux e Babylone*."[12] By definition, Joachim's system is, at least in some sense, inherently "post-Christian"—no matter how much Joachim himself would have been revolted by such a notion. Even without a displacement of the *parousia* as the conclusion of history, the structure of Joachim's new age is defined not by the leadership of Christ, but by a new figure, who was yet to emerge. Joachim established the framework of the characteristics of the modern age—indeed, the very concept of a modern age is essentially impossible apart from Joachimite doctrine.

10   Marjorie Reeves, *Joachim of Fiore and the Prophetic Future—A Medieval Study in Historical Thinking*, (Phoenix Mill, England: Sutton Publishing, 1999) p. 8.
11   Löwith, p. 148.
12   Voegelin, *Science Politics and Gnosticism*, p. 70.

Thus, in Voegelin's assessment, the threefold periodization was what gave rise to the notion of a Renaissance:

> The first of these symbols is that of the Third Realm—that is, the conception of a third world-historical phase that is at the same time the last, the age of fulfillment. An extensive class of gnostic ideas comes under the symbol of the three phases. First and foremost would be the humanistic periodization of world history into ancient, medieval, and modern.[13]

The Renaissance would be neither the first nor the last ideological movement to attach itself to a Joachimite vision of the ages of man. In fact, from the time of Joachim, an astounding array of heresies and ideologies have found their basis in Joachim's three ages.

Three other symbols arose from Joachim's vision which would mark movements he helped to inspire. According to Voegelin, "The second symbol Joachim developed is that of the leader, the *dux,* who appears at the beginning of a new era and through his appearance establishes that era."[14] Given Joachim's vision of the third age being one which was distinguished by monasticism, the more fanatical adherents of St. Francis of Assisi saw him as the coming *dux*—but he was by no means the last man to be 'cast' in this role. Igor Shafarevich observes in *The Socialist Phenomenon* that Joachim of Fiore and Amalric of Bena were "two thinkers who were destined to exert a continuous influence on the heretical movements of the Middle Ages and the Reformation"[15] and Amalric "also saw history as a series of stages in divine revelation." As Shafarevich explains:

---

13   ibid.
14   ibid., p. 71.
15   Igor Shafarevich, *The Socialist Phenomenon,* trans. by. William Tjalsma, (New York: Harper & Row, 1980) p. 24–25.

In the beginning there was Moses' law, then Christ's which superseded it. Now the time of the third revelation had come. This was embodied in Amalric and his followers, as previously revelation had been embodied in Christ. They had now become as Christ. Three basic theses of this new Christianity have been preserved. First of all: "God is all." Second: "Everything is One, for everything that is is God." And third: "Whoever observes the law of love is above sin." These theses were interpreted in such a way that those who followed the teachings of Amalric could attain identity with God through ecstasy. In them, the Holy Spirit became flesh, just as in Christ. Man in this state is incapable of sin, for his deeds coincide with the will of God. He rises above the law.

Thus the followers of Amalric perceived the Kingdom of the Spirit more in terms of a spiritual state of the members of the sect than in terms of a world to be actively transformed. The second interpretation was not entirely foreign to them, however.[16]

The immediate utility of Joachim's notion in the development of heresy should have been lost on no one. That one of his own contemporaries immediately developed a form of heresy incorporating (1) immediate inspiration, (2) libertinism, (3) blind devotion to a cult leader, and (4) at least a willingness to establish a 'heavenly' kingdom on earth should have been a warning to the coming generations that the Joachimite doctrine contained within it the seeds of destruction.

According to Voegelin, "the prophet" is the third of Joachim's symbols:

Joachim assumed that the leader of each age had a precursor, just as Christ had St. John the Baptist. Even the

---

16   ibid., p. 26.

leader out of the Babylonian captivity, who was to appear in 1260, had such a precursor—in this case, Joachim himself. With the creation of the symbol of the precursor, a new type emerges in Western history: the intellectual who knows the formula of salvation from the misfortunes of the world and can predict how world history will take its course in the future. … In the further course of Western history, the Christian tide recedes, and the prophet, the precursor of the leader, becomes the secularist intellectual who thinks he knows the meaning of history (understood as world-immanent) and can predict the future.[17]

No small number of such intellectuals present themselves, including Karl Marx—who claimed to know the whole future of mankind with 'scientific certainty.' Also prominent among pillars of 'modernity' who imagined they knew the course of human events in advance, and who bore the signs of manifest influence by Joachim is G. W. F. Hegel (1770–1831), whose search for a universal system of history, and belief in Progress, was aped by many—even his enemies.[18] Magee notes that the similarities between the thought of Joachim and that of Hegel are too clear to be ignored:

> The Joachimite influence is most apparent in Hegel's treatment of the Trinity. In his *lectures on the Philosophy of Religion*, Hegel deals in detail with the Trinity as constituting the "moments" of God (universality, diremption, and reconciliation). In the 1831 version of the lectures, Hegel introduces a new twist: he begins calling Father, Son and Holy Spirit the "King-

17   Voegelin, *Science, Politics and Gnosticism*, p. 73.
18   For example, one need only consider the widespread notion of the Hegelian dialectic (thesis-antithesis-synthesis) to begin appreciating how pervasive Hegel's influence—both directly, and in various simplified or corrupted forms—actually is.

dom [*Reich*] of the Father," "Kingdom of the Son," and "Kingdom of the Spirit." This use of "Kingdom" for the persons of the Trinity was employed widely by followers of Joachim. ... However, Hegel's treatment of the Trinity is, like Joachim's, temporal: he holds that the reconciliation of the diremption in God takes time; only at a certain point in human history is this accomplished. ... Once it is realized that the Concept, as the crowning conception of the Logic, contains three moments which correspond to the Christian Trinity, the similarity to Joachim is striking: both Hegel and Joachim see the hand of God, Providence, playing out in history according to the pattern of the Trinity.[19]

It is not without significance that Joachim's interpretation of the creation is linked to his beliefs regarding its Creator. In fact, Joachim's views concerning the doctrine of the Trinity were subject to censure by the Fourth Lateran Council in A.D. 1215. Joachim was opposed to the trinitarian teaching of Peter Lombard, and Lombard's defenders accused Joachim of falling into Tritheism—dividing the Persons of the Holy Trinity as to consider them as three gods. In the words of Reeves, "Because so much emphasis was later placed on the Abbot's doctrine of the three *status*, it has often been assumed that Joachim was most deeply influenced by the Greek approach to the Trinity through a stress on the Three Persons"[20] and although more recent scholarship has cleared Joachim of any Eastern influence in this regard, it is unsurprising that Joachim's unorthodox view of history, which was inextricably linked to his Trinitarian theology, would raise questions concerning his views regarding that article of the

19   Glenn Alexander Magee, *Hegel and the Hermetic Tradition,* (Ithaca and London: Cornell University Press, 2001) p. 240.

20   Marjorie Reeves, *The Influence of Prophecy in the Later Middle Ages—A Study of Joachimism,* (Notre Dame and London: University of Notre Dame Press, 1993) p. 31.

faith, as well. Thus, according to Reeves, the condemnation rendered by the Fourth Lateran Council, although it targeted only his *teaching*, and did not specifically condemn him as a heretic, colored the view which future generations would have of the man:

> None the less, to theologians of succeeding generations this condemnation placed Joachim in a definite category of one who had erred in his theological doctrine. It obviously influenced both St. Bonaventura and St. Thomas Aquinas, for instance. The verdict hung like a millstone on his reputation and earned him a place in catalogues of heretics. It has, indeed, be a matter of controversy right down to the present day as to whether Joachim did or did not err in his Trinitarian doctrine, and all too seldom have the judgements been dispassionate.[21]

Given the heretical notions which became widespread among Joachim's followers, it is little surprise that his Trinitarian doctrine would draw such concerns. And the fact that the fourth "symbol" (as so identified by Voegelin) further removed adherents from the discipline of the Church did little to assuage the fears of the orthodox:

> The fourth of the Joachitic symbols is the community of spiritually autonomous persons. In the spirit of the monasticism of the time, Joachim imagined the Third Realm as a community of monks. In our context, the importance of this image lies in the idea of a spiritualized mankind existing in community without the mediation and support of institutions; for, according to Joachim's view, the spiritual community of monks was to exist without the sacramental supports of the Church.[22]

---

21   Marjorie Reeves, *The Influence of Prophecy in the Later Middle Ages—A Study of Joachimism,* (Notre Dame and London: University of Notre Dame Press, 1993) p. 33.
22   Voegelin, *Science, Politics and Gnosticism,* p. 74.

The near universality of such a Joachimite "symbol" should be readily apparent; it is now simply taken for granted that the individual pursues his or her own 'piety' with as much (or little) interaction with the Church as he or she deems necessary. As Magee observed:

> There is a strong similarity between Joachim's conception of spirituality in the third age and the Pietist movement that arose in Germany centuries later. Both involve a rejection of the church as an intermediary between ordinary men and God and the claim that the lay community of worshippers can achieve salvation and knowledge of God unaided. Hegel explicitly identifies his Kingdom of the Spirit with the community of worshippers. ... Further, as O'Regan notes, both Hegel and Joachim make the unusual move of locating the eschaton in time, Joachim believing that it is at hand, Hegel believing that it has already happened.[23]

The modern age—which we thus see is, in its fundamental conception, one which has 'moved on' from the Age of Christendom—is one which is in fundamental revolt against the received Christian intertwining of secular and sacred history. Secular history is no longer sublimated to the concerns of sacred history; secular history becomes a new form of sacred history in which the former sacred history is overthrown. The Augustinian ambivalence to the rise and fall of worldly kingdoms no longer reigns; instead, each such secular event is perceived to be a matter of profound spiritual significance. On occasion, such notions approach the absurd, with concerns for one nation or another—one revolution or another—being interpreted as *the* blessed moment in the initiation of a profound new age of the human race. The concern for the emergence of a worldly 'Kingdom of the Spirit'—to borrow the phraseology of Hegel—is then allowed

23   Magee, p. 240.

to trump the Christian pilgrimage, which awaits the Last Day. The perception of a divinely-given "most favored nation" status becomes the *modus operandi* of the latter-day Joachimites, and men are no longer torn between "looking up" as the apostles once did, and going about the work of proclaiming the Christ in the midst of their earthly vocations. Rather, whether by means of the 'dictatorship of the proletariat,' the foundation of a 'thousand year reich,' or 'making the world safe for democracy' through a perpetual war for perpetual peace, the Joachimites have confused the sacred and secular in history, and have immanentized the eschaton, seeking to build a worldly blessed kingdom and the 'end of history' by means of the labors of their own hands. Thus, Joachim has provided a new mythological structure: he has recast the way in which men perceive themselves, their age, and the reason for living. In the words of John Gray, "The prevailing idea of what it means to be modern is a post-Christian myth."[24]

---

24   John Gray, *Al Qaeda and What It Means to Be Modern*, (New York and London: The New Press, 2003) p. 103.

CHAPTER 6.
TIME AND ETERNITY.

n our "modern" age, there are few more controversial words that those with which the Holy Scriptures begin: "In the beginning God created the heavens and the earth." (Gen. 1:1) An almost immeasurable well of ink has been spilled on debate of what was created and when, but our concern here is not one of cosmology and biology, but horology.[1] Our concern is not the means by which God created, but the fact that God's act of creation included the creation of time itself. Before the first moment of creation, there is no time; in short, there were no endless ages prior to God creating heaven and earth. *Space* and *time* and the raw *matter* of the created order come into existence "at the beginning." The first fact of all history is set forth in the first verse of Genesis. God makes a beginning of all things, and thus creates the context for history. History begins with a word which is spoken, and the unfolding of that history is recorded in words. "The earth was without form, and void; and darkness was on the face of the deep. And the Spirit of God was hovering over the face of the waters." (v. 2) The raw material of the created order—time, space and matter—has a joint moment of origin; the account of history since that first moment has been one of divine Providence acting directly and instrumentally on time, space and matter since that first moment of creation.

There is no time outside the divinely-given narrative. The divine act of 'beginning' establishes the chronological context for measuring all activity. Actions occur in time, and the record of divine action clearly establishes that the Lord begins

---

1   The word "Horology"—the study of time—is derived from Greek words ὥρα ("hour, time") and λόγος ("study, speech").

time as He begins to act in that time which He has created. In the words of J. A. A. Quenstedt (one of the 17th century Lutheran dogmaticians):

> It is ἀκυρολογία [incorrect phraseology] to say that at one time the world was not. For τὸ [the word] *aliquando* [at one time] is the same as *aliquo tempore* [at a certain time], but it cannot be said that at a certain time the world was not, because there was no time before the world was established. One who says that the world was not always speaks more carefully.[2]

According to Jackelén, "Israel never understood time as something separate from the respective event; in this sense, it knew only 'filled time,' that is, 'every event has a definite place in the time-order; the event is inconceivable without its time, and *vice versa*."[3] All time is *narrated* and *observed*: with each act of the creation, Holy Scripture declares that God *said*, and that He *saw that it was good*. The Lord's act of creation occurs according to a sequence of events—time is structured and sequential from its first moment. And the creation is always observed—even when the only observer is the Lord God Himself. All of human existence is perceived by the Lord; thus we read in one of the Psalms of David:

> Where can I go from Your Spirit?
> Or where can I flee from Your presence?
> If I ascend into heaven, You *are* there;
> If I make my bed in hell, behold, You *are there.*
> *If* I take the wings of the morning,
> *And* dwell in the uttermost parts of the sea,
> Even there Your hand shall lead me,

2   J. A. Quenstedt, *Creation—Theologia Didactico-Polemica Part I, Chapter X,* ed. and trans. by Luther Poellot. Unpublished manuscript. P. 37.

3   Antje Jackelén, *Time and Eternity—The Question of Time in Church, Science and Theology,* (Philadelphia and London: Templeton Foundation Press, 2005) p. 65.

And Your right hand shall hold me.
If I say, "Surely the darkness shall fall on me,"
Even the night shall be light about me;
Indeed, the darkness shall not hide from You,
But the night shines as the day;
The darkness and the light *are* both alike *to You.*

(Psalm 139:7–12 NKJV)

All time in Sacred Scripture is thus "filled time" and it is "observed time." The whole course of time is fulfilled according to the divine will. Thus, again, David wrote in the Psalm:

Your eyes saw my substance, being yet unformed.
And in Your book they all were written,
The days fashioned for me,
When *as yet there were* none of them.

(Psalm 139:16 NKJV)

To understand the relationship of the Creator to His creation, it is vital that we understand not only the concept of *time*, but also that of *eternity*. The nature of *eternity* is markedly different from that of *time*; eternity is more than simply 'endless time.' As Jackelén declares, "The eternity of God should not be understood as timelessness, but rather as the fullness of time and power over time."[4] With this conception, one may understand the *eternality* of the Triune God to be more than the assertion that He is without beginning and without end—that statement is true, but it does not exhaust the notion of His *eternality*. The concept of being "without beginning and without end" still speaks in relation to *time*, which is part of the Lord's good creation. *Eternality* places the Holy Trinity above and beyond time; *time*, like all the rest of God's good creation, is utterly inferior to God, together with *space* and *matter*. Contrary to the Calvinists,

---

4   Jackelén, p. 65.

who seek to make the Lord subject to the "laws of nature,"[5] the Lord is not subject to the restrictions of *time, space*, and *matter*, because all these aspects of creation are His work, accomplished through His Word. Thus He is not subject to any chain of causation, and His divine foreknowledge and predestination are certainly not precluded by the 'laws' of time.

Eternality is thus conceptually different from *immortality*; *eternality* is not simply an *immortality* which extends infinitely into the past and future. Although that which is immortal has infinite expansion forward in time, it is still subject to creation in time. Immortality and mortality are not excluded categories of existence for man as a creature of God. That which is immortal is still rooted within the created order as something which has a moment of beginning; for the immortal, there was still a time when it was not. Even if an immortal thing began with the first instant of creation, it is still merely creature because it came into existence within the created order of time. Eternality is of a fundamentally different character, because that which is eternal is not subject to time; time is subject to eternity.

The wonder of the Incarnation is thus further known when one considers the wondrous act of the eternal Son of God becoming Man in *time*. When the Jews confronted Jesus in the temple, they said to Him, "You are not yet fifty years old, and have You seen Abraham?" "Jesus said to them, 'Most assuredly, I say to you, before Abraham was, I AM.'" (John 8:57–58) Both in time, and in His essential eternality, the Son of God was before Abraham, as well as above and and beyond time. In the Athanasian Creed, the Church confesses the Christ to be, "Equal

---

5   Thus, for example, the Formula of Concord rightly condemns John Calvin for teaching, "That, because of the property of His human nature, it is impossible for Christ to be able to be at the same time in more than one place, much less to be everywhere with His body." (FC SD: VIII:30)

to the Father, as touching His Godhead: and inferior to the Father, as touching His Manhood," for the created human nature began in time; there is a moment of His conception, and thus a beginning to His incarnation. In the same creed, the Church also confesses, the Christ to be "One; not by conversion of the Godhead into flesh: but by taking the Manhood into God"—there has been no diminution of the Godhead, but the two natures in Christ participate in the essential eternality of the Holy Trinity by the communication of attributes. Thus, the human nature is, of itself, immortal, because the Son of God is coeternal with the Father and the Holy Spirit, the human nature is made a partaker of this eternality because of the communication of attributes— just as the human nature is omnipresent and omnipotent and omniscient because of the union of the two natures in Christ.

Because in the Incarnation, the union of the divine and human natures occurs "not by conversion of the Godhead into flesh; but by taking the Manhood into God," we may better understand the gift which is ours by grace through faith in Christ, when it is promised that "the righteous" go "into eternal life."[6] (Mat. 25:46 NKJV) That which is attributed to the Lord (e.g. Rom. 16:26) is credited as the gift of God to those who are partakers of salvation in Christ: "For the wages of sin is death, but the gift of God is eternal life in Christ Jesus our Lord." (Rom. 6:23 NKJV) St. Paul teaches that "… as we have borne the image of the man of dust, we shall also bear the image of the heavenly Man. Now this I say, brethren, that flesh and blood cannot inherit the kingdom of God; nor does corruption inherit incorruption. … For this corruptible has put on incorruption, and this mortal has put on immortality, then shall be brought to pass the saying that is written: 'Death is swallowed up in victory.'" (1 Cor. 15:49–50, 53) Although St. Paul declares that the King of kings and Lord of lords "alone has immortality" (1 Tim. 6:16), still the

---

6   "εις ζωην αιωνιον"

immortality of the Christ is given to each Christian by virtue of baptism in the resurrection. That "immortality" (αθανασια) and eternal life (ζωην αιωνιον) are both referred to the Lord and to the Christian teaches the Christian bow to the Word of God, and put aside such speculations as to the manner in which the Lord will thus bestow such blessings upon man; as St. John wrote: "Beloved, now we are children of God; and it has not yet been revealed what we shall be, but we know that when He is revealed, we shall be like Him, for we shall see Him as He is." (1 John 3:2 NKJV)

For the redeemed, the moment which they await is the Last Day—the *eschaton* in which the Christ returns in glory. Jesus refers to the Last Day as the day of the resurrection: "And this is the will of Him who sent Me, that everyone who sees the Son and believes in Him may have everlasting life; and I will raise him up at the last day." (John 6:40 NKJV)[7] The reference to that day being the "last" at the very least implies a fundamental change in the perception of time following the return of the Christ—a point to which we shall return shortly.

For now, mankind lives out his history in the interim between Creation and the Last Day. Andrea Nightingale describes such an existence in history in Augustinian terms as a life lived in tension between *psychic time* and *earthly time*:

> In my analysis of Augustine, I focus on two temporalities that govern human embodiment. First, I examine his discussion of inner time-consciousness in *Confessions* II, which focuses on the psyche: I call this *psychic time*. As Augustine argues, the mind is always "distended" ("stretched") into the past and the future through memory and expectation. The very word *distention* denotes something "swelling outward" from a central point. For

---

7   See also John 6:44, 6:54, 11:24, 12:48.

Augustine, the human mind distends outward from the present moment into the past and the future. It therefore has no grasp on the present. Ontologically and psychologically, it always has memory and expectation and is thus distended into different temporal periods. ...

In addition to his theory of psychic time, Augustine also conceived of a temporality that features the birth, aging, and death of all living organisms in the natural world. I call this *earthly time*. Augustine offers detailed discussions of the deterioration and death of the human body as time passes in the earthly world. ... In Augustine's theory, humans have bodies that are subject to earthly time and minds that distend in psychic time.[8]

Therefore, fallen man exists in a state of tension. Man is naturally a historian, living with the memory of his own past, and seeking to relate his own history to the broader history of man. The enduring questions "*Who* am I?," "*Where* am I?," and "*When* am I?"—cannot be answered meaningfully without reference to one's context. Living in psychic time perpetually takes man outside of himself. But earthly time is constantly rooting man in the present, obsessed with immediate concerns related to his mortality. It is in such earthly time that Jesus teaches His Church to pray, "Give us this day our daily bread," (Mat. 6:11) but He also teaches her:

"Therefore do not worry, saying, 'What shall we eat?' or 'What shall we drink?' or 'What shall we wear?' For after all these things the Gentiles seek. For your heavenly Father knows that you need all these things. But seek first the kingdom of God and His righteousness, and all these things shall be added to you. Therefore do not worry about tomorrow, for tomorrow will worry about

8   Andrea Nightingale, *Once Out of Nature—Augustine on Time and the Body*, (Chicago and London: The University of Chicago Press, 2011) p. 7–9.

its own things. Sufficient for the day is its own trouble." (Mat. 6:31–34)

Living in psychic time, the temptation to project earthly needs forward in time tempts man to sin. Thus we learn from one of the Lord's parables that the rich man unwisely sought to establish his temporal security at great spiritual harm:

> "The ground of a certain rich man yielded plentifully. And he thought within himself, saying, 'What shall I do, since I have no room to store my crops?' So he said, 'I will do this: I will pull down my barns and build greater, and there I will store all my crops and my goods. And I will say to my soul, "Soul, you have many goods laid up for many years; take your ease; eat, drink, and be merry."' But God said to him, 'Fool! This night your soul will be required of you; then whose will those things be which you have provided?' So is he who lays up treasure for himself, and is not rich toward God." (Luke 12:16–21)

Man is now tempted to idolize the past, or to despise the fathers, or he is tempted to covetousness and an idolatry of those things which are perceived to be needful in the future. Being subject to earthly time, and conscious of his decay and approaching death, man born of Adam wanders deeper into sin. And history, that good gift of knowing the past times which the Lord granted unto men, can be one more gift so corrupted by the sin of man. In Nightingale's words:

> Augustine offers a theological as well as a philosophical analysis of temporality. In his view, the human experience of time is not a value-neutral fact of life. Being temporalized is a punishment for original sin: Adam and Eve "fell" into mortal bodies and distended minds. In the Fall, they lost both self-presence and divine presence. Since the body changes all the time and the mind

stretches away from the present moment, human beings cannot experience the physics or the metaphysics of presence. Augustine laments over this condition: "I have been scattered in times [*in tempora dissilui*] whose order I do not understand. My thoughts—the very inmost bowels of my soul—are torn in pieces in tumultuous vicissitudes, until that day when, purged and made liquid by the fire of Your love, I will flow into You." Here, he refers to the scattered and tearing apart of the unified edenic psyche that once enjoyed a (near) timeless presence. The human mind is "scattered in times," pulled into a multitude of memories and expectations and thus denied self-presence.[9]

And Nightingale notes that, for Augustine, even in the anticipated eternal life, man will still retain a sense of the past, if no longer an anticipation of the future, for the knowledge of his redemption will keep him ever mindful of the redemption which he has received in Christ Jesus.[10] Thus man will remain a historian, for whom the sacred and secular history have become one. The events of life will be seen from the standpoint of eternity; the moments which may have seemed mundane will at last be beheld in their true context. Man will want, will lack, nothing— and thus may exist outside of anticipation of the future. But the past will remain.

---

9   Nighingale, p. 57.
10   ibid., p. 53.

CHAPTER 7.
AXIAL AGES, THE POWER OF MYTH
AND THE END OF AN AGE.

he emergence in recent years of the notion of mankind having entered a "post-modern" age raises, as we have noted previously, fundamental questions about the nature of such periodization within human history. Acknowledging that the emergence of the concept of a "modern" age draws upon Joachimite notions of the divisions of human history into discrete ages, in which the "modern"—or third—age is "post-Christian," the further development of a "post-modern" age is even more conceptually challenging. If modernity was to be the age of mankind's maturation—the final age—what does it mean to have moved *beyond* that age?

Our purpose has been, and remains, to understand man in relationship to sacred history, secular history, and mythology. If mankind has arrived at a "post-modern" age—or a time in which such an ideological construct holds a significant number of intellectuals under its sway—we need to understand how that construct shapes one's understanding of history and mythology. In the final chapter of his *magnum opus*, *The Myth of the Eternal Return*—a work first published in 1954—Mircea Eliade wrestled with the implications of this problem:

> In short, it would be necessary to confront "historical man" (modern man), who consciously and voluntarily creates history, with the man of traditional civilizations, who, as we have seen, had a negative attitude toward history. ... [T]he man of the traditional civilizations accorded the historical event no value in itself; in other words, he did not regard it as a specific category of his

own mode of existence. … We are nevertheless forced to touch upon the problem of man as consciously and voluntarily historical, because the modern world is, at the present moment, not entirely converted to historicism; we are even witnessing a conflict between two views: the archaic conception, which we should designate as archetypical and anhistorical; and the modern, post-Hegelian conception, which seeks to be historical.[1]

In short, for men of what Eliade calls "traditional civilizations," a mythological understanding of the world was the only meaningful frame of reference. "Historical" events fundamentally lacked enduring relevance; in fact, the meaning of life was found only in myth. Now, Eliade's "modern man" imagines that he has no place for mythology—and is likely inclined to reduce all sacred history to mythology, which he sees as a quaint fiction. Modern man believes that history is a field of scientific study of human events in which there is no place for transcendent meaning—let alone that it should be placed in service of a more enduring sacred history. For the "traditional" man, history is fundamentally cyclical, with all events repeating endlessly; for the "modern" man time is linear, but lacking in meaning, and while post-modern men may endeavor to "find" or "create" meaning, they are not drawing on something greater than man, but trying to simply import a supposedly-ennobling meaning into the mundane facts of history. The Christian verity comprehends in God's Word the relationship between those aspects of history which are cyclical (as taught in Ecclesiastes), and those aspects of history—especially salvation history—which are most certainly linear, and which will never be repeated. The Christian knows the relationship between sacred history, secular history, and mythology in a way which neither the "traditional" pagans nor the "modern"

1   Mircea Eliade, *The Myth of the Eternal Return,* trans. by Willard R. Trask, (Princeton and Oxford: Princeton University Press, 2005) p. 141.

post-Christians can comprehend.

For Eliade, the great challenge of the end of modernity—the "post-modern" era, if you will—is the "terror of history":

> The terror of history becomes more and more intolerable from the viewpoints afforded by the various historicistic philosophies. ... Heidegger had gone to the trouble of showing that the historicity of human existence forbids all hope of transcending time and history.
>
> For our purpose, only one question concerns us: How can the "terror of history" be tolerated from the viewpoint of historicism? Justification of a historical event by the simple fact that it is a historical event, in other words, by the simple fact that it "happened that way," will not go far toward freeing humanity from the terror that the event inspires. Be it understood that we are not here concerned with the problem of evil, which, from whatever angle it be viewed, remains a philosophical and religious problem; we are concerned with the problem of history as history; of the "evil" that is bound up not with man's condition but with his behavior toward others. ... And in our day, when historical pressure no longer allows any escape, how can man tolerate the catastrophes and horrors of history—from collective deportations and massacres to atomic bombings—if beyond them he can glimpse no sign, no transhistorical meaning; if they are only the blind play of economic, social, or political forces, or, even worse, only the result of the "liberties" that a minority takes and exercises directly on the stage of universal history?[2]

Robbed of mythology and sacred history in the Promethean rebellion against the divine order of creation, man has created an

---

2   ibid., p. 149–151.

anti-mythology of doctrines which shall be explored further in the second portion of this book as the "seven deadly values" of our culture.

Lacking the received wisdom of sacred history, men now consciously or unconsciously endeavor to create their own "backstory" for history. The advocates of Progressive historicisms (e.g. Marxism) thought that they had discovered a meaning to history which unified the whole of the story, without ever transcending man. But when these modernist idolatries of ideology—the great explanatory 'systems' such as Darwinism or Marxism, for example—proved themselves lacking in explanatory power when it came to mankind's fundamental need for a truly transcendent meaning, "post-modern" man began to flail around looking for a solution to the "terror of history" which had resulted from the anti-Christian agenda of modernism. Thus, as John Carroll declares in his book, *The Wreck of Western Culture*, the failure of modernism is the death of Renaissance humanism taken to its end:

> The twentieth century turned into a parody of humanism. While the confident *I* of the Renaissance had been *me*–centered, it had been geared to a higher end. It strived to use reason and free will to create the human world anew—Michelangelo his *Moses*, Newton his laws of motion, Kant his ethics, and the cumulative development of the modern metropolis. After Nietzsche, this collapsed into *me* the last man, in a rootless mania for consumption, stimulated by the consolations of regular therapy, massaging the insecure self, telling its diminutive being how great it is. ...
>
> Not only is the human individual not creature nor creator in one. He is not, as Darwin would have us believe, a highly evolved and supercharged fish. ...
>
> Under the humanist constellation, Death rules.

But this metaphysics of man, a fish endowed with consciousness, sets him too low. It is the dregs of humanism. Consciousness is mind, it is intellect, it is reason—it is Descartes. It is not the fragment of divinity, the soul. The soul creates the guilt that ruins Brutus, countermanding his freedom to kill Caesar. In fact, it makes him human, although Shakespeare may not realize this, so blurred has his consciousness become by the cruse of humanism.[3]

The sacred history which Joachim of Fiore used to knock aside that of the Christian verity led to the creation of new mythologies, which were not understood for what they were. And the end of his labors has been the systemic despair which is called the 'end of history.'

The world has been emptied of meaning by the hydra-headed ideologies of the modern age. In fact, the deadly values of our culture have left men unable to account for their *need* for meaning in their lives. The end of humanism—Nietzschean nihilism—imagined it would make man into a god and has instead reduced him to nothing. In Eliade's words:

It is by no means mere fortuitious coincidence that, in this philosophy, despair, the *amor fati*, and pessimism are elevated to the rank of heroic virtues and instruments of cognition. ...

... There is also reason to foresee that, as the terror of history grows worse, as existence becomes more and more precarious because of history, the positions of historicism will increasingly lose in prestige. And, at a moment when history could do what neither the cosmos, nor man, nor chance have yet succeeded in doing—that is, wipe out the human race in its entirety—it may be

3   John Carroll, *The Wreck of Western Culture—Humanism Revisited,* (Wilmington, Delaware: ISI Books, 2010) p. 257–258.

that we are witnessing a desperate attempt to prohibit the "events of history" through a reintegration of human societies within the horizon (artificial, because decreed) of archetypes and their repetition.[4]

What Eliade beheld nearly six decades ago is essentially what has transpired in the "post-modern" mentality. The historicisms of Marxism and Darwinism and Progress are petty idolatries that have failed to give meaning to life and human history, and the efforts of infuse mythological transcendence into such constructs has remained the lifeless clay of a failed homunculus. Seeking to generate history—sanitizing it of any truly sacred element, expunging every act of Providence, and mocking all transcendence—historical man is has placed himself in a butterfly jar, ready to be mounted and cataloged, and to gather dust. As Eliade observes:

> It is becoming more and more doubtful, he might say, if modern man can make history. On the contrary, the more modern he becomes—that is, without defenses against the terror of history—the less chance he has of himself making history. For history either makes itself (as the result of the seed sown by acts that occurred in the past, several centuries or even several millennia ago...) or it tends to be made by an increasingly smaller number of men who not only prohibit the mass of their contemporaries from directly or indirectly intervening in the history they are making (or which the small group is making), but in addition have at their disposal means sufficient to force each individual to endure, for his own part, the consequences of this history, that is, to live immediately and continuously in dread of history.[5]

---

4   Eliade, p. 152–153.
5   ibid., p. 156.

Modernism having reduced the production of history into an item of terror—and, in fact, a tool of coercion—the "postmodern" minds emptied the world of meaning. In fact it seems likely that absurd creeds such as that of Marxism have endured as long as they have because the need for meaning remains, even as the transcendent sources have been systematically denied. Thus, it has become common to speak of a new "Axial Age."

The concept of an "Axial Age" was first stated in such terms in the writings of Karl Jaspers in the mid-twentieth century. As noted previously in his contentions with Bultmann, Jaspers recognized man's enduring need for myth. Jaspers maintained that there was a widespread phenomenon of spiritual development during the "axis-time of history," and Eric Voegelin gave voice to a somewhat similar concept with his concept of an "ecumenic age".[6] Karen Armstrong summarizes the concept of the "Axial Age' as follows:

> By the eighth century BCE, the malaise was becoming more widespread, and in four distinct regions an impressive array of prophets and sages began to seek a new solution. … It marks the beginning of religion as we know it. People became conscious of their nature, their situation and their limitations with unprecedented clarity. New religious and philosophical systems emerged: Confucianism and Taoism in China, Buddhism and Hinduism in India; monotheism in the Middle East and Greek rationalism in Europe. These Axial traditions were associated with such men as the great Hebrew prophets of the eighth, seventh and sixth centuries; with the sages of the *Upanishads*, and the Buddha (c. 563–483) in India; with Confucius (551–479) and the author of the *Dao De Jing*

---

6   see, for example, Eric Voegelin's essay, "Configurations of History," in his *Published Essays, 1966–1985*, (Baton Rouge and London: Louisiana State University Press, 1990) p. 98ff.

in China; and with the fifth-century tragedians, Socrates (469–399), Plato (c. 427–347) and Aristotle (c. 384–322 BCE) in Greece.[7]

For proponents of the concept of an Axial Age, the recognition of the existence of such an age is of critical importance for understanding the emergence of the various major religious groups in the world today:

> It is to date the most ambitious effort to understand one of the most important transformations in world history. This is the appearance, with relative simultaneity in high cultures of Eurasia in the centuries around the middle of the first millennium BCE, of new forms of reflexivity and historical consciousness. A profound ontological change marked, or so the proponents of the idea of the Axial Age argue, a new chapter in the history of humanity characterized by a new sense of the potentials for humans to change the world, to act and to reach beyond the limits of the immediately given and taken for granted.[8]

Adherents of the notion of such an Axial Age maintain that core concept that these developments occurred throughout these broad historical areas at virtually the same time, and usually reject the notion of a diffusion of ideas between cultures. Thus, the notion of an Axial Age is built upon the foundational belief in a *late* origin of Scripture; the literature is replete with references to Deutero-Isaiah as the basis for an Axial Age conception of God among the Hebrews. For example, if one maintains the belief that the 'historical Moses' wrote the Pentateuch and that he lived in the 13th century B.C., clearly the heart of

7   Karen Armstrong, *A Short History of Myth,* (Edinburgh and New York: Canongate, 2005) p. 79–80.
8   Bjorn Wittrock, "The Meaning of the Axial Age," in *Axial Civilizations and World History,* ed. by Johann P. Arnason, S. N. Eisenstadt and Björn Wittrock, (Leiden and Boston: Brill, 2005) p. 51.

the Old Testament would have been written centuries before the supposed-Axial Age—giving primacy to the Hebrew Scriptures over the mythologies and philosophies of the Gentile nations. Even more dangerous to the inherent philosophical/historical egalitarianism of the Axial Age theory, such a Hebrew primacy could lead to the view that the Axial Age occurred among the Gentile nations at a time when the writings of Moses and many of the Prophets could have been distributed throughout the Gentile world during, and following, the years of the Babylonian Captivity in the sixth century B.C.

It is not uncommon for adherents of the theory of an Axial Age to believe that another such age is coming, or is already here. Armstrong's assessment certain views later modernism as establishing a new mythology, just as she believes the Axial Age civilizations had done:

> Instead of looking back to the past and conserving what had been achieved, as had been the habit of the premodern civilisations, Western people began to look forward. ... The new hero of Western society was henceforth the scientist or the inventor, who was venturing into uncharted realms for the sake of his society. He would often have to overthrow old sanctities—just as the Axial sages had done.[9]

But she also recognizes that the spirit of modernism has not resulted in a healthy mythological foundation: "As early as the sixteenth century, we see more evidence of a numbing despair, a creeping mental paralysis, and a sense of impotence and rage as the old mythical way of thought crumbled and nothing new appeared to take its place. We are seeing a similar anomie today in developed countries that are still in the earlier stages of modernisation."[10]

---

9   Armstrong, p. 120–121.
10   ibid., p. 122.

Alienated from what C. S. Lewis referred to as the "myth that is fact"—the Christian verity—post-moderns attempt to build a new mythology. And, although there is little in her analysis which is supportive of orthodox Christianity, Amstrong notes that, "We are myth-making creatures and, during the twentieth century, we saw some very destructive modern myths, which have ended in massacre and genocide. These myths have failed because they do not meet the criteria of the Axial Age."[11] This should not be surprising, for the modern age has been a rebellion against Christendom, and it has laid waste the ancient survivals of paganism in the process. What cannot be suffered by the modern is the survival of the pre-modern, and thus all traditional societies are assaulted, beginning (and ending) with the remnants of Christendom. The idolatries of the hour—the ideologies of our modern age—despise the Christian verity, and seek a doctrine of Babel to put in its place. It falls to the poet to speak the truth:

> Why should men love the Church? Why should they love her laws?
> She tells them of Life and Death, and of all that they would forget.
> She is tender where they would be hard, and hard where they like to be soft.
> She tells them of Evil and Sin, and other unpleasant facts.
> They constantly try to escape
> From the darkness outside and within
> By dreaming of systems so perfect that no one will need to be good.
> But the man that is will shadow
> The man that pretends to be.[12]

---

11   ibid., p. 136.
12   T. S. Eliot, "Choruses from 'The Rock,'" in *The Complete Poems and Plays, 1909–1950,* (New York: Harcourt Brace & Company, 1971) p. 106.

Modern man has become disconnected from time and place by seeking to sever time from all sacred significance, and by endeavoring to empty the world of myth. Endeavoring to rid the world of the inherited myths, modern man has blindly become a builder of systems and patterns of myth the spirit of which is as fervent as any Gnostic of old, with the arcana of his cosmologies and evolutionary systems every bit as complicated—and absurd—as those produced by the Valentinian Gnostics in the second century A.D. Such modern men are the fitting fulfillment of G. K. Chesterton's anticipations in *The Ballad of the White Horse*—written just over a century ago—when he concluded his epic poem with his observation regarding the nature the pagans of these latter days:

"They shall come mild as monkish clerks,
With many a scroll and pen;
And backward shall ye turn and gaze,
Desiring one of Alfred's days,
When pagans still were men. ...
"What though they come with scroll and pen,
And grave as a shaven clerk,
By this sign you shall know them,
That they ruin and make dark;

"By all men bond to Nothing,
Being slaves without a lord,
By one blind idiot world obeyed,
Too blind to be abhorred;

"By terror and the cruel tales
Of curse in bone and kin,
By weird and weakness winning,
Accursed from the beginning,
By detail of the sinning,
And denial of the sin;

"By thought a crawling ruin,
By life a leaping mire,
By a broken heart in the breast of the world,
And the end of the world's desire;

"By God and man dishonoured,
By death and life made vain,
Know ye the old barbarian,
The barbarian come again—

"When is great talk of trend and tide,
And wisdom and destiny,
Hail that undying heathen
That is sadder than the sea."

The new heathens truly are sadder than the sea, brought low by the despair at the very heart of their nihilistic doctrine. Slaves without a lord—rejecting submission to the saving Truth—they are subject to lies of their own devising, including the wretched half-truth of secularized history. The cynical sneer which looks to the generations of men, and recasts all that has been as but a struggle over capital, or progress, or some other doctrine of men, breaks asunder that which has held together the West across two millennia. Whatever truth was possessed by the various systems of the 'Axial Age' came from the light of reason, or by such dim communications from the oracles of God (Rom. 3:2) as might be made known among the nations during the scattering of the Remnant of God's people among the Gentile nations.

The rootless doctrines of men have wormed deep within the bosom of the visible Church, for many Christians do not know how to number their days (Psa. 90:12), and remain foolish in many regards pertaining to the course of this world. The "myth that is fact" comes to men in Word and Sacrament; as even secular scholars recognize that the myths are only rightly encountered 'liturgically,'[13] so the Christian believes that to receive Christ as He comes to His Church through Word and Sacrament is the very heart of his life in this vale of tears. The 'cycle' of the Christian Church Year is the ritual life of the Christian as he moves through the allotted days of his life, living in anticipation of the return of the Christ on the Last Day, and living in that cycle of seasons and days, he has hope in the midst of the vanity of the passing seasons and generations of men.

We have seen that the question, *"When* am I—*what time* is it?,"* is of vital significance to the Christian walk. We reject the Joachimite phantasy of a third age; we know that our "time" is that period of the senescence of the world; thus our Augsburg Confession acknowledges that "man's nature is gradually growing weaker" (AC XXIII:14) as the last age of this fallen world draws steadily to its close. The darkness of man's vain chasing after novel doctrines is but an echo of the darkness which nearly consumed all in the days leading up to the flood. (2 Pet. 3:3–9)

The disordering of priorities is found among those who pursue their vocations as if they were primary. Jesus spoke of those who mistakenly placed vocation in a higher place than the faith as those who rejected the summons to the wedding feast:

> But they all with one *accord* began to make excuses. The first said to him, 'I have bought a piece of ground, and I must go and see it. I ask you to have me excused.' And another said, 'I have bought five yoke of oxen, and I am going to test them. I ask you to have me excused.' Still another said, 'I have married a wife, and therefore I can-

---

13   Thus Armstrong: "Mythology is usually inseparable from ritual. Many myths make no sense outside a liturgical drama that brings them to life, and are incomprehensible in a profane setting." (p. 3)

not come.' So that servant came and reported these things to his master. Then the master of the house, being angry, said to his servant, 'Go out quickly into the streets and lanes of the city, and bring in here *the* poor and *the* maimed and *the* lame and *the* blind.' (Luke 14:18–21 NKJV)

When our lives are disordered, we have the wrong answers—or, at least, incomplete answers—to the questions which really matter: *"Who* am I?," *"Where* am I?," *"What time* is it?" If we truly believe the answer to the first question is defined by our baptism into Christ, the rest of our priorities begin to be conformed to that new life which is in us in Christ Jesus. Of course, living lives which still carry the corrupting influence of original sin guarantees that we will remain torn between the vanities of this fallen world, and the living hope which we have in Christ Jesus. But our participation in the life of Christ's Church—being immersed in the cycle of the Church Year, partaking regularly of the Word and Sacrament—transforms us. Where the Christian walk is defined by the flow of Advent into Christmas, into Epiphany, and thus to end with contemplation of the Last Day provides a very different frame of reference than when one's life is beholden solely to the flow of personal events, national holidays and the saccharin sweetness of 'days' defined by greeting card companies. Thus defined by life in Christ, in harmony with the walk of our brethren contending for the faith, our perception of the world is reshaped through the light of the Word. We begin, intermittently, to know the contentment of a harmony of lives shaped by sacred history, living in these last days of the world, as the baptized children of God.

The Seven Deadly Values of Contemporary Culture: The Shape of the Enemy's Weapons against Our People Today

INTRODUCTION.

"When an unclean spirit goes out of a man, he goes through dry places, seeking rest, and finds none. Then he says, 'I will return to my house from which I came.' And when he comes, he finds it empty, swept, and put in order. Then he goes and takes with him seven other spirits more wicked than himself, and they enter and dwell there; and the last state of that man is worse than the first. So shall it also be with this wicked generation."
(St. Matthew 12:43–45 NKJV)

In preparation for the Fifth Annual Conference of The Augustana Ministerium[1], the author was invited to speak on the topic, "The Seven Deadly Values of Contemporary Culture: The Shape of the Enemy's Weapons against Our People Today."[2] In the aftermath of that presentation, he was approached by one of the attending pastors, who encouraged him to expand the work so that its themes could be explored at greater length. This text is the result of such protracted ruminations, which (one may hope) shed further light upon the themes previously set forth in that essay.

There were clearly several ideas at work behind such an evaluation of our culture as was first conceived in the essay for The Augustana Ministerium, and now more fully-formed in this current work. First, the entirety of the conference was devoted to engaging the struggles which confront the Church in the modern (or, more accurately, post-modern) age; in such a discussion several underlying presuppositions are present: One must oper-

---

1 The conference was hosted by Charity Lutheran Church in Burleson, Texas.
2 This essay was included in the volume, *Lives in the Balance* (The Augustana Ministerium, 2011), edited by Dr. Steven Hein.

114

ate under the assumption that there is continuity in the so-called 'human condition'—a teaching of Holy Scripture which also firmly upholds that the unchanging apostolic doctrine speaks to this age as surely as it has in past generations of man. However, our examination of our current circumstances is also predicated on the understanding that there is also something in the character of this time which merits reflection.

Holy Scripture certainly testifies to the continuity of human nature—and that continuity is not very flattering to the vanity of men. After the Lord preserved believing Noah and his family through the waters of the Flood, the Lord "said in His heart, 'I will never again curse the ground for man's sake, although the imagination of man's heart is evil from his youth; nor will I again destroy every living thing as I have done.'" (Gen. 8:21 NKJV³) The Lord knew that the human heart would not fundamentally change itself as long as this sinful world endures, and that a defining characteristic of the heart of man is an evil imagination "from his youth." This assessment is reiterated in the New Testament, when St. Paul wrote to the Church in Rome that "the carnal mind is enmity against God; for it is not subject to the law of God, nor indeed can be." (Rom. 8:7) Thus, as "the Preacher, the son of David" (Ecc. 1:1) teaches, anyone looking for an innovation in the ways of man will be disappointed:

That which has been is what will be,
that which is done is what will be done,
and there is nothing new under the sun.
Is there anything of which it may be said, "See, this is new"?
It has already been in ancient times before us.
There is no remembrance of former things,
Nor will there be any remembrance of things that are to come
By those who will come after. (Ecc. 1:9–11)

---

3   All Scriptural citations are from The New King James Version.

Man is always seeking after innovation, but all that he finds is more of the same, with part of that constant repetition being his own ignorance of those things which have transpired in the past.

Still within this repeating pattern of human activity, there is still an alternation of appointed "times". Thus we read in Ecclesiastes 3: "To everything there is a season, a time for every purpose under heaven". (v. 1) Man rarely faces the alternation of "times" with equanimity; "a time to love, and a time to hate; a time of war, and a time of peace" (v. 8)—to cite just a few of the appointed "times"—are hardly received alike with a spirit of joy by the masses of men. But the Word teaches us that different ages will be marked by the spirit of the times—and this is no mere *Zeitgeist* operating apart from divine Providence; instead, the will of the Triune God is shaping and directing all things in heaven and earth according to His will.

Thus, when speaking of "contemporary culture" it is asserted that there remain distinctive particularities to the time in which we live which differentiate it as a meaningfully discernible *age*. Although such particularities account only for limited aspects of our *age*, nevertheless they are remarkable enough in their influence and their pervasive character to permit a differentiation of this time from that which came before and which will (if the Lord so wills it) mark it as distinct from the *age* which shall follow our own.

Second, in the process of undertaking an evaluation of the present age, the enumeration of seven 'deadly values' calls to mind centuries of Christian thought in the realm of moral theology. There is a readily apparent allusion to the designation of seven deadly sins, which are generally numbered as pride, avarice, envy, wrath, lust, gluttony and sloth. Against these deadly sins stand the seven virtues, which include the four cardinal virtues of prudence, justice, temperance and courage, and the theological virtues of faith, love and hope, or alternately, the seven heavenly virtues of humility, charity, kindness, patience, chastity, temperance, and diligence.

A crucial distinction between the "deadly values" and the "deadly sins" is that while the classification of such sins is of an unchanging character as long as this world endures, the "deadly values" are, to a certain extent, peculiar to this age. As this study progresses, one may see that such 'values' are related to the 'sins'—and thus the 'deadly values' share, to an extent, something of the longevity of the enumerated 'sins.' However, they are not identical, and as the fatal flaws of each age and of each civilization thus vary, so, too, does the manner in which temptations take form.

As we consider the seven deadly values of contemporary culture we are actually addressing values which spring from the font of all sin, located in the "horrible, dreadful hereditary malady" (FC SD I.5[4]) which has come down through the generations from the Fall. The holy apostle instructs the Church: "No temptation has overtaken you except such as is common to man; but God is faithful, who will not allow you to be tempted beyond what you are able, but with the temptation will also make the way of escape, that you may be able to bear it." (1 Cor. 10:13) The deadly 'values' which threaten the children of the Lord in this generation are such as have threatened in the past, and although various false doctrines wax and wane according to the generations of man, those which we confront at present are but the continuation of such as have troubled our civilization across the course of recent centuries.

---

4   All Confessional citations are from the H.E. Jacobs edition of *The Book of Concord.*

Sin and Self-Definition

In our discussion of the sins and temptations—the 'deadly values'—of this age, we must 'begin at the beginning.' That is to say, we must consider again and anew man's fall into sin in Paradise.

In Genesis 3, we read that the temptation which confronted Eve was threefold: "So when the woman saw [1] that the tree was good for food, [2] that it was pleasant to the eyes, and [3] a tree desirable to make one wise, she took of its fruit and ate." (v. 6) The immoderate desire for that which one deems necessary for the sustenance of the flesh, the appeal of the senses, and the pursuit of forbidden knowledge have been the ruin of man from the Garden to this day, but this threefold temptation also expresses a deeper revolt on the part of the woman: She elected to perceive the world not as the Lord had given instruction, but according to her own will. When Holy Scripture sets forth the three elements of Eve's self-justification for her sin, that self-justification is expressed in terms of self-will. This is to say that she perceived the tree of the knowledge of good and evil not as the Word of the Lord had proclaimed it to be, but according to her own criteria, apart from that Word. Her sin required such self-centered perception—it required an assessment of the tree and its fruit according to her own criteria, and not that criterion which had been given by the Lord. Her sin required the assertion of the individual will apart from, and outside of, the Word of the Lord.

That Eve's sin was rooted in self-definition is of profound importance because the identity of man within creation is something which is divinely-given, since man was made in the image of God (Gen. 1:27). The Word which the Lord speaks (Gen. 1:28–29[5]) and divine action assigning to man his place

5   "Then God blessed them, and God said to them, 'Be fruitful and

and role (Gen. 2:15[6]) thus defined man. The Lord had only to speak the Word once to define man, just as He spoke but once to the various forms of life and made all of creation to be fruitful and multiply. Eve's sin is that she speaks a new 'word' to herself which requires redefining her identity self-referentially—and such a manner of identification is reserved to God alone (Exo. 3:13–14[7]; John 8:58[8]).

Our "Hereditary Malady"

When our first parents rebelled against the Word of God, the whole of humanity was in Adam and Eve, and thus fell in their transgression. As noted previously, the Formula of Concord speaks of original sin as "the horrible, dreadful hereditary malady whereby the entire nature is corrupted" (FC SD I.5). Holy Scripture speaks clearly of this inherited sin as something which is present in man from the moment of his conception; thus we read the words of David in Psalm 51, "Behold, I was brought forth in iniquity, and in sin my mother conceived me." (v. 5) The death which came to Adam and Eve on account of their transgression has passed down through the generations of mankind because all of the human race was in Adam. St. Paul's language in his letter to the Romans clearly communicates the

---

multiply; fill the earth and subdue it; have dominion over the fish of the sea, over the birds of the air, and over every living thing that moves on the earth.' And God said, 'See, I have given you every herb that yields seed which is on the face of all the earth, and every tree whose fruit yields seed; and it you it shall be for food."

6   "Then the LORD God took the man and put him in the garden of Eden to tend and keep it."

7   Then Moses said to God, "Indeed, *when* I come to the children of Israel and say to them, 'The God of your fathers has sent me to you,' and they say to me, 'What *is* His name?' what shall I say to them?" And God said to Moses, "I AM WHO I AM." And He said, "Thus you shall say to the children of Israel, 'I AM has sent me to you.'"

8   Jesus said to them, "Most assuredly, I say to you, before Abraham was, I AM."

reality that Adam's sin was the means by which, and the moment in which, all of mankind fell. Thus he wrote in Romans 5:12, "Therefore, just as through one man sin entered into the world, and death through sin, and thus death spread to all men, because all sinned". That death *entered* and *spread*, and that all men *sinned* is clearly proclaimed in the Greek to be a one-time, completed action.[9] In other words, the universality of sin and death for the whole human race was complete in the first generation; no matter how many thousands of years separate the birth of any individual from the time of Adam and Eve, the sin and death into which that individual would one day be conceived and then born are already complete in Adam and Eve.

Thus, when the first generation was born to Adam, we are told in Holy Scripture, "And Adam lived one hundred and thirty years, and begot a son in his own likeness, after his image, and named him Seth" (Gen. 5:3)—paralleling the manner in which the Word speaks of man being created in the image and likeness of God. Adam, broken and twisted by sin, begot the next generation in conformity to the new image of man. This inherited image is dominated by the heritable malady; though the nature of man remains a good creation of the Triune God, still the damage wrought by the sin of Adam is far greater than human reason can grasp; as our fathers in the faith taught in the Formula of Concord: "...this hereditary evil is so great and horrible that it can be covered and forgiven before God only for Christ's sake, and in the baptized and believing. Human nature also, which is deranged and corrupted thereby, must and can be healed only by the regeneration and renewal of the Holy Ghost, which, nevertheless, is only begun in this life, but will at length be fully completed in the life to come." (FC SD I:14)

---

9   ...δι᾽ ἑνὸς ἀνθρώπου ἡ ἁμαρτία εἰς τὸν κόσμον εἰσῆλθεν καὶ διὰ τῆς ἁμαρτίας ὁ θάνατος διῆλθεν, ἐφ᾽ ᾧ πάντες ἥμαρτον.

The truth of our predicament may be summed up by a variation on the old idiom, "They broke the mold after they made him." Rather than sticking with such an egocentric expression of individualism, a better way to present our current state would be to say, "They—Adam and Eve—broke the mold, and then made us." Or, in the more dignified language of Lazarus Spengler (1479–1534):

> All mankind fell in Adam's fall,
> One common sin infects us all;
> From sire to son the bane descends,
> And over all the curse impends. (TLH 369:1)

Adam and Eve made an idol of their own will, and all the children of Adam are by nature self-willed to this day. The inherited rebellion against the Triune God is part of the legacy of sin in the Garden of Eden, and every one of their fallen children continues to idolize his own will to this day.

Idolatry: The Center of Man's Rebellion

All sin is fundamentally centered in idolatry; as Luther observed in the Large Catechism regarding the First Commandment, "it is of chief importance because, as before said, where the heart is rightly disposed toward God and this commandment is observed, all the rest follow." (LC I:48) That is, if man kept the First Commandment and worshiped only the one true God, man would keep the whole of the decalogue. Because the heart of man is *not* rightly disposed toward the Holy Trinity and the commandment is *not* observed, the entirety of fallen man's thoughts, words and deeds are marked by sin—even in matters which are not, of themselves, inherently sinful. This is because fallen man has the wrong god, and is thus born into idolatry.

The sin of Eve—with her attempted self-definition— necessarily involved idolatry, because she trusted in something which is not the one true God. As Luther rightly teaches in the Large Catechism:

> What is it to have a god? or, what is God? Answer: A god is that whereto we are to look for all good and to take refuge in all distress; so that to have a god is to trust and believe him from the whole heart; as I have often said that the confidence and faith of the heart alone make both God and an idol. If your faith and trust be right, then is your god also true. And, on the other hand, if your trust be false and wrong, then you have not the true God; for these two belong together, viz. faith and God. (LC I:2–3)

Eve trusted more in her own diabolically-inspired assessment of the forbidden fruit than she trusted the Word of the Triune God. Thus she made an idol of the devil's word and her own will. She listened to the devil's reviling accusation, and looked to establish her confidence not in the love of God and His divine Word; instead, she wanted to be well fed by something which the Lord had declared could bring nothing but death. That sums up pretty well what it means to have an idol.

What You Eat Can Say A Great Deal About What You Believe

"So when the woman saw that the tree was good for food, that it was pleasant to the eyes, and a tree desirable to make one wise, she took of its fruit and ate. She also gave to her husband with her, and he ate." (Gen. 3:6) What Adam and Eve believed was manifest in what they ate—the Holy Trinity gave them "every herb that yields seed which is on the face of all the earth, and every tree whose fruit yields seed" (Gen. 2:29). Adam and Eve ate that which was forbidden to them to express their idolatry.

What about our age? Is there still a connection between what you eat and what you believe?

Every Lent, our secular culture receives a reminder of the connection between faith and diet when all of the 'fast food' restaurants suddenly start serving fish items on their menu. But the connection between faith and food extends far beyond the Lenten fast.

When the author was an undergraduate student at Behemoth University in our nation's capital, it meant a number of cultural adjustments. Daily life was no longer defined by the rhythm of 'small town,' 'Protestant' life; with a large Muslim—and an even larger Jewish—population on campus, the dietary regulations of other religions loomed large every time one went to the cafeteria, especially during various seasonal religious observances. *What* you ate—and *when*—told everyone around you what you believe.

As observed previously, because the heart of man is *not* rightly disposed toward God and the commandment is *not* observed, the entirety of fallen man's thoughts, words and deeds are marked by sin—even in matters which are not, of themselves, inherently sinful. Jesus declared in Matthew 15, "Do you not yet understand that whatever enters the mouth goes into the stomach and is eliminated? But those things which proceed out of the mouth come from the heart, and they defile a man." (v. 17–18) As Christians, we recognize that no foods are forbidden to us—and yet, as mankind's fall into sin was linked to eating that which had been forbidden, the pervasive character of sin's corruption is seen the manner in which men misuse food to serve idols. Thus, as we consider man's idolatry, it is worth dwelling, at least for a moment, on the freedom of the conscience and the meat sacrificed to idols.

In 1 Corinthians 10 and Romans 14, St. Paul wrote of the meat which had been sacrificed to idols, and addressed whether or not a Christian could eat such meat. Paul wrote in 1 Corinthians 10:

> Eat whatever is sold in the meat market, asking no questions for conscience' sake; for *"the earth is the LORD's, and all its fullness."* If any of those who do not believe invites you *to dinner,* and you desire to go, eat whatever is set before you, asking no question for conscience' sake. But if anyone says to you, "This was offered to idols," do not eat it for the sake of the one who told you, and for conscience' sake; for *"the earth is the LORD's, and all its fullness."* "Conscience," I say, not your own, but that of the other. For why is my liberty judged by another *man's* conscience? But if I partake with thanks, why am I evil spoken of for *the food* over which I give thanks? Therefore, whether you eat or drink, or whatever you do, do all to the glory of God. (v. 25–31)

"Shut up and eat it," is the rule of the day, unless the heathen makes a point of conscience out of eating. There's nothing wrong with the food, but there is something very wrong with the person who would imagine you share his false faith if you conform with a menu which has been scripted to serve idols.

St. Paul was certainly no Gnostic, and therefore did not believe that the meat sacrificed to idols was 'unclean' simply because of its ritual association; therefore he wrote to the Romans: "I know and am convinced by the Lord Jesus that *there is* nothing unclean of itself; but to him who considers anything to be unclean, to him *it is* unclean." (v. 14) If a Christian were caught up in a spiritual confusion regarding such meat, and thus he imagined that to eat it was to have fellowship with demons, it would be unclean to him because he *thought* that eating it would mean such eating was an expression of fellowship; for such a person, eating would be unclean—even though the meat, of itself, was an indifferent thing. Thus St. Paul concluded, "But he who doubts is condemned if he eats, because *he does* not *eat* from faith; for whatever *is* not from faith is sin." (v. 23) Thus St. Paul used the example of such eating to illustrate a much larger principle: **That which is not from faith is sin**. This means that everything that the unbeliever thinks, says or does is, *ipso facto*, sinful. Furthermore, if the weak Christian is tempted to qualms of conscience in such matters, he needs for his conscience to receive further instruction from the divine Word; in the meantime, to use the words commonly attributed to Martin Luther at Worms, "To go against conscience is neither right nor safe."

What Eve ate was an expression of rebellion against the Triune God; it was a rebellion rooted in self-definition and idolatry. What Eve ate declared that she—and all the race which came forth from her—did not love and trust in God above all things. Eve's eating of the forbidden fruit was inherently sinful; now, the Christian knows that diet is a matter of *adiaphora*, for there is no longer any food which is inherently forbidden to us—eating may become sinful, when a matter of confession becomes attached to it. The principle of *adiaphora*—and the cases when such inherently indifferent things are no longer indifferent—will be of great importance in our consideration of the 'deadly values' of this age.

The Lord Has a Job for You to do… Well, Several Jobs, Actually.

As we continue our consideration of the the Fall, we must acknowledge, then, that the first idolatry is self-centered; the serpent's words, "... and you will be like God, knowing good and evil" (Gen. 3:4) drove Eve's rebellion, and such a temptation drives all appeals to choose one's own will over the divinely-given Word. As noted previously, Eve attempted to redefine herself, and thus mankind was plunged into sin. The Lord God had defined man in His assignation of a vocation—a calling—to man before the Fall: "Be fruitful and multiply; fill the earth and subdue it; have dominion over the fish of the sea, over the birds of the air, and over every living thing that moves on the earth." (Gen. 1:28) With these words, the Lord God defined man's role over against the rest of creation.

There are divinely-given changes in the vocation of man after the Fall; man and woman are described according to their fallen condition (Gen. 3:16–19), and mankind is driven from the place which had been appointed at the first for man's steward-ship, the garden of Eden. Various aspects of the vocation of man are now marked by the wages of sin. Thus, mankind was still to "Be fruitful and multiply; fill the earth and subdue it," but now the Lord God said to the woman: "I will greatly multiply your sorrow and your conception; in pain you shall bring forth children; your desire shall be for your husband, and he shall rule over you." (3:16) And the Lord said to Adam: "Cursed is the ground for your sake; in toil you shall eat of it all the days of your life. Both thorns and thistles it shall bring forth for you, and you shall eat the herb of the field. In the sweat of your face you shall eat bread till you return to the ground, for out of it you were taken; for dust you are, and to dust you shall return." (v. 17–19) Man would still multiply and fill the earth, but his labors would now be marked by the futility of returning to the earth, and the great joy of beholding his progeny would be accompanied by pain and alienation. Thus the words of the Preacher in Ecclesiastes 1: "And I set my heart to seek and search out by wisdom concerning all that is done under heaven; this burdensome task God has given to the sons of man, by which they may be exercised. I have seen all the works that are done under the sun; and indeed, all is vanity and grasping for the wind." (v. 13–14)

The Doctrine of Vocation in a Fallen World

With the adjustments in vocation after the Fall come other changes. It is after man's fall into sin, and the promise of the *protoevangelium* (Gen. 3:15), that relationship begins to be named: "And Adam called his wife's name Eve, because she was the mother of all the living." (Gen. 3:20) In Genesis 3:15, the "first Gospel" is proclaimed; the Lord says to the serpent: "And I will put enmity between you and the woman, and between your seed and her Seed; He shall bruise your head, and you shall bruise His heel." The promised Seed of the woman is Christ Jesus, who at the time appointed crushes Satan's power. Thus Jesus declared in Luke 11:

> But if I cast out demons with the finger of God, surely the kingdom of God has come upon you. When a strong man, fully armed, guards his own palace, his goods are in peace. But when a stronger than he comes upon him and overcomes him, he takes from him all his armor in which he trusted, and divides his spoils. He who is not with Me is against Me, and he who does not gather with Me scatters. (v. 20–23)

The 'stronger one'—the Messiah—has crushed Satan, and taken and divided his 'spoils.' And, as St. Paul wrote to the Church in Rome, this is a victory which the Church continues to witness: "And the God of peace will crush Satan under your feet shortly. The grace of our Lord Jesus Christ be with you. Amen." (v. 20) As often as the Gospel is proclaimed, Satan is crushed, for the Holy Spirit works through the Word to call men to the salvation which Jesus won through His suffering and death. Thus in Revelation 13, St. John refers to the Christ as "the Lamb slain from the foundation of the world" (v. 8); the redemption which Jesus accomplishes through His death on the cross is an atonement for all the sin of man, from Adam to the end of the age. When Adam and Eve heard the first proclamation of the Gospel—the Word recorded in Genesis 3:15—and they believed that Word by the work of the Holy Spirit, they were already partakers of Christ's victory, despite the fact that the crucifixion was still thousands of years in their future. By faith in the promised Seed of the woman, Adam and Eve believed the Gospel, and thus they were members of the Church.

Adam's decision to name his wife "Eve" emphasizes the earlier point regarding the unity of the human race in our first parents: Truly, she was the "mother of all the living." However, it is also a highly significant name which recognizes that identity and calling are inseparable. Name and vocation were joined from the beginning; many 'family' names were once vocational, and the very act of naming places one in relation to family and State, while the naming in holy Baptism places one in relationship to Christ and His Church. To this day, merely hearing a person's name can be quite informative concerning the national background and even socio-economic status of the individual. To those names with which we are born, we add titles and degrees acquired through education, service and various forms of labor. Each vocation adds further descriptive terms, so that an inquiry regarding a person's identity elicits a recitation of such vocational 'labels.' In fact, it is hard even to think of one's own identity apart from a list of vocations.

Beginning with Adam, every human being has his identity defined in terms of various vocations. In fact, each man's identity is found in relationship to the divinely-given Estates of Church, State and Home. As Ælfric of Eynsham (c. 955–c. 1010) wrote,

> When there is too much evil among humankind, wise men ought to consider with discerning thought which of the pillars of the throne might be broken, and immediately repair it. The throne stands on these three pillars:

laboratores, bellatores, oratores. Laboratores [workers] are those who labor for our sustenance, ploughmen and farmers devoted to that alone. *Oratores* [those who pray] are those who intercede for us to God and who promote Christianity among Christian nations in God's service. They are devoted to this alone, to spiritual warfare, for the benefit of us all. *Bellatores* [warriors] are those who protect our towns and our homeland, fighting against the roving army with weapons. As St. Paul the teacher of the Gentiles said in his teaching, 'The warrior does not bear his sword for no purpose. He is God's servant for your benefit, appointed for vengeance on those who do evil.' On these three pillars stand the throne, and if one is broken, the throne immediately falls to the detriment of the other pillars.[10]

It is in such a tradition of understanding the Estates that the Table of Duties was added to the Small Catechism, that from youth every Christian would be rightly instructed in the "various orders and conditions of men" (SC Appendix III.1). The various distinctions of vocation delineated in the Table of Duties are all centered on the three Estates of Church, State and Home; the Table is drawn from "certain passages of the Scriptures, selected for various orders and conditions of men, wherein their respective duties are set forth."[11] Thus we find the duties of men within the Church are expressed in terms of "Bishops, Pastors and Preachers" and "What Duties Hearers owe their Bishops," while those of the State are summarized in terms of "Magistrates" and "What Duties Subjects owe Magistrates," while the Estate of the Home is variegated under the headings of "Husbands," "Wives," "Parents," "Children," "Male and Female Servants, and Labor-

10   Paul Cavill, *Vikings—Fear and Faith*, (Grand Rapids: Zondervan, 2001) p. 130.
11   SC Appendix III:1.

ers," "Masters and Mistresses," "Young Persons in General," "Widows," and—finally—"Christians in General."

We are instructed in the Large Catechism that in the midst of these estates, "The parental estate God has especially honored above all estates that are beneath Him, so that He not only commands us to love our parents, but to honor them." (LC I:105) According to the parental estate, we find:

> Thus we have two kinds of fathers presented in this commandment, fathers in blood and fathers in office, or those to whom belongs the care of the family, and those to whom belongs the care of the nation. Besides these they are yet spiritual fathers; not like those in the Papacy, who have indeed caused themselves to be so designated, but have not performed the functions of the paternal office. For those only are to be called spiritual fathers who govern and guide us by the Word of God. Of this name St. Paul boasts (1 Cor. 4:15), where he says: "In Christ Jesus I have begotten you through the Gospel." Because they are fathers indeed they are entitled to honor about all others. But they are regarded of the least importance: for the only honor the world has to confer upon them is to drive them out of the country and to grudge them a piece of bread, and in short they must be (as says St. Paul, 1 Cor. 4:13) "as the filth of the world and the offscouring of all things."(LC I:158–160)

In other words, each of the three Estates is fundamentally paternal in character; regardless of whether one is a father "in office" or "in blood," one is still a father if serving in a paternal office related to each estate. It is worth noting that our Lutheran Confessions single out those men whom the Lord has called into the office of the holy ministry as "fathers indeed": our objection to the way in which Romanists have used the appellation is that their priests have failed to uphold the paternal responsibilities of the holy office. Also, as pertains to each of the Estates, Luther's observation regarding parents would apply:

> We must, therefore, impress it upon the young that they should regard their parents in God's stead, and remember that however lowly, poor, frail and strange they may be, nevertheless they are father and mother given them by God. And they are not to be deprived of their honor because of their mode of life or their failings. Therefore we are not to regard their persons, how they may be, but the will of God who has thus appointed and ordained. In other respects we are, indeed, all alike in the eyes of God; but among us there must necessarily be such inequality and distinction with respect to order, and therefore God commands that you be careful to obey me as your father, and that I have the precedence. (LC I:108)

The entirety of the authority exercised within the three Estates is thus found in offices which operate "in God's stead." But the right understanding of such authority is quite different from Roman Catholic notions of hierarchy. To correctly grasp what is being taught and confessed regarding the three Estates, one must have a correct understanding of the relationship of the three Estates to the two kingdoms.

The Two Kingdoms and the Three Estates

As Christians, we live in two kingdoms at the same time: The Kingdom of God, and the kingdom of this world. This reality has been the occasion of a great deal of confusion in the Church (and in the world), because men have been tempted to convert the one kingdom into the other. Roman Catholicism, for example, has sought to import the notion of vocational hierarchies into the Kingdom of God. As noted in the Apology of the Augsburg Confession, one of the vilest notions associated with the monasticism promoted by the papacy was that it maintains "that the monks merit eternal life the more abundantly" than ordinary Christians; the papacy teaches that such a vocation places one in a better standing before the Lord. What is expected of ordinary Christians is markedly less; thus, in the words of the current Roman Catholic Catechism: "The precepts of the Church are set in the context of a moral life bound to and nourished by liturgical life. The obligatory character of these positive laws *decreed by the pastoral authorities* is meant to guarantee to the faithful the indispensable minimum in the spirit of prayer and moral effort, in the growth in love of God and neighbor"[12]—a statement which continues to be worthy of the condemnation proclaimed in Apology XIII:

> Again, it has been laid down in the Confutation that the monks endeavor to live more nearly in accordance with the Gospel. Therefore it ascribes perfection to human traditions if they are living more nearly in accordance with the Gospel by not having property, being unmarried, and obeying the rule in clothing, meats and like trifles.
>
> … For Christ does not mean that to forsake parents, wife, brethren, is a work that must be done because it merits the remission of sins and eternal life. Yea such a forsaking is cursed. For if any one forsake parents or wife, in order by this very work to merit the remission of sins or eternal life, this is done with dishonor to Christ.
>
> There is, moreover, a twofold forsaking. One occurs without a call, without God's command; this Christ does not approve (Matt. 15:9). For the works chosen by us are useless services. But it appears the more clearly that Christ does not approve this flight from the fact that He speaks of forsaking wife and children. We know, however, that God's commandment forbids the forsaking

---

12   ¶ 2041, *Catechism of the Catholic Church* (Doubleday: New York, 1995) p. 548.

of wife and children. ... For the Gospel's sake we ought even to forsake our body. Here it would be ridiculous to hold that it would be a service to God to kill one's self, and without God's command to leave the body. So too it is ridiculous to hold that it is a service to God without God's command to forsake possessions, friends, wife, children. (¶ 39, 40-42)

The papists are ensnared by such confusions because they do not rightly discern the distinction between the kingdom of the world and the Kingdom of God. In his book, *Law and Protestantism— The Legal Teachings of the Lutheran Reformation*, John Witte makes a helpful distinction between Roman notions of hierarchy and the biblical, Lutheran doctrine:

> Luther's two-kingdoms theory was a rejection of traditional hierarchical theories of being, society, and authority. For centuries, the Christian West had taught that God's creation was hierarchical in structure—a vast chain of being emanating from God and descending through various levels and layers of reality. In this great chain of being, each creature found its place and purpose, and each human society found its natural order and hierarchy. It was thus simply the nature of things that some persons and institutions were higher on this chain of being, some lower. It was the nature of things that some were closer and had more ready access to God, and some were further away and in need of greater mediation in their relationship with God. This was one basis for traditional Catholic arguments of the superiority of the pope to the emperor, of the clergy to the laity, of the spiritual sword to the temporal sword, of the canon law to the civil law, of the Church to the state.
>
> Luther's two-kingdoms theory turned this traditional ontology onto its side. By distinguishing the two

kingdoms, Luther highlighted the radical separation between the Creator and the creation, and between God and humanity.[13]

A biblical understanding of the two kingdoms recognizes that the Christian is a citizen of both the Kingdom of God and the kingdom of this world. According to his citizenship in the Kingdom of God, there is no consideration of vocation; according to his citizenship in the kingdom of the world, every relationship is expressed in terms of vocation. As Gustav Wingren observed in his book, *Luther on Vocation*, "So vocation belongs to this world, not to heaven; it is directed toward one's neighbor, not toward God. This is an important preliminary characteristic. In his vocation one is not reaching up to God, but rather bends oneself down toward the world."[14]

When Scripture speaks of the Christian according to the Kingdom of God, the vocations of this world according to the three estates are not taken into consideration; thus, for example, we read in Galatians 3: "For you are all sons of God through faith in Christ Jesus. For as many of you as were baptized into Christ have put on Christ. There is neither Jew nor Greek, there is neither slave nor free, there is neither male nor female; for you are all one in Christ Jesus." (v. 26–28) This sonship is not dependent on, or related to, any worldly vocation. In Wingren's words, "When anyone, be he emperor or craftsman, turns to God in faith, or, more concretely, in prayer, he is without the outer support which 'station' gives in relation to others. Here one does not stand *in relatione*, or meet with another human being, as one does in his vocation. Each is alone before God."[15]

13   John Witte, Jr., *Law and Protestantism—The Legal Teachings of the Lutheran Reformation*, (Cambridge: Cambridge University Press, 2002) p. 6.
14   Gustav Wingren, *Luther on Vocation,* (Ballast Press: Evansville, Indiana, 1994) p. 10.
15   p. 13.

134

However, one's citizenship in the Kingdom of God is not something which annuls one's vocations in the kingdom of the world. Thus a Christian is also a citizen of the kingdom of this world, *and* his life is defined according to the various estates, and this reality is not changed by Baptism—except insofar as the Christian must flee such stations in life which are inherently sinful.[16] Thus St. Paul wrote to the Church in Corinth: "Let each one remain in the same calling in which he was called. Were you called while a slave? Do not be concerned about it; but if you can be made free, rather use it. For he who is called in the Lord while a slave is the Lord's freedman. Likewise he who is called while free is Christ's slave. You were bought at a price; do not become slaves of men. Brethren, let each one remain with God in that state in which he was called." (1 Cor. 7:20–24) As clearly confessed in the "Table of Duties" in the Small Catechism, one must also not limit such godly vocations to the sense often employed in English usage; as Wingren observes,

> It is important to emphasize the fact that vocation is not confined to an occupation, but includes also what Betcke calls biological orders: father, mother, son, daughter. Every attempt to differentiate between the sphere of the home, where personal Christian love rules, and the sphere of office, where the more impersonal rules of vocation hold sway, immediately runs afoul of Luther's terminology. The life of the home, the relation between parents and children, is vocation, even as is life in the field of labor, the relation between employer and employee. In anything that involves action, anything that concerns the world or my relationship with my neighbor, there is nothing, Luther holds, that falls in the private sphere lying outside of station, office, or vocation. It is only be-

16   Wingren, p. 4. Wingren offers as the difficulty of reconciling faith and life in the cloister an example of such a tension.

fore God, i.e., in heaven, that the individual stands alone. In the earthly realm man always stands *in relatione*, always bound to another.[17]

To understand the three Estates, one must therefore rightly believe the doctrine of the two Kingdoms. Christians are used to hearing of the distinction between the Kingdom of God and the Kingdom of Man, or between the kingdom of the world and the kingdom of heaven. However, despite the familiarity of the terminology, all too often this distinction is misunderstood; a misappropriation of terms may take place which leads to the conclusion that whereas the Christians knows that the kingdom of heaven is 'good,' this means that the kingdom of the world is 'bad.' After all, Jesus said to Pontius Pilate, "My kingdom is not of this world," (John 18:36) and Scripture tells us that the devil took Jesus "up on a high mountain, showed Him all the kingdoms of the world in a moment of time," and then said, "All this authority I will give You, and their glory; for this has been delivered to me, and I give it to whomever I wish." (Luke 4:5, 6)

The disordering of sin wars against the divinely-established relational character of our existence; like Eve, the temptations which confront us are self-referential. Thus, rather than man's identity being defined according to the estates of Church, State and Home (as in Table 1 below), the temptation to Individualism is to an existence which is *curvatus in se*—that is, turned in on oneself. This **Individualism** is related to an entire constellation of other "deadly values": **Gnosticism, Nominalism, Progress, Democratism, Scientism** and **Tolerance** (see Table 2 below). All of these "deadly values" are related to one another, and although it may be mistaken to seek to express their connections in genitive terms (as if one were simply the source of the others), they are certainly related to one another, and mu-

---

17   p. 4–5.

tually reenforce one another. Furthermore, as is most often the case with deadly temptation, the danger which they pose is all the greater because they are popularly conceived to be virtues.

The difficulties attendant with speaking of the various "deadly values" is compounded by the inherently (and, perhaps, ironically) relational character of said values. As the influence of **Gnosticism**, **Nominalism** and **Progress** rose to prominence in Western thought at the dawn of the Modern Age at a point prior to **Democratism**, **Scientism** and **Tolerance**, it is beneficial to treat of them as a group, before turning to the remainder of the values under consideration. Lastly, we will return to the topic on which we have begun, **Individualism**, which one may hope can be better understood once its relationship to the other six "deadly values" may stand in relief.

Table 1
THE INDIVIDUAL IN RELATION TO THE THREE ESTATES

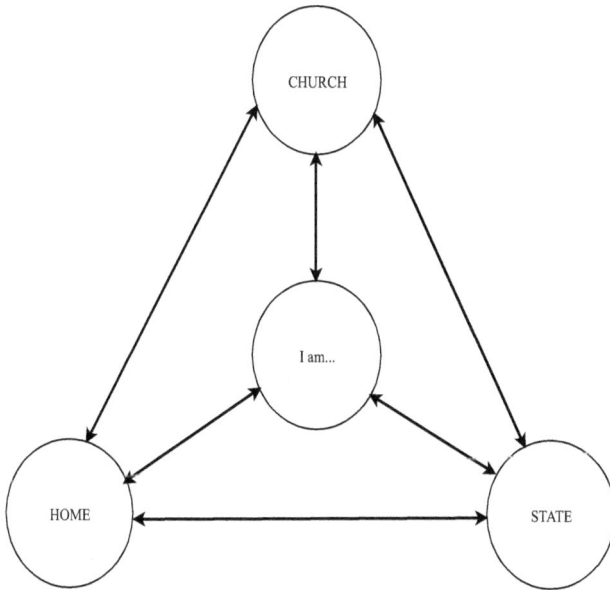

Table 2
THE SEVEN DEADLY "VALUES" IN RELATIONSHIP TO ONE ANOTHER

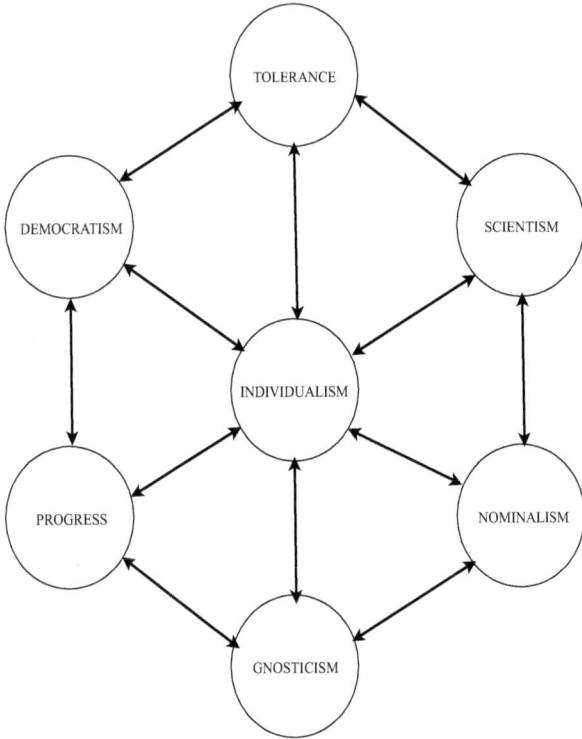

GNOSTICISM, NOMINALISM, AND THE DOCTRINE OF PROGRESS.

"O Timothy! Guard what was committed to your trust, avoiding the profane and idle babble and contradictions of what is falsely called knowledge [της ψευδωνυμου γνωσεως]—by professing it some have strayed concerning the faith. Grace be with you. Amen."
(1 Tim. 6:20–21)

That which has been is what will be, that which is done is what will be done. And there is nothing new under the sun. (Ecc. 1:9)

he terms "**Gnosticism**" and "**Nominalism**" need not be widely known, or easily defined by the "man in the street" (or the pew, for that matter), for the influence of the doctrines associated with those terms to have had a widespread, deleterious influence on our entire culture. "**Progress**" is, of course, a term which is broadly used to cover an almost limitless array of doctrines, technological developments, and aberrant endeavors to 'reform' society according to ideological constructs.

"**Gnosticism**" takes its name from the Greek word γνῶσις (gnõsis) which is translated as "knowledge." The "Gnostic" is one who purports to have a secret knowledge which has been acquired by means of direct inspiration, or by access to a secret tradition which has been handed on from generation to generation from ancient teachers. St. Paul's warning to St. Timothy appears to be directed against such "Gnostics," as they were understood by the Apostle to be purveyors of "what is falsely called knowledge"—and whose doctrines have led some to stray from the catholic and apostolic doctrine.

The term "**Nominalism**" is perhaps even more obscure in the common mind, except among students of philosophy. Broadly defined, "Nominalism" is the doctrine that there is no correspondence between the name which is given to a thing and the reality, the essence, of the thing so named. Thus, for example, in the realm of biology, the Nominalist would maintain (in proper Darwinian fashion) that the identification of species is an abstraction; there is no such thing as a "horse," for example—each one of the creatures which we might call a horse is simply one of many potential transitional creatures which, despite a high degree of similarity between various individual creatures, do not represent a fixed type.[1] Nominalism is the root of the chain of reasoning which has led to Post-Modern declarations that ultimately all meaning is that which is ascribed by men alone.

Lastly, our use of the term "**Progress**" incorporates various aspects of such popular definitions, but is also concerned for a teleological notion which lurks behind many common usages: The idea that mankind is steadily perfecting himself in a process which is leading toward a higher state of being, or more perfect social order.

One more preliminary point should be stated before beginning an analysis of the impact of Gnosticism, Nominalism and belief in Progress: The emergence of each of these "deadly values" occurred within the confines of the visible Church. These doctrines were not secular in origin; their proponents were not considered enemies of Catholic verity or piety. In their time, each one of the men who were primarily responsible for

1   There is a similarity between such reasoning and that which Plato attributes to Heraclitus of Ephesus, who purportedly maintained that one cannot step into the same river twice. Philosophers will occasionally engage in a type of philosophizing which is so utterly vacuous that its worthlessness may be grasped quite easily by anyone but a philosopher.

the spread of these errors was considered a faithful Christian[2] and most of these men served as teachers of the Church. In fact, all were profoundly influential during their own generations and later through their writings and their disciples—a point which should be obvious, after all, since the entire point of our examination of their doctrines is not an antiquarian endeavor.

The Rebirth of Gnosticism at the Beginning of the Modern Age

In speaking of Gnosticism, our primary concerns are regarding the source of knowledge of the truth, and the goal of man; in short, our concern is epistemological. Gnosticism, with its fundamental, historic reliance on a secret body of knowledge is antithetical to the Christian tradition. Secret teachings and hidden wisdom are not the way in which the Lord has taught His Church in either the Old Testament or the New; as we read in Isaiah 45:

> For thus says the LORD,
> Who created the heavens,
> Who is God,
> Who formed the earth and made it,
> Who has established it,
> Who did not create it in vain,
> Who formed it to be inhabited:
> "I am the LORD, and there is no other.
> I have not spoken in secret,
> In a dark place of the earth;
> I did not say to the seed of Jacob,
> 'Seek Me in vain';
> I, the LORD, speak righteousness,
> I declare things that are right." (v. 18–19)

2　　The possible exception here would be Giovanni Pico della Mirandola, who was excommunicated for heresy for a time. However, he was later restored to the communion of the Church by Pope Alexander VI in 1493.

And Jesus declared when He was brought before Caiaphas: "I spoke openly to the world. I always taught in synagogues and in the temple, where the Jews always meet, and in secret I have said nothing." (John 18:20) It has been the intimation of the evil one that true knowledge is hidden away in secret; the serpent tempted Eve by directly denying the revealed Word of God, and offering her a hidden 'gnosis': "You will not surely die. For God knows that in the day you eat of it your eyes will be opened, and you will be like God, knowing good and evil." (Gen. 3:4b–5) God's Word, therefore, does not contain hidden 'Bible codes' or secret messages, as the Kabbalists (and others) dream—imagining that the Lord has hidden a 'deeper' and more profound, meaning beneath the literal meaning.

In his second epistle, St. Peter declared: "And so we have the prophetic word confirmed, which you do well to heed as a light that shines in a dark place, until the day dawns and the morning star rises in your hearts; knowing this first, that no prophecy of Scripture is of any private interpretation, for prophecy never came by the will of man, but holy men of God spoke as they were moved by the Holy Spirit." (2 Pet. 1:19–21) The continuity of the apostolic faith is not found in hidden teachings or private interpretations, but in a body of doctrine set forth in Holy Scripture. Rather than importing one's own teachings into Scripture—as Kabbalists are inclined to do—one seeks to receive that which is openly taught in Holy Writ. Thus St. Paul wrote to the Church in Corinth: "Now I praise you, brethren, that you remember me in all things and keep the traditions just as I delivered them to you." (1 Cor. 11:2) The true knowledge proclaimed in the Word of God is that which faithful servants of the Word proclaim; as St. Paul wrote to the Romans: "How then shall they call on Him in whom they have not believed? And how shall they believe in Him of whom they have not heard? And how shall they hear without a preacher?" (10:14) And Jesus declared concerning those whom He sent to proclaim His Word: "He who hears you hears Me, he who rejects you rejects Me, and he who rejects Me rejects Him who sent Me."

The divine Word—the *true* knowledge—proclaims salvation by grace through faith in Christ Jesus, and the Church confesses that which St. Peter proclaimed by inspiration of the Holy Spirit, "Nor is there salvation in any other, for there is no other name under heaven given among men by which we must be saved." (Acts 4:12) Thus the true knowledge of salvation comes only through the Word of God. Gnosticism, by contrast, does not proclaim a *savior*; instead, each individual is his own 'savior,' with salvation coming through *knowledge*. As Hans Jonas wrote in his classic study of ancient Gnosticism: "The emphasis on *knowledge* as the means for the attainment of salvation, or even as the form of salvation itself, and the claim to the possession of this knowledge in one's own articulate doctrine, are common features of the numerous sects in which the gnostic movement historically expressed itself."[3] According to Jonas,

> The Church Fathers considered Gnosticism as essentially a Christian heresy and confined their reports and refutations to systems which either had sprouted already from the soil of Christianity (e.g., the Valentinian system), or had somehow added the figure of Christ to their otherwise heterogeneous teaching (e.g., that of the Phrygian Naassenes), or else through a common Jewish background were close enough to be felt as competing with and distorting the Christian message (e.g., that of Simon Magus).[4]

The historical origins of Gnosticism are probably beyond recovery—a fact which is an artifact of the very nature of Gnos-

---

3   Hans Jonas, *The Gnostic Religion*, (Beacon Press: Boston, 1958) p. 32.
4   ibid.

ticism. The stunning array of Gnostic sects may be attributed in no small part to the phenomenon which drew the ire of the Church Fathers: the Gnostic propensity to mold other religions to the purposes of Gnosticism. Gnosticism, as it concerns us within the current context, is syncretic, borrowing disparate elements of various traditions and melding them according to the idiosyncrasies of the Gnostic system builders.[5] For the Gnostic, there is no contradiction in borrowing disparate elements from different religions and mixing those elements with doctrines drawn from his own depraved mind.

On occasion, individuals from the earliest centuries of the New Testament era expressed sympathy for non-Christian writers, and when they found pagans who affirmed some aspect of the Truth, did not hesitate to acknowledge it, and urged such pagans to convert, and come to a true, complete knowledge, which comes from the Word alone. Thus, for example, one may read in the *Exhortation to the Greeks* written by Clement of Alexandria ca. A.D. 200:

> Wherefore it seems to me, that since the Word Himself came to us from heaven, we ought no longer to go to human teaching, to Athens and the rest of Greece, or to Ionia, in our curiosity. If our teacher is He who has filled the universe with holy powers, creation, salvation, beneficence, lawgiving, prophecy, teaching, this teacher now instructs us in all things, and the whole world has by this time become an Athens and a Greece through the

---

5   In the words of Jonas, "Modern scholars have advanced in turn Hellenic, Babylonian, Egyptian and Iranian origins and every possible combination of these with one another and with Jewish and Christian elements. Since in the material of its representation Gnosticism actually is a product of syncretism, each of these theories can be supported from the sources and none of them is satisfactory alone; but neither is the combination of all of them, which would make Gnosticism out to be a mere mosaic of these elements and so miss its autonomous essence." (Ibid., p. 33.)

Word. For surely, after believing in a poetic legend which records that Minos the Cretan was "a familiar friend of Zeus," you will not disbelieve that we, who have become disciples of God, have entered into the really true wisdom which leaders of philosophy have only hinted at, but which the disciples of Christ have both comprehended and proclaimed abroad.[6]

Even a man such as Clement recognized that there was no room for mixing the Truth with falsehood; any aspect of truth which the Gentiles had come to know should simply lead them to renounce all pagan error and embrace the Christian verity.

However, the modern gnosticizing teachers were not of one mind with men such as Clement. Instead, they sought out pagan antiquity for a separate revelation from the Lord, and desired to syncretize the pagan and Christian teachings into a common doctrine. For purposes of this presentation, our models for such Gnostic syncretism are Gemistos Plethon (1355–1454), Marsilio Ficino (1433–1499) and Giovanni Pico della Mirandola (1464–1494).

The complexities of Gnostic influence on the Church extend far beyond what can be explored in this context. The conflict between teachers of the early Church and various schools of Gnosticism has been the basis for a great deal of academic study. Many church fathers (including, most notably, St. Irenaeus of Lyons) vigorously contended against Gnosticism because such labors were necessitated by their duty to teach the Church. Indeed, Irenaeus' *Adversus Haereses (Against Heresies)* is a model of such works of Christian apologetics.

---

6   trans. by G. W. Butterworth, (Harvard University Press: Cambridge, 2003) p. 239.

In fulfillment of St. Paul's warning in 1 Timothy 6, Gnostic writers sought to lead Christians astray by producing various false 'gospels'—and the pernicious influence of such blasphemous works is by no means at an end. Although these pseudepigraphal 'gospels' were written long after the four canonical Gospels, various 'scholars' continue to treat such obvious forgeries as if they are simply 'alternative gospels' written by 'different Christianities' that simply lost out in some cosmic lottery.[7]

Much of the argumentation offered in defense of such Gnostic pseudepigrapha is absurd, given even a passing familiarity with the actual history of the early church. For example, the proponents of Gnostic texts having a place within some 'different Christianity' ignore the fact that the doctrine already contained in the Old Testament would exclude central tenets of the Gnostic doctrines; in the words of Kostenberger and Kruger:

> Thus, right from the outset, certain "versions" of Christianity would have been ruled out of bounds. For example, any Gnostic version of the faith that suggests the God of the Old Testament was not the true God but a "demiurge"—as in the case of the heretic Marcion—would have been deemed unorthodox on the basis of these Old Testament canonical books alone. As Ben Witherington has observed, "Gnosticism was a non-starter from the

---

7   Thus, for example, Bart Ehrman peddles his books, *Lost Christianities* and *Lost Scriptures,* under the false claim that "only one set of early Christian beliefs emerged as victorious in the heated disputes over what to believe and how to live that were raging in the early centuries of the Christian movement. These beliefs, and the group who promoted them, *came to be thought of as 'orthodox'...*" (*Lost Scriptures,* [Oxford University Press: Oxford, 2003] p. 2.) A thorough refutation of such nonsense may be found in *The Heresy of Orthodoxy: How Contemporary Culture's Fascination with Diversity Has Reshaped Our Understanding of Early Christianity*, by A. Kostenberger and Michael Kruger (Crossway: Wheaton, Illinois, 2010).

outset because it rejected the very book the earliest Christians recognized as authoritative—the Old Testament."[8]

Ultimately, Gnosticism failed in its effort to win a broad popular adherence to its tenets—if, indeed, its purveyors ever actually intended to achieve such an appeal.[9] The bleakness of Gnosticism—which rejected the world as inherently evil, and a prison which one sought to escape—and the elitist pretensions of its teachers no doubt contributed to the slow demise of Gnosticism in the West.

However, the seeming-death of Gnosticism proved only to be temporary. No doubt the shelter which the doctrine found within the boundaries of the Eastern Church (and beyond), allowed for a survival of its doctrines, and its eventual export back to Western Christendom.

Malcolm Lambert observes in his book, *Medieval Heresy,* that Gnostic sects seem to erupt full-grown in the West not long after A.D. 1000. The reemergence of Gnosticism is so sudden in Western Christendom that Lambert notes, "The radical nature of the denials of the adherents, of the doctrines of incarnation and resurrection, have led some historians to argue that the heresy was imported, to some degree ready-made, and that it represents a fragmentary influence from the developed heretical tradition of the movement of the Bogomils, then spreading from its cradle-land in Bulgaria into other parts of the Byzan-

8   *The Heresy of Orthodoxy*, p. 156.

9   In *Gnosis—The Nature & History of Gnosticism*, Kurt Rudolph maintains that Mandeans are the only ancient Gnostic sect to survive to the present age: "Only one gnostic sect has survived to the present day... It is the community of the Mandeans, a baptist sect, comprising about 15,000 followers, and to be found especially in the southern region of the Euphrates and Tigris in the Republic of Iraq." (trans. by Robert McLachlan Wilson, [HarperSanFrancisco: San Francisco, 1987) p. 343.

tine Empire."[10] Certainly the later Cathar heresy of the eleventh through thirteenth centuries was heavily influenced by Gnosticism, though its teachers sought to conceal their heterodoxy from neophytes until they had been thoroughly seduced by error.[11]

But the early Gnostic sects, and the later, more widespread, Cathar heresy were suppressed by the Church and continued to be understood as *extra Ecclesiam*. The influence of Gnosticism within the Church developed later, at the very beginning of the modern age, through the influence of Gemistos Plethon (1355–1454), a man obsessed with reconciling pagan doctrines with Christian doctrine.[12] For Plethon, the openness to the notion of a divine revelation given to the pagans began with a fascination with Zoroaster, a Persian thinker so mysterious that scholars are still debating over which century it was in which he lived. Although Plethon never learned the Persian language, and only gleaned knowledge of Zoroastrian teaching from Greek writers, he nonetheless believed him to have been divinely inspired.

According to his contemporaries, Plethon appears to have been led to his heretical notions regarding Zoroastrianism through one of his teachers in Byzantium, a Jew named 'Elisha' who was schooled in Averroistic philosophy.[13] Plethon believed that Zoroaster was divinely inspired, and thus represented another line of true revelation from God which was equal to the Scriptures.[14]

---

10   (Cambridge: Blackwell Publishers, 1992) p. 15.

11   p. 118.

12   C. M. Woodhouse's *Gemistos Plethon—The Last of the Hellenes* (Oxford: Oxford University Press, 2000) is a good introduction to Plethon's thought and influence.

13   Moshe Idel, "Prisca Theologia in Marsilio Ficino," in *Marsilio Ficino: His Theology, His Philosophy, His Legacy.* Ed. by Michael J. B. Allen and Valery Rees with Martin Davies, (Leiden, Boston, Köln: Brill, 2002) p. 143–4.

14   Current scholarship makes it clear that Plethon was, in fact, what

The danger which Plethon's incipient Universalism posed to the Church was apparent to his contemporaries. As Woodhouse notes, George of Trebizond (1395–1473) "considered Gemistos no less dangerous a heretic than Muhammad himself, reported him as saying that not many years after his death men would adopt a universal religion, which would be neither Christianity nor Islam but a revived paganism."[15] And Gennadius Scholarius—a scholar who was at the Council of Florence with Plethon, favored union with West on theological grounds, and would later serve as Patriarch of Constantinople—saw the origins of Plethon's false teachings in the darkest of terms:

> Before he had acquired the maturity of reason and education and the capacity of judgment in such matters—or rather, before he had even devoted himself to acquiring them—he was so dominated by Hellenic ideas that he took little trouble about learning traditional Christianity, apart from the most superficial aspects. In reality it was not for the sake of the Greek language, like all Christians, that he read and studied Greek literature—first the poets and then the philosophers—but in order to associate himself with them; and so in fact he did, as we know for certain from many who knew him in his youth.

It was natural in the case of a man under such influence, in the absence of divine grace, that through

---

could rightly be called a neo-pagan; his adherence to the writings of Zoroaster was accompanied by a belief in the pagan gods of the Greek pantheon. For example, in his *Summary of the Doctrines of Zoroaster and Plato*—a work which Plethon kept to himself, but which still survives—Plethon maintained: "(1) The gods really exist; Zeus is chief among them and 'altogether apart'; Poseidon is second; and the rest of the gods are produced by those two, without mothers but with the help of Hera." (Woodhouse, p. 319.) Regarding Plethon's views regarding Zoroaster, see Woodhouse, p. 24–25 and p. 355–356.

15   Woodhouse, p. 26.

the demons with whom he associated there should have come a tendency toward an ineradicable adherence to error, as happened to Julian and many other apostates. The climax of his apostasy came later under the influence of a certain Jew with whom he studied, attracted by his skill as an interpreter of Aristotle. This Jew was an adherent of Averroes and other Persian and Arabic interpreters of Aristotle's works, which the Jews had translated into their own language, but he paid little regard to Moses or the beliefs and observances which the Jews received from him.

This man also expounded to Gemistos the doctrines of Zoroaster and others. He was ostensibly a Jew but in fact a Hellenist [pagan].[16]

Plethon was a representative of the Eastern Church at the Council of Ferrara/Florence (also known as the Council of Union) in 1438 and 1439, and it was in that capacity that he met the *de facto* ruler of Florence, Cosimo de'Medici.[17] Plethon's "multilinear"[18] notion of inspiration was then given a life in Western thought by Cosimo de'Medici's establishment of the Platonic Academy,[19] and his patronage of a young scholar, Mar-

16   ibid., p. 24.

17   ibid., p. 155-156.

18   The term is borrowed from the previously cited article by Idel.

19   Ficino describes Plethon's influence in the rise of the Platonic Academy at Florence: "At the time when the Council was in progress between the Greeks and the Latins at Florence under Pope Eugenius, the great Cosimo, whom a decree of the Senate (*Signoria*) designated *Pater patriae*, often listened to the Greek philosopher Gemistos (with the cognomen Plethon, as it were a second Plato) while he expounded the mysteries of Platonism. And he was so immediately inspired, so moved by Gemistos' fervent tongue, that as a result he conceived in his noble mind a kind of Academy, which he was to bring to birth at the first opportune moment. Later, when the great Medici brought his great idea into being, he destined me, the son of his favourite doctor, while I was still a boy, for the great task." (quoted in *Gemistos Plethon—*

silio Ficino (1433–1499), to carry out translations from pagan antiquity and to teach the rising generation of Italian Renaissance thinkers.

As detailed in *Prisci Theologi and the Hermetic Reformation in the Fifteenth Century*,[20] Ficino wholeheartedly adhered to the Plethonic notion of "multilinear inspiration," and believed that there existed a succession of six perfect teachers of pagan antiquity whose doctrine constituted a *prisci theologi* ("ancient theology") which was not dependent upon the prophetic and apostolic Scriptures for its truth claims. Ficino believed that the mythical figure of "Hermes Trismegistus" was the *primus auctor theologiae*[21] and thus placed a number of Gnostic writings attributed to Hermes on a par with Holy Scripture. Thus the rediscovery of a book of hermetical works, and Ficino's translation of those works into Latin—for the first time—was intended to open the minds of the West to an entirely different body of 'scripture.' As Ficino wrote in the preface to his translation of the *Corpus Hermeticum*:

> At the time when Moses was born flourished Atlas the astrologer, brother of the natural philosopher Prometheus and maternal grandfather of the elder Mercurius, whose grandson was Mercurius Trismegistus. … They called him Trismegistus or trice-greatest because he was the greatest philosopher and the greatest priest and the greatest king. … Thus, he was called the first author of theology, and Orpheus followed him, taking second place in the ancient theology. After Aglaophemus, Pythagoras came next in theological succession, having been initiated into rites of Orpheus, and he was followed by Philo-

---

The Last of the Hellenes, p. 156.

20   James D. Heiser, *Prisci Theologi and the Hermetic Reformation in the Fifteenth Century*, (Malone, Texas: Repristination Press, 2011).

21   ibid., p. 36.

laus, teacher of our divine Plato. In this way, from a wondrous line of six theologians emerged a single system of
ancient theology, harmonious in every part, which traced
its origins to Mercurius and reached absolute perfection
with the divine Plato. Mercurius wrote many books pertaining to the knowledge of divinity, ... often speaking
not only as philosopher but as prophet. ... He foresaw
the ruin of the old religion, the rise of the new faith, the
coming of Christ, the judgement to come, the resurrection of the race, the glory of the blessed and the torments
of the damned.[22]

Despite the radical character of his views, Ficino served as a
priest at the Duomo in Florence. His writings and private teaching were well-received by a wide audience of Renaissance
theologians and humanists, and those who can now be counted
among his students include Pope Leo X (1475–1521)—who,
ironically, excommunicated Martin Luther for false doctrine—
as well as Hebraist Johannes Reuchlin (1455–1522), a proponent of Kabbalistic studies, uncle of Lutheran Reformer Philip
Melanchthon, and ally of Johannes Eck in opposing the Reformation. Arguably the most 'famous' of Ficino's students was
Giovanni Pico della Mirandola (1463–1494) who, despite the
brevity of his life, remains the stereotypical 'Renaissance Man'
in the minds of many students of that age.

Thoroughly committed to the Gnostic syncretism of
Christian and pagan doctrine, Ficino and Pico promulgated a
doctrine drawn from such disparate sources as the Zoroastrian
Chaldean Oracles and the Gnostic-Hermetic *Corpus Hermeticum* to the Neoplatonic works of Iamblichus, Proclus and Plotinus. Pico built on the Ficino's syncretic melding of Christian

22   quoted in *Prisci Theologi and the Hermetic Reformation in the Fifteenth Century*, p. 42–43.

and pagan 'inspiration' so that in both his famous *Oration on the Dignity of Man* and *900 Theses* Pico's syncretism merged Kabbalah, magic, Neoplatonism, Hermetical Gnosticism, Zoroastrianism, Platonism and Aristotelean teaching into a set of doctrines opposed to that which was taught by the medieval scholastic doctors. As Pico declared in his *Oration*:

> For these reasons, I have not been content to repeat well-worn doctrines, but have proposed for disputation many points of the early theology of Hermes Trismegistus, many theses drawn from the teachings of the Chaldeans and the Pythagoreans, from the occult mysteries of the Hebrews [i.e., Cabala] and, finally, a considerable number of propositions concerning both nature and God which we ourselves have discovered and worked out.[23]

In point of fact, both Ficino and Pico called for a 'reformation' of the Church in keeping with their syncretic theology. Ficino's *Platonic Theology* is a thoroughgoing effort to merge Neoplatonic, Gnostic, and Christian theology into one doctrine—an effort which fails, at least insofar as the result is undeniably far removed from the pale of the apostolic and catholic faith.

In brief, what Plethon, Ficino and Pico bequeathed to future generations was a syncretic approach to truth which was drawn from Gnostic influences. The writings and influence of these men gave birth to notions which are now taken for granted by many individuals in the West: That 'truth' is personal, and therefore relative; that God speaks to men through different religions and offers many paths to a common 'salvation'; and that it is the responsibility of each individual to find his or her path

---

23   Giovanni Pico della Mirandola, *Oration on the Dignity of Man*, trans. by A. Robert Caponigri (Washington, D.C.: Regnery Publishing Co., 1956) p. 49.

to God—these syncretistic notions are a Gnostic legacy which is essentially accepted axiomatically in our contemporary culture. They are, however, antithetical to Christianity, as Philip J. Lee observes in *Against the Protestant Gnostics*:

> Syncretism is not like other categories delineating gnostic faith; it is not an object of faith but a method. It is the method of achieving the various gnostic goals. Gnostic faith can exist within Christianity, indeed can thrive within Christianity, so long as the Incarnation is accepted as only one image among many. Through purposeful syncretism the one image becomes diffused, a mere element in the gnostic mix. In this sense, gnostic syncretism involves not only an acceptance of many beliefs and practices, but a denial of the particular belief and the particular practice that make Christianity, Christianity. Many ideas, all lacking in subordination, aid and abet the gnostic cause; particularity, a single focus, represents a threat to the gnostic thought pattern.[24]

The Gnostic influences thus reinforce, and are reinforced by, **Individualism**, and interact with the other two deadly values under consideration in this section; that is, **Nominalism** and **Progress**.

Nominalism—What's in a Name?

Turning to a consideration of **Nominalism**, our concerns are more ontological, because of the fundamental challenge which it poses to the received order of nature. As noted previously, broadly defined, Nominalism is the doctrine that there is no correspondence between the name which is given to a thing and the reality, the essence, of the thing so named. Although the doctrine of Nominalism may reside in seemingly-abstruse medieval discussions of philosophy, the implications of Nominalism

24 Philip J. Lee, *Against the Protestant Gnostics,* (New York and Oxford: Oxford University Press, 1987) p. 176–177.

surround us every day. Because it denies the existence of Universals—that is, the existence of a divine 'blueprint' or 'plan' according to which the things of this world are created and sustained, by its very nature, Nominalism maintains that order and species within the created realm are illusory; such concepts are, at most, an artifact of observation. For the consistent Nominalist, only individuals exist, and all appeals to Universals must be only crude generalizations.

Several important articles of the Nominalists' creed are that God is ultimately unknowable and 'mankind' is a meaningless concept, other than as a means for describing the aggregate of individuals. William of Occam (ca. 1288–ca. 1348) is usually deemed to be the pivotal figure in the early development of Nominalism, though it may be argued that the system later progressed in directions far beyond the intended scope of his argument. Richard Weaver poignantly sets forth the dilemma of man in the Nominalist Age:

It was William of Occam who propounded the fateful doctrine of nominalism, which denies that universals have a real existence. His triumph tended to leave universal terms mere names serving our convenience. The issue ultimately involved is whether there is a source of truth higher than, and independent of, man; and the answer to the question is decisive for one's view of the nature and destiny of humankind. The practical result of nominalist philosophy is to banish the reality which is perceived by the intellect and to posit as reality that which is perceived by the senses.[25]

Nominalism assaults the Christian verity at several key points. Several of the most crucial assaults include Nominal-

---

25   Richard M. Weaver, *Ideas Have Consequences,* (Chicago and London: The University of Chicago Press, 1984) p. 3.

ism's attendant obligatory **Individualism**, and also its rejection of formal and final causes, and ultimately calls into question what man may actually know about God. What this means is that because Nominalists maintain that God is ultimately unknowable, and therefore His will is unknowable, then that which is revealed in Holy Scripture does not reveal the entirety of God's purposes. If the "final cause" (the plan for man's salvation, for example) set forth in Holy Scripture is called into question by the possibility of a different "final cause" existing in the hidden will of the hidden God, man's faith in the Christian verity may be shattered. Thus, for example, John Calvin's belief in a double predestination on the part of the "hidden God" ultimately rests on such Nominalist notions: Calvinists ignore the clear meaning of passages such as John 3:16, which affirms that God so loved "the world" that He gave His only-begotten Son, declaring that, in essence, while God may *say* He loves the world in His revealed will, according to His hidden will, He is willing something else. As Gillespie explains in *The Theological Origins of Modernity,*

> Most nominalists were convinced that human beings could know little about God and his intentions beyond what he reveals to them in Scripture. Natural theology, for example, can prove God's existence, infinity, and supremacy, according to Ockham, but it cannot even demonstrate that there is only one God. ...
>
> Ockham also rejected the scholastic understanding of nature. Scholasticism imagined nature to be teleological, a realm in which divine purposes were repeatedly realized. ... The nominalist rejection of universals was thus a rejection not merely of formal but also of final causes. If there were no universals, there could be no universal ends to be actualized.[26]

---

26   Michael Allen Gillespie, *The Theological Origins of Modernity,* (Chicago and London: The University of Chicago Press, 2008) p. 24.

While the Nominalists may have begun by affirming Scripture, ultimately their speculations calling into question the correspondence of Scriptural doctrine with divine reality undermines faith in that revelation. Thus the 'young Calvinist,' who begins to stray by challenging certain articles of the faith based on his Nominalist preconceptions, becomes the 'old Unitarian,' denying whatever aspects of the divine revelation do not conform to his personal theological convictions about the hidden God.

Nominalism is also a fundamental assault on the doctrine of Creation. The denial of the final cause is something specifically refuted in the Word; Jesus affirms that even those things of little worth or significance to sinful man are ordered according to the divine will: "Are not two sparrows sold for a copper coin? And not one of them falls to the ground apart from your Father's will. But the very hairs of your head are all numbered. Do not fear therefore; you are of more value than many sparrows." (Mat. 10:29–31) In all of its apparent futility, all of creation is moving according to the purposes which the Lord has ordained: "For the creation was subjected to futility, not willingly, but because of Him who subjected it in hope; because the creation itself also will be delivered from the bondage of corruption into the glorious liberty of the children of God. For we know that the whole creation groans and labors with birth pangs together until now." (Rom. 8:20–22) That which is unimaginable to human reason is made clear in the divine Word: even futility manifested in that which has been created serves the will of God. Ordained futility serves the divinely established *telos* of the created order.

The necessary denial of reality implicit in subscription to the Nominalist doctrine inflicts grave spiritual damage to man. Subjecting himself to the Nominalist ideology, modern man denies what he knows to be true. Richard Weaver poignantly describes the plight of the Nominalist as follows:

There is no term proper to describe the condition in which he is now left unless it be "abysmality." He is in a deep and dark abysm, and he has nothing with which to raise himself. His life is practice without theory. As problems crowd upon him, he deepens confusion by meeting them with *ad hoc* policies. Secretly he hungers for truth but consoles himself with the thought that life should be experimental.[27]

Deeming God to be ultimately unknowable, man, too, becomes unknowable—and true knowledge is ultimately banished from the entire created order. According to the reasoning of experiential Nominalism, the soul was not visible under the microscope, and thus it never existed—anything which is not measured or comprehensible to human reason and sensation is ultimately unknowable, or—at the very least—uncertain, which is just as bad as "unknowable," when it concerns matters pertaining to the faith. With the Universals banished by the brands and spears of ideology, the radical **Individualism** of Transmutationism and (later) Darwinism was inevitable: Species became an illusion; all that actually exists are individuals, and every individual is a transitional form on the way to the next form.[28]

---

27   Weaver., p. 6–7.

28   Thus Gillespie's observation: "Nominalism destroyed the ontological ground of medieval science by positing a chaotic world of radically individual beings. Indeed, for the nominalists, the world itself is only a higher order sign, an aid to the understanding that does not correspond to any reality. Nominalism thus seems to make science impossible. In fact, however, modern science develops out of nominalism as the result of a reconsideration of the meaning of nominalist ontology. ... The existence or nonexistence of God is irrelevant for the understanding of nature, since he can neither increase nor decrease the chaos of radical individuality that characterizes existence. Science thus does not need to take this God or Scripture into account in its efforts to come to terms with the natural world and can rely instead on experience alone. 'Atheistic' materialism thus has a theological origin in the nominalist revolution. Materialism, it is true, also draws upon ancient atomism and

But God, in every sense which is truly meaningful to man, is knowable in His Word; Holy Scripture is a divine revelation provided by the Holy Trinity, whereby man may truly know the one true God. The Nominalist obsession with the hiddenness of God has time and again shipwrecked on the notion that somehow what God has made known concerning Himself in Holy Scripture is less than man is capable of knowing in this fallen world, and even has fallen into the blasphemy that somehow what the Lord reveals concerning Himself in Holy Scripture is not true to His hidden nature. In fact, at their foundation, all of the various Reformed heresies are based in such a Nominalist dichotomy between, on the one hand, the revealed Triune God of Holy Scripture and, on the other hand, the hidden God of the Reformed imagination.

Speculations about the hidden will of God have been inherent in the Nominalist view from the point when it was first propounded. Thus the Formulators of Concord made it clear that there is no room for speculations concerning a hidden will of God when speaking of matters of faith and salvation.

> But that many are called and few are chosen is not owing to the fact that the meaning of the call of God, made through the Word, is as though God were to say: "Outwardly, through the Word, I indeed call to my kingdom all of you to whom I give my Word, yet in my heart I intend it not for all, but only for a few; for it is my will that the greatest part of those whom I call through the Word should not be enlightened or converted, but be and remain lost, although, through the Word in the call, I declare myself to them otherwise." For this would be to assign to God contradictory wills. That is, in such a

---

Epicureanism, but both of these are received and understood within what was already an essentially nominalist view of the world." (p. 35, 36)

manner it would be taught that God, who is, however, eternal truth, would be contrary to himself; and yet God also punishes the fault when one thing is declared and another is thought and meant in the heart (Ps. 5:9 and 12:2 sq.). Thereby, also, the necessary consolatory foundation is rendered altogether uncertain and of no value, as we are daily reminded and admonished, that only from God's Word, whereby he treats with us and calls us, should we learn and conclude what his will to us is, and that that, to which he gives his Word and which he promises, we should certainly believe and not doubt. (FC SD XI:34–36)

The Formula of Concord thus argues that as the Lord has made known His will for man (that man would not be double-minded, Psa. 5:9[29] and 12:2[30]) we thus know the character of God in this regard. Nominalist speculations regarding what God might *actually* will—in place of what He has made known in His divine Word—are strictly forbidden. In Article II of the Solid Declaration of the Formula of Concord, the pastoral counsel offered by the Formulators is that weak, dejected Christians whose hearts may be filled with Nominalist fears regarding the question of whether the Lord actually wills that they would be saved should be sent to the Word and Sacraments as the sure testimony of God Himself regarding His will; in fact, it is through those means of grace that the Holy Spirit creates and sustains faith: "For this reason we will not relate still further from God's Word how man is converted to God, how and through what means (namely, through the oral Word and the holy Sacraments) the Holy Ghost

29   Lead me, O LORD, in Your righteousness because of my enemies; Make Your way straight before my face. For *there is* no faithfulness in their mouth; Their inward part *is* destruction; Their throat *is* an open tomb; They flatter with their tongue. (v. 8–9)
30   Help, LORD, for the godly man ceases! For the faithful disappear from among the sons of men. They speak idly everyone with his neighbor; *With* flattering lips *and* a double heart they speak. (v. 1–2)

is efficacious in us, and is willing to work and bestow in our hearts, true repentance, faith and new spiritual power and ability for good, and how we should act ourselves toward these means, and [how] use them." (¶48) Again, we read in Article XI of the Formula of Concord:

Therefore no one who would be saved should trouble or harass himself with thoughts concerning the secret counsel of God, as to whether he also is elected and ordained to eternal life; for with these miserable Satan is accustomed to attack and annoy godly hearts. But they should hear Christ [and in him look upon the Book of Life in which is written the eternal election], who is the Book of Life and of God's eternal election of all God's children to eternal life; who testifies to all men without distinction that it is God's will that all men who labor and are heavy laden with sin should come to him, in order that he may give them rest and save them (Matt. 11:28).

According to this doctrine of Christ, they should abstain from their sins, repent, believe his promise, and entirely entrust themselves to him; and since this we cannot do by ourselves of our own powers, the Holy Ghost desires to work repentance and faith in us through the Word and Sacraments. And in order that we may attain this, and persevere and remain steadfast, we should implore God for his grace, which he promised us in holy baptism, and not doubt he will impart it to us according to his promise as he has said (Luke 11:11 sqq.): "If a son shall ask bread of any of you that is a father, will he give him a stone? or if he ask a fish, will he for a fish give him a serpent? or if he shall ask an egg will he offer him a scorpion? If ye then, being evil, know how to give good gifts unto your children, how much more shall your heavenly Father give the Holy Spirit to them that ask him?" (FC SD XI:70–72)

Again, the Confessions argue from a divinely-given analogy between the Lord and men who have been made in the image and likeness of God; even fallen men know what good things a father gives to his children. The Nominalist contention of a radical disjuncture between the hidden God and the creation which He has fashioned is refuted from the Word. And men are again counseled not to listen to satanic doubts concerning the will and Word of the Lord, but instead to listen to the Gospel as it comes to us through the Word and Sacraments. God's Word counsels total reliance upon that Word to speak Truth to us; Nominalism teaches men to doubt the Word (and thus doubt all communication) to convey Truth. The position of the Nominalists is akin to that of Humpty Dumpty in *Through the Looking Glass*:

> 'When *I* use a word,' Humpty Dumpty said in rather a scornful tone, 'it means just what I choose it to mean -- neither more nor less.'
>
> 'The question is,' said Alice, 'whether you *can* make words mean so many different things.'
>
> 'The question is,' said Humpty Dumpty, 'which is to be master - - that's all.'

Nominalism seeks precisely such mastery; it is the fruit of a spirit which does not wish to be subject to definition, but which wishes to redefine at whim. Nominalism imagines that exercising such a mastery over language will make one a god, capable of reshaping creation according to one's own imagination. Again, in the words of Weaver,

> Here begins the assault upon definition: if words no longer correspond to objective realities, it seems no great wrong to take liberties with words. From this point on, faith in language as a means of arriving at truth weakens, until our own age, filled with an acute sense of doubt, looks for a remedy in the new science of semantics.[31]

31   Weaver, p. 7–8.

Current examples of such Nominalist word games undertaken by theological Humpty Dumptys can be seen in the argumentation for women's ordination or homosexual marriage. 'Calling' and 'ordaining' a woman to the office of the ministry is an impossibility because the Word of God excludes such a thing (e.g., 1 Tim. 2:12–13; 1 Cor. 14:34–36). Pronouncing two men or two women to be 'married' is also an impossibility because it is excluded by the divine institution (e.g., Gen. 2:24; Mat. 19:4–6). In all such matters, the attempt of Nominalists to redefine reality are in vain.

In truth, the error of the Nominalists' denial of Universals is refuted from the second chapter of Genesis. It is not a matter of speculation whether there is a Universal: all of man was in Adam; the helper "made comparable to him" is taken from his side.

> This is now bone of my bones
> and flesh of my flesh;
> She shall be called Woman,
> Because she was taken out of Man. (Gen. 2:23)

Adam was all mankind; thus in Adam's fall we sinned all. The Universals are established in Adam, who was created in the image of God; "in the image of God He created him; male and female He created them." (Gen. 1:27) After the Fall, when Seth was born to Adam and Eve, Scripture declares that Adam "begot a son in his own likeness, after his image" (Gen. 5:3). To speak of man is not an abstraction; the Universal of "man" walked in the Garden of Eden, and bestowed the names of every living creature. Thus the names given by Adam "to all cattle, to the birds of the air, and to every beast of the field" (Gen. 2:20) are not empty terms, or rough approximations. The Universal man bestowed these names according to the essence of each created species, even as we are told that he first called Eve "Woman, because she was taken out of Man," (2:23) and later gave her the name "Eve, because she was the mother of all living." (3:20) The naming is not an empty labeling: to speak of Mankind is not a meaningless term, or a mere contrivance or convenience. So, too, in the redemption accomplished by Christ Jesus the Universal is not an empty labeling. "For if by the one man's offense many died, much more the grace of God and the gift by the grace of the one Man, Jesus Christ, abounded to many." (Rom. 5:15)

That such establishment of Universals is not limited to man among the created things was certainly reaffirmed at the time of the Flood, when Noah was commanded, "And of every living thing of all flesh you shall bring two of every sort into the ark, to keep them alive with you; they shall be male and female." (Gen. 6:19) There was a time when the Universals of every living thing were thus confined within the Ark in the midst of the deluge. It would also appear that Noah and his faithful sons were not Nominalists, either, for they understood what it meant for them to "bring two of every sort into the ark"; the Nominalist, seeing only a mob of discrete individuals, would have either despaired of accomplishing the task because it would have meant gathering *every* living being into the ark (because there are no "sorts"—no species) or he would have complained in his heart that God was using such imprecise terminology.

But it is unnecessary to press this argument this far: All has been proven in this regard from Matthew 10: "Are not two sparrows sold for a copper coin? And not one of them falls to the ground apart from your Father's will. But the very hairs of your head are all numbered. Do not fear therefore; you are of more value than many sparrows." (v. 29–31) That each created thing has its life and purpose according to the will of its Creator stands sufficient to negate Nominalist speculations.

The interaction of **Nominalism, Gnosticism** and **Individualism** would seem, then, readily apparent. **Nominalism** wars against any certainty of meaning and divine definition; the interplay of such a corrosive view with the syncretism of **Gnosticism** is readily evident in the relativized ethics and "do-it-yourself" religious system-building and the cafeterial creeds which post-Modern Western man takes for granted. Fallen man wants to define himself, and build a religion according to his own "felt needs" and specifications. Such is the way that leads to death.

The Perilous Path of "Progress."

As pertains to the doctrine of **Progress**, our concern is of a teleological nature. Even as **Gnosticism** and **Nominalism** were busy defining away any knowable divinely-established end for man, men were busy fashioning a new end for themselves. Thus the notion of the Progress of Man was born, albeit initially as a means of expressing a further unfolding of divine purpose. And the teacher of this novel doctrine preceded those who inaugurated the other two movements which we have explored thus far: Joachim of Fiore (ca. 1134–1202) is the chief culprit in this development of the modern notion of Progress and his influence was felt before William of Occam and Marsilio Ficino launched their own errors. As historian Eric Voegelin observed regarding Joachim and his doctrine of historical "Progress":

> Joachim's historical speculation was directed against the then reigning philosophy of history of St. Augustine. According to the Augustinian construction, the phase of history since Christ was the sixth, the last earthly age—the *saculum senescens,* the time of the senility of mankind. The present had no earthly future; its meaning was exhausted in a waiting for the end of history through eschatological events. ... But twelfth-century

western European man could not be satisfied with the view of a senile world waiting for its end; for his world was quite obviously not in decline, but, on the contrary, on the upsurge. ...

Like Joachim himself, his speculation arose out of the thriving religious orders. He projected his view of history on a trinitarian scheme. World history was a consequence of three great ages—those of the Father, the Son, and the Holy Spirit. The first age lasted from the Creation to the birth of Christ; the second, that of the Son, began with Christ. But the age of the Son was not, as Augustine had it, mankind's last; rather, it was to be followed by an additional one, that of the Holy Spirit. We can recognize, even in this thoroughly Christian context, the first symptoms of the idea of a post-Christian era. Joachim went further and indulged in concrete speculations about the beginning of the age of the Holy Spirit, fixing its inauguration at 1260. And the new age, like the preceding ones, was to be ushered in by the appearance of a leader. As the first age began with Abraham and the second with Christ, so the third was to begin in the year 1260 with the appearance of a *dux e Babylone.*[32]

Voegelin's point is well-taken: Man in the time of Joachim was no longer as willing to believe that the most important chapter in human history had already been written. Twelve centuries after the resurrection of the Christ, man looked to create new meaning for himself, and a further earthly development in the Kingdom of God. In the Joachimite system, the importance of the atonement and resurrection is not negated; but a Third Age of Man is nonetheless anticipated as adding something necessary.

---

32   Eric Voegelin, *Science, Politics & Gnosticism,* (Wilmington, Delaware: ISI Books, 2004) p. 69–70.

The subversive power of the notion of Progress is hard to overestimate. The flurry of Progressive ideologies which have marched to and fro in the earth since the Enlightenment (and earlier) seeking whom they may devour may be laid at the feet of Joachimite speculations. Writing in his profoundly important work, *The Pursuit of the Millenium,* Norman Cohn declares:

> Joachim was not consciously unorthodox and he had no desire to subvert the Church. It was with the encouragement of no less than three popes that he wrote down the revelations with which he had been favoured. And nevertheless his thought had implications which were potentially dangerous to the structure of orthodox medieval theology. ... However mindful Joachim might be of the doctrines and claims and interests of the Church, he had in effect propounded a new type of millenarianism—and moreover a type which later generations were to elaborate first in an anti-ecclesiastical and later in a frankly secular sense.[33]

The change which Joachim brought to man's understanding of the order of the universe is difficult to overstate. Belief in Progress, which was impossible to ancient man, has become the an article of faith addressed to the idol of this age.

Why was belief in Progress impossible for mankind before the Modern Age? And what changed to allow such a belief to arise at all? J. B. Bury explored the roots of the doctrine in his 1920 book, *The Idea of Progress—An Inquiry into its Origin and Growth.*[34] Bury noticed that beyond those ideas which "depend for their realisation on human will," there is:

> ...another order of ideas that play a great part in deter-

33   Norman Cohn, *The Pursuit of the Millennium,* (Oxford: Oxford University Press, 1970) p. 109.
34   (London: MacMillan and Co., 1920).

mining and directing the course of man's conduct but do not depend on his will—ideas which bear upon the mystery of life, such as Fate, Providence, or personal immortality. Such ideas may operate in important ways on the forms of social action, but they involve a question of fact and they are accepted or rejected not because they are believed to be useful or injurious, but because they are believed to be true or false.

The idea of the progress of humanity is an idea of this kind, and it is important to be quite clear on the point.[35]

For the ancient pagans and or the early and medieval church, belief in progress was essentially impossible. The doctrine of Progress is not merely the belief that things have gotten better than they have been in the past (whether one is speaking philosophically, morally, materially, etc.). In Bury's words, "you have not got the idea of Progress until you go on to conceive that it is destined to advance indefinitely in the future"[36]—and that "destiny" must rest in hands no greater than those of men.

According to Bury, belief in the alternation of Golden and Iron Ages preserved the pagans from arriving at a doctrine of Progress:

The theory of world-cycles was so widely current that it may almost be described as the orthodox theory of cosmic time among the Greeks, and it passed from them to the Romans. According to some of the Pythagoreans each cycle repeated to the minutest particular the course and events of the preceding. If the universe dissolves into the original chaos, there appeared to them to be no reason why the second chaos should produce a world differing

---

35   p. 1.
36   ibid., p. 7.

in the least respect from its predecessor. The nth cycle would be indeed numerically distinct from the first, but otherwise would be identical with it, and no man could possibly discover the number of the cycle in which he was living.[37]

And, in agreement with the assessment of Voegelin which was cited previously, Bury believed that the Augustinian understanding of the current age categorically excluded the notion of Progress:
> The idea of the universe which prevailed throughout the Middle Ages, and the general orientation of men's thoughts were incompatible with some of the fundamental assumptions which are required by the idea of Progress. According to the Christian theory which was worked out by the Fathers, and especially by St. Augustine, the whole movement of history has the purpose of securing the happiness of a small portion of the human race in another world; it docs not postulate a further development of human history on earth. …
> Again, the medieval doctrine apprehends history not as a natural development but as a series of events ordered by divine intervention and revelations. … A belief in Providence might indeed, and in a future age would, be held along with a belief in Progress, in the same mind; but the fundamental assumptions were incongruous, and so long as the doctrine of Providence was undisputedly in the ascendant, a doctrine of Progress could not arise. And the doctrine of Providence, as it was developed in Augustine's *City of God*, controlled the thought of the Middle Ages.
> There was, moreover, the doctrine of original sin, an insuperable obstacle to the moral amelioration of the race by any gradual process of development. For since, as long as the human species endures on earth, every child

---
37   ibid., p. 12.

will be born naturally evil and worthy of punishment, a moral advance of humanity to perfection is plainly impossible.[38]

An important point which must be grasped is that for Progress to exist as a doctrine, it cannot be as a corollary to that of Providence. In Bury's words, "The process must be the necessary outcome of the psychical and social nature of man; it must not be at the mercy of any external will; otherwise there would be no guarantee of its continuance and its issue, and the idea of Progress would lapse into the idea of Providence."[39] It is not hard to see, then, that in this sense Joachim's doctrine is still a precursor to a true "doctrine of Progress," because it still was under Providence. Nevertheless, Joachimism—in the narrowest possible sense—still functionally overturned the purportedly Augustinian view of history. Thus, having cleared away the notion of the current age being the *last* age, adherents of Progress began to speculate wildly regarding the ends to which mankind—no longer conceived of in terms of Providence—could establish for himself. And, for Progress to commence, the notion of fallen man's inherent imperfectability had to be disregarded. It is small wonder that by the time of Reformation, the doctrine of original sin had been so profoundly eroded: the same Romanist theology which demanded the perfectibility of the saints so that they should have works of supererogation (more good works than necessary to deliver them from the flames of Purgatory) played to the notion of perfectibility which attends the doctrine of Progress.

Following Joachim, man began looking for the "next big thing," and a shockingly large number of popular (and not-so-popular) intellectual and religious movement since the thir-

---

38   ibid., p. 21–22.
39   ibid., p. 5.

teenth century have proclaimed themselves to be the realization of Joachim's Third Age of Man. Man was not now simply awaiting the return of the Christ in glory at the end of the age; instead, there was an expectation of the revealing of an entire new age of man which was previously unanticipated. The connection of Joachim's doctrine of Progress to modern Millenarianism of many stripes is too obvious to miss, of course; but the influences of the doctrine of Progress extend far beyond the confines of such heterodox movements.

The Joachimite doctrine had a profound, and deleterious, effect on European Christianity. Regardless of Joachim's intentions, his ideas lead to the eruption of revolutionary, Millenarian movements which shook the continent with sedition—and often slaughter, as we shall see. Despite Joachim's commitment to the Roman papacy and monasticism, his influence spread as easily within Protestantism as it did among the early followers of St. Francis of Assisi (whom they interpreted to be the leader of the Third Age). Majorie Reeves, an expert on Joachim's thought, wrote in *Joachim of Fiore & the Prophetic Future* of the power which Joachim still had over the minds of Protestants in the seventeenth century:

> The strength of the Joachimist element in this inherited tradition lay in its affirmation of a coming new age in history which would be one of illumination and liberty. … All have certain themes in common: an expectation of immediate catastrophe in the near future, coupled with an optimistic attitude toward the future beyond; an ecumenical belief in the possibility of a *concordia mundi*, both ecclesiastical and political; an affirmation of 'progress' towards the light, as seen in the recent development of learning, printing, geographical discovery, illumination of the Scriptures and evangelical preaching. Their affirmation was basically one about further revela-

tion from God, not about the innate capacity of men to progress; furthermore, it would seem that they expected change to stop in the final state of immutable beatitude. Nonetheless, their ideas could become a seedbed for future hopes: a new illumination of the Spirit, a reign of peace, an ecumenical gathering into one sheepfold, a blossoming of the gifts of men, a richer yield from the earth, all these expectations, detached from their eschatological setting, could be translated into purely human hopes within history, that is, into a doctrine of human progress.[40]

Nor did Joachim's influence end there, for Reeves traces his influence to figures of the German Enlightenment such as Gotthold Lessing (1729–1781) and F. W. Schelling (1775–1854), whose writing influenced G. W. F. Hegel (1770–1831). In fact, Schelling was an early advocate of concept which has now become commonplace among the post-modern intellectual elite: the notion that the West would enter a "post-Christian" age, as the fulfillment of a third age of religion: "The first stage was that of Catholicism, the second of Protestantism, but the third will be the perfect religion of mankind."[41] Thus, Reeves concludes that the revolutionary, "Progressive" character of Joachim's thought has cast a long shadow over the intellectual history of the West: "Thus it is not the devout biblical exegete who has lingered longest in the historical memory, but the imaginative, artistic apostle of a bold new spirit... The Abbot who submitted all his writings to the authority of the Pope has become transformed into a symbol of anarchy and revolutionary change."[42]

---

40   (Gloucestershire, England: Sutton Publishing, 1999) p. 165.
41   ibid., p. 170.
42   ibid., p. 174–175.

Our Lutheran understanding of history substantially holds with the received, Augustinian understanding of the history of the Church. Nevertheless, even Luther and other early Lutheran reformers were not utterly immune to such Joachimite, three-fold divisions of history; as Headley observes, "Without claiming for Luther an implicit scheme of periodization, one can discover a certain pattern by observing the continual return of his attention to crucial moments in the Church's past. The rise of the Papacy and the eschatological significance of his own time distinguish three periods: the early Church, Antichrist, and the last times."[43] The anticipation of the "Last Things" of the history of this world has been a common feature of Christian theology and piety; the problem is that some of the Lutheran reformers attempted to apply Joachim's vision for the coming leader of the Third Age to none other than Martin Luther!

Robin Bruce Barnes' book, *Prophecy and Gnosis— Apocalypticism in the Wake of the Lutheran Reformation*, documents the readiness of people at the time of the Reformation to assume that the "Last Days" were close at hand. In Barnes' words,

> More effectively than any previous interpreter, he [Luther] gave a world-historical, indeed a world-transcending significance to contemporary events by placing them in an eschatological framework; everything pointed to the coming Day of Redemption. Luther found little or no comfort in contemplating the earthly future; hope lay in the discovery that his generation was witnessing and participating in the critical closing acts of history.[44]

43   John M. Headley, *Luther's View of Church History,* (New Haven and London: Yale University Press, 1963) p. 154.

44   Robin Bruce Barnes, *Prophecy and Gnosis—Apocalypticism in the Wake of the Lutheran Reformation*, Stanford University Press: Stanford, 1988) p. 4.

Barnes' last point is of crucial significance: It was the "optimism" of Joachim, and "Progressives" down to the current hour, which drove the development of various fanatical ideologies. Confident that they are building a better world, the proponents of various "Progressive" theologies and ideologies have justified murder and rapine. The "apocalyptic"/prophetic concerns of Luther and Lutheran reformers did not revolve around any worldly improvement or new "Golden Age"—they were looking for the signs that demonstrated that this sin-weary world was drawing to a close.

Nevertheless, even Lutherans would occasionally make use of Joachim in their studies of the Last Days. In the case of Matthias Flacius (1520–1575), the identification of Joachim's prophetic leader of the Third Age of Man was simple: Martin Luther "filled the bill." Flacius was, and remains, a controversial figure in the history of the Reformation—even his defenders admit that he was an acerbic lay theologian whose errors regarding the doctrine of original sin were later justly condemned by the Church in Article I of the Formula of Concord. But Barnes draws particular attention to Flacius as one among those 'Lutherans' who made use of the writings of a man whose theology was far removed from that of the Reformation:

> The greatest example of the search for prophetic truth through the ages was the *Catalogus testium vertatis* of Matthias Flacius Illyricus, published in 1556. Flacius had gathered some 400 witnesses who had spoken against the papacy and its errors. Many of these figures were obscure or entirely unknown to the sixteenth century before Flacius brought them to light again, but the work also included such major writers as Joachim of Fiore. Flacius cited various supposed prophecies of Joachim that could be read as antipapal, but he was apparently also willing to see Luther's movement as the

fulfillment of Joachim's expected world Reformation. Certainly Flacius entertained no thought of a new historical dispensation; he used only what suited his purposes. Yet his work did show remarkable openness to this and to many other sources that, without their prophetic character, would have been of little use to defenders of biblical Protestantism.[45]

Arguably, the Reformation era's greatest example of Joachimite "Progressive" theology can be seen in Thomas Müntzer (1488–1525) and his activities during the Peasants War (1524–1525). Although Müntzer at first appeared to share some of the same concerns regarding the Papacy which motivated Luther and other Reformation theologians, his Joachimite/"Progressive" tendencies quickly metastasized. Norman Cohn offers the following analysis:

> What Müntzer needed if he was to become a new man, sure of himself and of his aim in life, was not indeed to be found in Luther's doctrine of justification by faith alone. It was to be found, rather, in the militant and bloodthirsty millenarianism that was unfolded to him when in 1520 he took up a ministry in the town of Zwickau and came in contact with a weaver called Niklas Storch. … [Storch] proclaimed that now, as in the days of the Apostles, God was communicating directly with his Elect; and the reason for this was that the Last Days were at hand. First the Turks must conquer the world and Antichrist must rule over it; but then—and it would be very soon—the Elect would rise up and annihilate all the godless, so that the Second Coming could take place and the Millennium begin. What most appealed to Müntzer in this programme was the war of extermination which the righteous were to wage against the unrighteous. Aban-

45   ibid., p. 76–77.

176

doning Luther, he now thought and talked only of the
Book of Revelation and of such incidents in the Old Testament as Elijah's slaughter of the priests of Baal, Jehu's
slaying of the sons of Ahab and Jael's assassination of
the sleeping Sisera. Contemporaries noted and lamented
the change that had come over him, the lust for blood
which at times expressed itself in sheer raving.[46]

Müntzer's raving blood lust was directed toward establishing
a primitive Communist "utopia." His purpose for fanning the
flames of rebellion in the Peasants War was, Müntzer admitted,
that "all Christians should become equal and the princes and
lords reluctant to serve the Gospel be driven out or put to death."
According to Shafarevich, "The motto of the Allstedt union
[Müntzer's organization] was *Omnia sunt communia* (Everything in common). Everyone was to share with others 'as much
as he could.' And if a prince or a count refused to do so, 'he was
to be beheaded or hanged.'"[47] The result of Müntzer's Communist, Millenarian rebellion was the slaughter of his followers.
Müntzer's rebellion, however, was far from the last; the Communist, Millenarian takeover of the town of Münster[48] (which
was briefly renamed "New Jerusalem") in 1534–35 was the next
link in the chain of "Progressive" efforts to reshape the world
according to fanatical visions of ideologues.

The Augsburg Confession clearly rejects any Progressive notion of history; the argument is made that priests should
be allowed to marry precisely because human nature is becoming weaker even as the world grows old: "Seeing also that, as
the world is aging, man's nature is gradually growing weaker,

---

46   Cohn, *The Pursuit of the Millennium*, p. 235-236.
47   Igor Shafarevich, *The Socialist Phenomenon,* (New York: Harper &
Row, 1980), p. 53.
48   See, for example, Shafarevich, p. 59–66.

it is well to guard that no more vices steal into Germany." (AC XXIII:14) And the *Augustana* concisely dispels all notions of millennial kingdoms: "They condemn also others, who are now spreading certain Jewish opinions that, before the resurrection of the dead, the godly shall take possession of the kingdom of the world, the ungodly being everywhere suppressed [exterminated]." (AC XVII:5) In this regard, a confessional Lutheran approach to the history of the world and the Church could not be more removed from that of Joachim, who foresaw the rise of a monastic elite in the last age, the Age of the Spirit: Far from supporting the medieval monasticism at the heart of Joachimism, the *Augustana* upheld the understanding that man was less well-fitted for such a life than he had been previously.

The rebellion and slaughter unleashed by the madness of Thomas Müntzer in the Peasants' War (1525), and the Communist, Millenarian state of "New Jerusalem" in Münster (1534/35) were powerful lessons of the dangers loosed on the world in the notion of a New Age of Man prior to the return of the Christ in glory. In time, the Progressive ideology took on a secular mantle, as Cohn briefly summarizes:

> For the long-term, indirect influence of Joachim's speculations can be traced right down to the present day, and most clearly in certain 'philosophies of history' of which the Church emphatically disapproves. Horrified though the unworldly mystic would have been to see it happen, it is unmistakably the Joachite phantasy of the three ages that reappeared in, for instance, the theories of historical evolution expounded by the German Idealist philosophers Lessing, Schelling, Fichte and to some extent Hegel; in Auguste Comte's idea of history as an ascent from the theological through the metaphysical up to the scientific phase; and again in the Marxian dialectic of three stages of primitive communism, class society

and a final communism which is to be the realm of freedom in which the state will have withered away. And it is no less true—if even more paradoxical—that the phrase 'the Third Reich', first coined in 1923 by the publicist Moeller van den Bruck and later adopted as a name for that 'new order' which was supposed to last a thousand years, would have had but little emotional significance if the phantasy of a third and most glorious dispensation had not, over the centuries, entered into the common stock of European social mythology.[49]

The connection between Progress and **Gnosticism** was not long in developing. According to Shafarevich's study of the origins of Socialism, a theologian at the University of Paris, Amalric of Bena (d. ca. 1204-7), "was ideologically linked to Joachim of Flore.

He also saw history as a series of stages in divine revelation. In the beginning there was Moses' law, then Christ's which superseded it. Now the time of the third revelation had come. This was embodied in Amalric and his followers, as previously revelation had been embodied in Christ. They had now become as Christ. Three basic theses of this new Christianity have been preserved. First of all: "God is all." Second: "Everything is One, for everything that is is God." And third: "Whoever observes the law of love is above sin." These theses were interpreted in such a way that those who followed the teachings of Amalric could attain identity with God through ecstasy.[50]

In the thirteenth and fourteenth centuries, the sect of the "Free Spirits" carried on such views:

The key doctrine of this sect was belief in the possibil-

---

49   Cohn, p. 109.
50   Shafarevich, p. 26

ity of "transfiguration into God." Since the soul of each man consists of divine substance, any man in principle can achieve a state of "Godliness." To attain this end he must pass through many years of novitiate in the sect, renounce all property, family, will, and live by begging. Only then does he attain the state of Godliness and become one of the "Free Spirits." ... In other words, the Free Spirit was liberated from all moral constraints. He was higher than Christ, who was a mortal man who attained Godliness only on the cross. The Free Spirit was the complete equal of God, "without distinctions." Hence his will is the will of God, and to him the notion of sin becomes meaningless.[51]

Thus one begins to comprehend in the examination of each of these ideological structures—**Gnosticism**, **Nominalism** and **Progress**—the deadly danger which any one of them poses to adherents of the Christian verity. In conjunction, meeting as they do in a common idolization of the Individual, they have proven lethal to this civilization. They are all mutually reinforcing elements of a larger system. And they are not the full extent of the problem.

---

51   ibid.

SCIENTISM, DEMOCRATISM, AND TOLERANCE.

ur survey of the seven "deadly values" of our culture requires that we visit three remaining values which generally follow from, and build upon, those which have already been examined. The first which we shall examine is **Scientism**, an ideological construction which certainly owes much to the empiricism latent in **Nominalism**. What this means is that Nominalism's insistence on relying only on observable data—that which man may know by applying his reason to the data provided by his senses—has become an ideology which demands that only such observable data can be known to be *true*. The moment one encounters the categorical exclusion of knowledge which is divinely revealed, one is contending which the ideology of Scientism.

Scientism is not to be confused with science—though both proponents and opponents of Scientism often engage in such a confusion. Scientism is an ideology which is fundamentally materialistic; that is, it is the belief that the realm of the senses and the capacities of human reason establish the limits of what can be known—and, indeed, of all that there is to know. Therefore, Scientism leaves no room for spiritual considerations whatsoever.

Democratism is not to be confused with democracy—though, once again, both proponents and opponents of Democratism engage in such confusion. The relationship of democracy and Democratism is a confusion of *means* for *ends*. Democracy is a method of decision making, and although often dominated by cantankerous individuals and rancorous debate, it is a method which has demonstrated a measure of usefulness—as have all other forms of government. Democratism, however, worships the very methodology as an end in itself. Democratists challenge the validity of non-democratic forms of government, and they also tend to be ambivalent to the *outcome* of the 'democratic process.' Democratism is the temple of Sisyphus, where endlessly rolling the stone of public opinion uphill is worshipped as the very essence of man's existence.

Tolerance is the attendant consequence of adherence to **Democratism**. Because Democratists worship the very process of democracy, it is necessary that all parties partake of the sacred rites of measuring public opinion and exercising one's suffrage. For adherents of the doctrine of Tolerance, it is necessary, for the sake of consistency, that no person nor opinion may be excluded from the processes of Democratism, save for those which question any of the seven "deadly values." Tolerance exists in a perpetual war against those who would challenge any of those "values" because such a challenge calls Tolerance into question.

Scientism—Worshiping the Man in the Mirror
In the previous section, reference was made to Michael Gillespie's book, *The Theological Origins of Modernity,* on account of his insights into the origins and effects of Nominalism. In tracing such theological origins, Gillespie also offers some helpful analysis for our examination of **Scientism.**

In Gillespie's analysis of the theological origins of our modern age, the charge that René Descartes (1596–1650) is the father of Scientism might be defended because of Descartes' designation of the scientist as the wisest of men. In the words of Gillespie, "The scientist therefore will be the master not of [a] single area of knowledge but of all knowledge. His knowledge will be a *mathêsis universalis,* a universal science or universal mathematics. He will thus be not merely the wisest human being but also the best technician and the best lawgiver in both political the [sic] theological matters."[1]

Descartes' conclusion is only possible when one has already removed divine revelation from consideration of the higher realms of knowledge. Claims concerning the existence or nature of God are automatically excluded since (it is maintained by the scientistically-minded) there is no sensory evidence to substantiate such claims. Science assumes a lofty standing by resting on the proclamation that *only* the empirical is true, and that therefore, by definition, no higher knowledge can exist. Of course, such an assertion is usually accompanied by a near total ignorance of those fields which might challenge the empirical. It is also a delightfully self-contradictory assertion, since for one to maintain that only the empirical is true is a non-empirical assertion; that is, it cannot be negated on the basis of evidence from the senses, but must be accepted axiomatically.

In fact, despite Descartes' claims for his own objectivity, the truth of the matter is that, by his own account, his crucial scientific breakthrough came in a dream which he allegedly experienced on November 10, 1619. Allen Debus writes of this dream:

> ... he dreamed of a universal science of nature to which the key would be mathematics and the mathematical method. The account is reminiscent of the dreams so prominent in the contemporary alchemical literature. And in fact we do know that Descartes was then aware of the educational and scientific reforms being proposed by those neo-Paracelsian authors who wrote under the name of the "Rosicrucians." Further, on Descartes's return to Paris in 1623 he found that his friends feared that he had become a Rosicrucian while he had been away— an opinion that he found necessary to refute. This epi-

---

1   Gillespie, p. 187.

sode may only be accorded a footnote in most accounts of the work of Descartes, but it once more illustrates the difficulty faced by historians who seek absolutely to demarcate the "rational" from the "irrational" in the early seventeenth century.[2]

As implausible as it seems, the man who insisted on an absolutely "mechanical" view of the universe,[3] invoked the imagery of divine revelation by insisting such an awareness came to him in a dream, and he chose such an invocation in the context of various **Gnostic** organizations (e.g., the Rosicrucians) using similar imagery to peddle their 'secret knowledge.'

Having eliminated divine revelation as a source of knowledge concerning the Lord who fashioned man and the world, Scientism drives a **Progressive** agenda which denies that "human nature" has a fixed, unalterable (humanly-speaking) character which must be accommodated, rather than reengineered. (Remember: for those who are adherents of the doctrine of **Progress**, belief in original sin is categorically eliminated.) Scientism, being inherently **Nominalistic**, only sees individuals, for whom "mankind" is a hollow descriptive. In the analysis of Russell Kirk:

> To resume, nevertheless the typical ideologue thinks of himself as perfectly objective. The core of his belief is that human nature and human society may be improved infinitely—nay, perfected—by the application of the techniques of the physical and biological sciences to the governance of men. Nearly all nineteenth and twentieth-century radical movements drew their inspiration in considerable part from this positivistic as-

---

2   Allen G. Debus, *Man and Nature in the Renaissance,* (Cambridge & New York: Cambridge University Press, 1978) p. 105–6.
3   ibid., p. 106.

sumption; Marxism is only one of the more systematic products of this view of life and thought. For the convinced positivist-ideologue, traditional religion has been a nuisance and a curse, because it impedes the designs of the ideological planner. Science, with a Roman S, should supplant God. The religious teacher would give way to the "scientific" manager of the new society.

This rather vague claim that society ought to be regulated on "scientific" principles has held an appeal for some physical and biological scientists; and the less such scientists have known of humane letters, history, and political theory, the more enthusiastic they have tended to be for a new order which would sweep away all the errors and follies of mankind by a radical application of scientific theory and method. The high achievements of physical and biological sciences in the nineteenth century gave powerful reinforcement to advocates of "scientism" in sociology and politics. Religion, moral tradition, and the complex of established political institutions were irrational and unscientific and subjective, it seemed; surely the scientists must show the preachers and politicians the way to a better world.[4]

The way of Progressivist ideology has often been the path of fire and sword since those days immediately following the death of Joachim. Man is centered in the Three Estates in a manner which does not easily allow him to be dislodged; the bonds of fathers in blood and fathers in office are not easily severed, nor is the inherent love of one's own land and people. The wisdom of Ælfric—that "When there is too much evil among humankind, wise men ought to consider with discerning thought which of the pillars of the throne might be broken, and immediately

---

4   Russell Kirk, "The Drug of Ideology," in *The Essential Russell Kirk*, (Wilmington, Deleware: ISI Books, 2007) p. 354–355.

repair it. The throne stands on these three pillars: *laboratores, bellatores, oratores*"—endured even after the words were forgotten because the Table of Duties expresses the divine order established for life in this world. Thus the satanic fury of the ideologists has raged against these Estates, assaulted the pillars of civilization, and sought to sever the ancient bonds and remake man—as if any man were ever, could ever, be a *tabula rasa*. The demonic character of the war against the Estates must be recognized; in the words of Philip Melanchthon's hymn regarding the war between the angels and demons:

> The ancient Dragon is their foe;
> His envy and his wrath they know.
> It always is his aim and pride
> Thy Christian people to divide.
> As he of old deceived the world
> And into sin and death has hurled,
> So now he subtly lies in way
> To ruin school and Church and State. (TLH 254:4–5)

Science v. Scientism

While reflecting on the pernicious influence of Scientism, a point which must be emphasized is that the interest in science which developed in the late Middle Ages and blossomed in the Lutheran Reformation was firmly opposed to Scientism, and sought simply to improve man's knowledge of God's creation. In fact, the origins of modern science can clearly be seen in a rejection of certain strictures of Greek philosophy which had become common in the early universities.[5] In fact, the development of the sciences in the West took place as an unanticipated consequence of rattling, and finally breaking, certain fetters imposed upon the Western mind by Aristotelean philosophy.

---

5   The following is drawn from the author's essay, "Faith and Community: Moving Beyond LEO," in *Civilization and the New Frontier* (Malone, Texas: Repristination Press, 2010), p. 57–74.

The development of the university is uniquely an artifact of Christendom. As Edward Grant noted in his book, *The Foundations of Modern Science in the Middle Ages*, the universities established by the Church were of foundational significance for the rise of the sciences:

> ...a scientific revolution could not have occurred in Western Europe in the seventeenth century if the level of science and natural philosophy had remained what it was in the first half of the twelfth century, that is, just prior to the translation of Greco-Arabic science that was under way in the latter half of that century. Without the translations, which transformed European intellectual life, and the momentous events that followed from them, the Scientific Revolution in the seventeenth century would have been impossible.[6]

However, the translations undertaken in the late-twelfth century were only the first of three factors which gave rise to the sciences:

> A second precondition was the formation of the medieval university, with its corporate structure and varied activities. The universities that had emerged by the thirteenth century in Paris, Oxford, and Bologna were different from anything the world had ever seen. Nothing in Islam, China, or India, or in the ancient civilizations of South America, was comparable to the medieval university. It is in this remarkable institution, and its unusual activities, that the foundations of modern science must be sought.[7]

As Grant observes, the Church could have chosen to suppress Greek learning in the fourth century, but elected not to, and

---

6   (Cambridge & New York: Cambridge University Press, 1996) p. 170.
7   ibid., p. 172.

instead made the trivium and quadrivium the core of learning.[8] But it was not only the presence of translations, and a university setting, which was necessary for the development of the sciences: a class of theologically-trained natural philosophers provided the third necessary element for the rise of the sciences:

> The third, and final, pre-condition for the Scientific Revolution was the emergence of a class of theologian-natural philosophers, that is, a class of individuals who were not only trained in theology—most had theological degrees—but who also had previously attained the degree of master of arts or its equivalent and were therefore thoroughly trained in that discipline. Their importance cannot be overestimated. If theologians at the universities had decided to oppose Aristotelean learning as dangerous to the faith, it could not have become the focus of study in European universities. Without the approval and sanction of these scholars, Greco-Arabic science and Aristotelean natural philosophy could not have become the official curriculum of the universities.[9]

In fact, it appears that what transpired in the late twelfth century was a balance between church and university which allowed for just enough—but not too much—influence for Aristotle. When the University of Paris allowed too much latitude to the teachings of Aristotle, the bishop of Paris issued a series of condemnations in A.D. 1277 which provided theological impetus to consider an order of nature which Aristotelean science had deemed impossible.

The bishop of Paris, Etienne Tempier, determined that a formal condemnation of certain Aristotelean doctrines would be necessary because they placed limitations on the Triune God—

8   ibid., p. 4, 5, 15.
9   ibid., p. 174.

they were, in essence, an assault on the Lord's omnipotence. One of the most important of the Aristotelean dogmas was the notion that it was "impossible" for the God to create more than one world. In the science of Aristotle, the Earth is the bottom/center of creation where the heaviest of the elements must naturally settle; to allow for multiple worlds would allow for multiple 'centers'—which would be a logical impossibility. The belief "That the First Cause cannot make several worlds" was directly enunciated and condemned in the bishop's decree. [10] As a leading expert on the decree has written:

> The decree of 1277 therefore marks a complete reversal in the opinion of the Parisian masters about the plurality of worlds. Before the decree, they accumulated reasons derived from Peripatetic physics in order to establish that the existence of several worlds is an impossibility; therefore they refused God the power to multiply worlds. They endeavored to prove that this refusal was not a limitation on God's creative omnipotence. After the decree, all theologians held for certain that God can create multiple worlds, if He wishes to. They endeavored to destroy the reasons given from physics that were pitted against this proposition, or at least to interpret them in such a way that they were no longer objections. [11]

According to Duhem, "After the ban formulated by Etienne Tempier, the masters of Oxford also accepted this decision". [12] Because of the bishop's condemnation, Grant declares, "By emphasizing God's absolute power to do anything short of a logical contradiction, the articles condemned in 1277 had a curious, and probably unintended, effect: they encouraged speculation about

10   Pierre Duhem, *Medieval Cosmology—Theories of Infinity, Place, Time, Void, and the Plurality of Worlds*, ed. and trans. by Roger Ariew, (Chicago and London: The University of Chicago Press, 1985) p. 450.
11   ibid., p. 455.
12   ibid.

natural impossibilities in the Aristotelean world system, which were often treated as hypothetical possibilities."[13] In short, the Church's defense of the omnipotence of God allowed the nascent sciences to explore a more extensive range of God's possible works in creation.

The University of Wittenberg became an important center for the new science during the Reformation era. From his inaugural lecture in 1518, Philip Melanchthon played an important role in reforming education in the sciences.[14] Although both Luther and Melanchthon were initially quite critical of Aristotle, after publication of Melanchthon's commentary on Colossians in 1527, Wittenberg moved in the direction of more overt support for sciences. In the assessment of Kusukawa:

> Melanchthon's message was always the same: the studies of astrology, astronomy, arithmetic and geometry are necessary because they all aim at the same goal of knowing God the Ruler and Creator; the inseparable studies of astrology and astronomy had to be studied because they were key to knowledge of God's government of the heavens; geometry and arithmetic had equally to be learnt because they were necessary preparations for this knowledge of God's government.[15]

The study of natural philosophy was undertaken for a benefit which today would be called "apologetic":

> Instead of systematically resolving questions by logical distinctions, definitions and syllogisms, Melanchthon proceeded by providing definitions of pre-selected and pre-ordered *loci*, in order effectively to teach the Provi-

---

13   Grant, p. 81.

14   Sachiko Kusukawa, *The Transformation of Natural Philosophy— The Case of Philip Melanchthon*, (Cambridge: Cambridge University Press, 1995) p. 37.

15   ibid., p. 142.

dential design of God in this physical world.

Melanchthon's natural philosophy never rationally proved the central tenets of Lutheran theology. Theological points were introduced always with Scriptural grounding. Melanchthon's natural philosophy offered *a posteriori* arguments in order to confirm a single point about the divinity, that God created and sustains everything in this physical universe with Providential design.[16]

It should also be noted that the Lutheran approach to natural philosophy was markedly different from that of **Nominalist** Calvinism. Again, in the words of Kusukawa: "Calvin too understood that all the works of God clearly demonstrated their Creator, but he differed from Melanchthon in insisting that human reason is so impaired by sin that it misperceives God's revelation. That is, there was no reliable natural knowledge of God for Calvin."[17] But then, given Calvin's double predestination, it would seem that he did not believe that Holy Scripture provided "reliable" knowledge concerning the will of God, since Calvin posited a hidden divine will which was radically in opposition to His revealed will.

In the aftermath of the Thirty Years War, with the rise of Descartes' scientistic pretensions, the earlier Lutheran contributions to the place of the sciences within the realm of human knowledge was steadily eclipsed. The bloodless calculations of the scientistically-bent mind built on the foundation laid by Joachim, William of Occam and Marsilio Ficino, harmonizing these mutually-reenforcing rebellions against the divine order into a juggernaut aimed at the heart of civilization. Thus Weaver notes: "The history of our social disintegration began with the

---

16   ibid., p. 202.
17   ibid., p. 205.

unfixing of relationships in the fourteenth century, but the effort to do away with society entirely did not become programmatic until the nineteenth, when it appeared as a culmination of the prevailing nature philosophy."[18] It took time for the critical mass necessary for this rebellion to take shape; having infiltrated Church, State and Home, in time and through subversion the pillars were assaulted and the bonds broken toward the end that atomized individuals could stand before a self-deified State. A man is a mere *datum* in the calculations of the pseudo-science of the ideologists. Political philosophy degraded to "Political Science," and metaphysics and theology relegated to mere antiquarian interest or obscurantist intention, the **Progressive**, **Scientistic** agenda is also a leveling agenda—a **Democratist** agenda—and thus we are brought to our next point under examination.

Descent into Democratism

One tragic effect of the decline from political philosophy to "Political Science" is that the practitioners of the latter know virtually nothing of the former. If such a woeful ignorance did not predominate, the would-be molders of men would approach their task with greater trepidation, and would at the least not be ignorant of the disdain which wise men of earlier generations expressed toward those who appealed to mass sentiment. Thus, for example, the defenders of the American Republic among the ranks of the Federalists declared in 1787 in the celebrated *Federalist No. 10* that the capitulation of law to mass sentiment— which is the essence of Democratism—was injurious to good government.

> A common passion or interest will, in almost every case, be felt by a majority of the whole; a communication and concert results from the form of Government itself; and there is nothing to check the inducements to

18   Weaver, p. 36.

sacrifice the weaker party, or an obnoxious individual. Hence it is, that such Democracies have ever been spectacles of turbulence and contention; have ever been found incompatible with personal security, or the rights of property; and have in general been as short in their lives as they have been violent in their deaths. Theoretic politicians, who have patronized this species of Government, have erroneously supposed, that by reducing mankind to a perfect equality in their political rights, they would, at the same time, be perfectly equalized and assimilated in their possessions, their opinions and their passions.

A Republic, by which I mean a Government in which the scheme of representation takes place, opens a different prospect, and promises the cure for which we are seeking.[19]

Democratism, the founders realized, was given to a factious party spirit which is inherently dangerous to ordered liberty, and thus to the Estates which are vital to the essence of civilization. Again, in the words of *Federalist No. 10*, one may see that the Federalists' Republican cure to Democratism was to limit the ability of the mass of men to seize authority over the whole of the body politic:

The influence of factious leaders may kindle a flame within their particular States, but will be unable to spread a general conflagration through the other States: a religious sect, may degenerate into a political faction in a part of the Confederacy; but the variety of sects dispersed over the entire face of it, must secure the national Councils against any danger from that source: a rage for paper money, for an abolition of debts, for an equal division of property, or for any other improper or wicked project, will be less apt to pervade the whole body of

19   *The Federalist Papers,* (New York: Bantam Books, 1982) p. 46.

the Union, than a particular member of it; in the same proportion as such a malady is more likely to taint a particular county or district, than an entire State.[20]

But one may see that the very egalitarianism which drove fear into the heart of "Publius" as he penned the above cited argument quickly triumphed, for Democratism is consistent with the other deadly values of this culture. In short, belief in **Individualism** and **Progress** will drive a Democratist spirit because once one has conceded such notions, the search for Progress through the pooling of the fatuous sentiments has a Darwinian character: The viciousness of the political marketplace will determine 'winners' whose opinions are what passes for law. And the leveling of political power inherent in Democratism is also expressed in egalitarianism in the distribution of goods. The discovery of this linkage of vices was no new discovery on the part of the founding fathers; it has been known since classical antiquity. Thus Aristophanes predicted in his 4th century B.C. play, *Ecclesiazusae*, when the women seize power and declare a communist state. The leader of the communistic scheme, Praxagora, announces her "scheme" as follows:

> Briefly my scheme is: mankind should possess
> In common the instruments of happiness.
> Henceforth private property comes to an end—
> It's all wrong for a man to have too much to spend,
> While others moan, starving; another we see
> Has acres of land tilled prosperously,
> While this man has not enough earth for his grave.
> You'll find men who haven't a single lean slave
> While others have hundreds to run at their call. ...
> That's over: all things are owned henceforth by all.[21]

---

20   ibid., p. 48–49.
21   *The Complete Plays of Aristophanes,* (New York: Bantam Books, 1981) p. 438.

When one (Blepyros) dares to ask, "Can your scheme touch the man rich in coin? Can't he block it?," the threat of violent leveling permeates Praxagora's response: "He must hand gold all in." Blepyros raises a further objection, complaining of the 'free love' which Praxagora would make an element of her 're-form,' he asks, "But where love has run wild who will know his own child?," only to be told: "He won't; and why should he? Now children will say *Father* to any man older than they."[22] The new form of household will be "In one common to all—easy and free, mingling with beautiful liberty: All family restrictions abolished."[23] The abolition of different levels of authority being allotted to different standings within the Estates has been understood for thousands of years to lead to a leveling which destroys all responsibility and authority within society.

In *The Rise of Totalitarian Democracy*,[24] J. L. Talmon's analysis of Totalitarian movements from the 18th to the 20th centuries draws on the connection between Democratism (which he terms "totalitarian democracy") and the other "deadly values" which we have under consideration. Specifically, Talmon connects Democratism to the doctrines of **Progress** (which had become overtly post-Christian by the time period under consideration in his study) and **Individualism**:

> Men were gripped by the idea that the conditions, a product of faith, time and custom, in which they and their forefathers had been living, were unnatural and had all to be replaced by deliberately planned uniform patterns, which would be natural and rational.

> This was the result of the decline of the traditional order in Europe: religion lost its intellectual as well as

---

22   ibid., p. 439, 440.
23   ibid., p. 442.
24   (Boston: The Beacon Press, 1952).

its emotional hold; hierarchical feudalism disintegrated under the impact of social and economic factors; and the older conception of society based on status came to be replaced by the idea of the abstract, individual man. ... The decline of religious authority implied the liberation of man's conscience, but it also implied something else. Religious ethics had to be speedily replaced by secular, social morality. With the rejection of the Church and of transcendental justice, the State remained the sole source and sanction of morality. This was a matter of great importance, at a time when politics were considered indistinguishable from ethics. ...

... In the past it was possible for the State to regard many things as matters for God and Church alone. The new State could recognize no such limitations. Formerly, men lived in groups. A man had to belong to some group, and could belong to several at the same time. Now there was to be only one framework for all activity: the nation.[25]

Although Talmon does not express himself in terms of the Church's traditional language regarding the Estates, the "groups" to which he refers are indeed those divinely-established relationships in which all of mankind is ordered. One's standing in those Estates is fundamental to identity—to one's relationship with the entire created order. "Totalitarian democracy," or Democratism, idolizes the State because it becomes the sole authority; the soulless, faceless masses all have their equal—equally meaningless—"input"[26] into the endless calculations of a total State which demands unswerving obedience from all of its constituent parts.

25   p. 3, 4.

26   The general acceptance of such a mechanistic term as "input" to describe one's participation in Church, State and Home demonstrates how far the dehumanizing character of the seven deadly values have permeated the mindset of the public. Human beings are merely data generators, providing "input" for the calculations of the elite overseeing a presumably omnicompetent State.

To understand the subversive character of Democratism, one would be well-served by a reading of José Ortega y Gasset's *The Revolt of the Masses*, for one would quickly discover that the fruit of the all the movements outlined above could be found in what Ortega identified in 1930 as the "mass man." Ortega wisely understood that the coming of the masses represented an overthrow of the fathers in blood and office (whom he termed "select minorities") necessary to civilization:

> When one speaks of "select minorities" it is usual for the evil-minded to twist the sense of this expression, pretending to be unaware that the select man is not the petulant person who thinks himself superior to the rest, but the man who demands more of himself than the rest, even though he may not fulfill in his person those higher exigencies. For there is no doubt that the most radical division that it is possible to make of humanity is that which splits it into two classes of creatures: those who make great demands of themselves, piling up difficulties and duties; and those who demand nothing special of themselves, but for whom to live is to be every moment what they already are, without imposing on themselves any effort toward perfection; mere buoys that float on the waves.[27]

Civilization rests upon such a distinction, such a division, of mankind, and it falls to the "select minorities" to guide their respective Estates. Membership in such "select minorities" carries obligations which may not be shirked without potential temporal and eternal ramifications. Mass man resents the authority which such minorities may exercise over him, but he does not desire the responsibilities which are concomitant with such authority.

---

27   José Ortega, *The Revolt of the Masses*, (New York and London: W.W. Norton, 1993) p. 15.

Where the Estates exercise their divinely-given authority, or-dered liberty is possible. The paternal 'rule' which takes place within the three Estates is not one which is established through coercion; in Ortega's words:

> By "rule" we are not here to understand primarily the exercise of material power, of physical coercion. ... The stable, normal relation amongst men which is known as "rule" *never rests on force*; on the contrary, it is because a man or group of men exercise command that they have at their disposition that social apparatus or machinery known as "force."[28]

Legitimate rule has force at its disposal: Parents disciple their children, Pastors excommunicate the impenitent, and Rulers punish criminals with death or imprisonment. One's paternal authority within the three Estates is not established by force, though it may exercise its responsibilities through coercion. But when and where Democratism abolishes any authority but its own, rule descends into tyranny because its very existence runs counter to the Estates and can only be established and main-tained through the use of violence.

Now, the subversion of right and godly order had culmi-nated in the revolt of the masses; in the words of Ortega:

> ...the mass had decided to advance to the foreground of social life, to occupy the places, to use the instruments and to enjoy the pleasures hitherto reserved to the few.
>
> It is evident, for example, that the places were never intended for the multitude, for their dimensions were too limited, and the crowd is continuously over-flowing; thus manifesting to our eyes and in the clearest manner the new phenomenon: the mass, without ceasing to be mass, is supplanting the minorities.

---

28   p. 126.

No one, I believe, will regret that people are to-day enjoying themselves in greater measure and numbers than before, since they have now both the desire and the means of satisfying it. The evil lies in the fact that this decision taken by the masses to assume the activities proper to the minorities is not, and cannot be, manifested solely in the domain of pleasure, but that it is a general feature of our time. Thus—to anticipate what we shall see later—I believe that the political innovations of recent times signify nothing less that the political domination of the masses. The old democracy was tempered by a generous dose of liberalism and of enthusiasm for law. By serving these principles the individual bound himself to maintain a severe discipline over himself. Under the shelter of liberal principles and the rule of law, minorities could live and act. Democracy and law—life in common under the law—were synonymous. To-day we are witnessing the triumphs of a hyperdemocracy in which the mass acts directly, outside the law, imposing its aspirations and its desires by means of material pressure.[29]

But the "mass man" is no mere Proletarian—in a Marxist sense of the term, anyway. Already eighty years ago Ortega identified the 'scientific' specialist as the quintessential "mass man":

For it is necessary to insist upon this extraordinary but undeniable fact: experimental science has progressed thanks in great part to the work of men astoundingly mediocre, and even less than mediocre. That is to say, modern science, the root and symbol of our actual civilisation, finds a place for the intellectually commonplace man and allows him to work therein with success. The reason for this lies in what is at the same time the greatest advantage and the gravest peril of the new sci-

29   ibid., p. 16–17.

ence, and of the civilisation directed and represented by it, namely mechanisation.

... The specialist "knows" very well his own tiny corner of the universe; he is radically ignorant of all the rest.[30]

For those who have eyes to see, such an analysis is, in retrospect, undeniably true. The terrible imagination of the **Progressives** who would remake the world according to their vision is uncomplicated by such things as a knowledge of history or the long, twisting paths of political philosophy. With gleaming eyes and flashing knives, every tradition, aspect of the human condition, or divinely established institution which would challenge their Democratist dreams is hewn down like so many Gordian Knots. As Paul Rahe has written, the forced egalitarianism which is at the heart of Democratism has been readily evident since the time of Alexis de Tocqueville (1805–1859):

> On this point, Tocqueville and our forebears were surely right. For in the course of the past seventy-five years, as our government has conferred on its citizens the extensive array of programmatic rights now called "entitlements," there has been a steady erosion of our political and our private rights. To grasp why this is so, one must begin with the recognition that there is one great—one might even say, insuperable—obstacle to guaranteeing the citizens of a nation "equality in the pursuit of happiness," and that obstacle is what Tocqueville calls "the inequality of intellect." As we have already noted ... the equality for which democratic peoples hunger cannot be achieved. No matter how "democratic the *etat social* and the political constitution of a people may be," thanks to the natural "inequality of intellect," the equality that they desire "retreats before them every day without ever concealing itself from view; and in withdrawing, it draws

---

30   ibid., p. 111.

them on in pursuit. Unceasingly, they believe that they are going to lay hold of it, and it escapes unceasingly from their grasp. They see it close enough to know its charms, they do not approach it close enough to enjoy it, and they die before having fully savored its sweetness." It is democratic envy, Tocqueville claims, that accounts for "the singular melancholy" displayed by the inhabitants of democratic countries "in the bosom of their abundance," and it explains as well "the disgust with life that comes at times to lay hold of them in the midst of an easy and tranquil existence" (*DA* II.ii.13, p. 125).[31]

The statesmen have been replaced by technocrats, men and women utterly lacking an elevated vision guided by the Word of God and the lessons of antiquity. They see in society a laboratory to try out various brands of ideological patent medicine. The fatherless modern home is Democratism enfleshed—the living nightmare of Aristophanes' *Ecclesiazusae*—and the infantile masses are herded by social workers through the stages of life until it falls to one such faceless bureaucrat to finally euthanize the individual who has outlived the period of productivity decreed by the holy depreciation calendar. Systematized inhumanity is sacramentally affirmed through the herding of the masses into places where they may cast ballots for distinctions without a difference. It must be so, for a vital principle of **Democratism** is that a meaningful distinction—a true difference if philosophy—is a deadly threat (in fact, the only threat) to the syncretistic whole. And this brings us to the doctrine of **Tolerance**.

The Tyranny of Toleration

Tolerance would seem to be intellectually inevitable, given the points discussed previously. The essence of 'intoler-

31   Paul A. Rahe, *Soft Despotism, Democracy's Drift,* (New Haven & London: Yale University Press, 2009) p. 262.

ance' is found in varying assertions concerning Truth.[32] 'Intolerance' is affirming that morality is not a plaything subject to opinion polls. 'Intolerance' is declaring that not every fevered delusion of sin-darkened souls is simply "another path to God" which is "just as good" (or, better yet, "just as spiritual") as the one holy catholic and apostolic faith.

To maintain that mutually exclusive assertions are actually mutually exclusive runs counter to the spirit of the age; with Gnostic syncretism ascendant, men would rather simply accommodate all views—heedless of the disjointed monstrosity which is the fruit of their labors—rather than confront the reality of the differences. Gnostic syncretism is assisted by **Nominalism's** thesis that definition is an assertion of human will; being undefined by God and lacking both formal and final cause, men are free to pursue the **Democratist** agenda of **Progress** unto a self-defined perfection. The cost has been that the much vaunted **Individual** has become virtually a meaningless concept, for the ideological straightjacket of **Scientism** endeavors to cut men off from knowledge of those parts of themselves which cannot be confined to a petri dish and slid under a microscope.

It is worth pausing to consider how inhuman the confluence of deadly values actually is. The notion of **Tolerance** is something which is at war with the very notion of 'society,' as Loren Samons observes:

32   It was not always so; without the other deadly values being in place, Tolerance need not arise. Samons observes Athenian Democracy did not bring Tolerance with it: "Yet the freedom with which Athenians addressed these issues should not lead us to conclude that they rejected cultural norms and embraced something like modern 'social tolerance.' ... [For example:] Far from demanding a particularly tolerant attitude toward sexual activity, the Athenians' treatment of sex in their popular media continually reinforced the prevailing moral code, which differed from other societies' conventions but was a moral code nonetheless." (Loren J. Samons II, *What's Wrong with Democracy?—From Athenian Practice to American Worship*, [Berkeley: University of California Press, 2004] p. 165.)

On the face of it, diversity per se as a goal seems inconsistent with the idea of a "society" as traditionally understood and as desired naturally, I am speculating, by human beings. The word *society* reflects the idea of alliance between individuals or groups based on shared goals (*socii* in Latin are "allies," those who share, follow, act together). ... As traditionally understood, a society seems incapable of comprising a set of individuals seeking diversity *as a goal* (while societies of certain types may produce diversity *as a result*). Nevertheless, many Americans would list diversity as one of America's particular identifying features and strengths.[33]

This is where the rebellion of Eve has led: Seeking to be like God, the mass man is terrified that anyone might assert that there is a God Who is beyond man's judgment but Who may yet be known according to His Word, and may even be known to a limited extent in His creation. Thus, what may not be tolerated is the assertion that there is one God, and He does not answer to the demands of focus groups and free elections. What may not be tolerated is the assertion that there is one Truth, for if Truth is one, and all that which opposes it is error, and there is One who will judge between men on the basis of the revealed Truth, then all of the seven 'values' guiding contemporary culture are a lie.

The late A.J. Conyers insightful book, *The Long Truce,* demonstrates that the development of, and intention behind, the doctrine of toleration has been the pursuit of power in the hands of the scientistic practitioners of Progress, and he thus points to the character of tolerance portrayed in Thomas Hobbes' *Leviathan*:

> In Hobbes we find in precise form the motivation for a modern idea of toleration. The engraving on the title page of the first edition of *Leviathan* depicts the gargan-

___
33   ibid., p. 167.

tuan figure of a man, with the crown of a king, bearing in one hand the sword of the ruler and in the other the crosier of a bishop, keeping watch over a peaceful city. The giant figure is, upon closer inspection, composed of a multitude of people who make up his body. This giant authority rules with the symbols of church and state and the two are no longer permitted to resist or correct each other. Theology has been set aside in the interest of the political task of ruling. Therefore, all groups, including the church, but not exclusively the church, are coopted into the general political enterprise. Groups no longer appear distinctly, only the multitude of individuals and the ruler himself.[34]

Leviathan will permit the shell of the Estates to remain, for a time; but it will not permit such Estates to challenge, or even question, its authority and its decrees. Thus the insight of Samons well describes the interaction of **Democratism** and **Tolerance**:

In the United States today, the anti-values of freedom, choice, and diversity have become so powerful (and dangerous) in part because—note the supreme irony—they admit of no philosophical opposition. One simply cannot oppose treating these ideas as society's appropriate goals without risking being labeled a reactionary, heretic, or worse, as if it had been empirically proven that only peoples or regimes that worship these deities can produce justice or happiness.[35]

The seven deadly values of contemporary culture end in precisely such idolatry. One will worship what the rebellion of man has wrought, or be destroyed. Like Narcissus, fallen man worships and lusts for his own fallen image—an idolatry which ends in death.

---

34   A. J. Conyers, *The Long Truce—How Toleration Made the World Safe for Power and Profit*, (Dallas: Spence Publishing Company, 2001), p. 63-4.
35   Samons, p. 184.

CONCLUSION.

In the aftermath of the developments survey above, the last state of post-modern man is worse than the first. Each of the deadly values came to prominence because it was believed to be addressing something that was *lacking* in pre-modern thought. In truth, what was sacrificed was a civilization which was Christendom. What has taken its place is a mass of men who do not even know who they are, or from whence they have come.

Gnostic syncretism found its appeal at a time when cultures (and religions) were in conflict—the engagement with Gnostic heresies which were imported into Western Europe from the East, and the centuries of ongoing conflict with the Mohammedans. The civilizational decay which was in evidence when Gnosticism flowed into Western Europe from the East not only once, but at least twice—first through the rise of the Albigensian heresy in the 13th century, and then through the Hermetic/Neoplatonic syncretism in the 15th century—indicates that the West steadily lost the ability to resist the tide of **Gnosticism** as syncretism became more and more acceptable. Confronted by different religions, there was a temptation to interpret such *false* paths as simply being *alternative* paths—an error in which **Tolerance** would be enshrined as one of the chief virtues of the modern age.

Nominalism emerged in Western thought because Greek notions of the Universals came into question; the new dogma was part of a general assault on the perceived weaknesses of Medieval Scholasticism. Nominalism brings alienation with it—an alienation not only from God, but from the rest of creation. The revealed will of God is called into question, and even the testimony of our own senses is called into question. A philosophy focused on one's self—Descartes' *cogito ergo sum*—is the desperate cry of the Nominalist vainly struggling to believe that anything is real, including himself. In a world in which every man is alienated from his fellow man by a fundamental sense of alienation, in which vocations are reduced to mere labels, and the ability to know one's Creator is ruled fundamentally impossible, one is left with a society which has gone mad—an endless row of Skinnerian boxes, left with no one to tend them, and no sure confidence that there is anything outside of one's 'box.'

Progress, as we have seen, developed as a force in European imagination in no small part because of the length of time which had passed since the Ascension; there was a readiness in the Western mind to believe that "something new" would transpire before the Last Days, and even those who remained fundamentally 'Augustinian' in their view of history sought for signs of the end in their own time with a fervor which had apparently not been seen in generations. However, what Joachim unleashed on the world has resulted in the mass of men abandoning making the hope of the resurrection the center of their life, and have turned away to the creation of a new Tower of Babel for their hope. As J.B. Bury wrote nearly a century ago:

> We may believe in the doctrine of Progress or we may not, but in either case it is a matter of interest to examine the origins and trace the history of what is now, even should it ultimately prove to be no more than an *idolum sæculi*, the animating and controlling idea of western civilization. For the earthly Progress of humanity is the general test to which social aims and theories are submitted as a matter of course. The phrase *civilization and progress* has become stereotyped, and illustrates how we have come to judge a civilization good or bad according

as it is or is not progressive. The ideals of liberty and democracy, which have their own ancient and independent justifications, have sought a new strength by attaching themselves to Progress. The conjunctions of "liberty and progress," "democracy and progress," meet us at every turn. Socialism at an early stage of its modern development, sought the same aid. The friends of Mars, who cannot bear the prospect of perpetual peace, maintain that war is an indispensable instrument of Progress. It is in the name of Progress that the doctrinaires who establish the present reign of terror in Russia profess to act. All this shows the prevalent feeling that a social or political theory or programme is hardly tenable if it cannot claim that it harmonises with this controlling idea.[1]

Now, with Progress being the assumed necessary frame of reference for any societal concern, the inherently anti-Providential character of the doctrine permeates all of society. Men have functionally abandoned the hope of the resurrection for a plastic 'heaven on earth.'

The emergence of **Scientism** was linked with the triumph of Western science following the seventeenth century. Key assumptions which are at the root of science—that the universe is intelligible to the human mind, that the human perception of cause and effect reflect reality, etc.—are drawn from Christian theology, as numerous historical works have demonstrated. Scientism need not have followed on the heels of the emergence of the historic preconditions which gave rise to the development of the sciences following the condemnations of 1277. If **Nominalism** and **Gnosticism** had not already undermined the credibility of theology and the perception of the reliability of divine revela-

---

1   J.B. Bury, *The Idea of Progress*, (London: MacMillan and Co., 1920) p. vii–viii.

tion, the arrogance of the fallen nature which manifested in Scientism after the Thirty Years War would have had a much harder time establishing itself.

Democratism also relied on those errors which had come before; without a notion of **Progress**, democratic notions would likely have centered on a particularly inefficient form of decision making, instead of becoming *the* means for measuring the Truth divined at the altar of Demos. Once the rest of the deadly values are in place, it seems almost unavoidable that **Tolerance** would arise, since Democratism is virtually inextricable from it. The moral authority to denounce 'toleration' has steadily atrophied, and the demand of the political and moral levelers has silenced most of those whose vocations would normally demand leadership, so that fathers in blood and office silently abdicate their offices. As Rahe observes:

> As a people, if we are to judge solely by attendance in church, Americans are still comparatively religious. But no one today would describe religion as "the first" of our "political institutions," as Tocqueville once did (II.ii.9, p. 227), for it is no longer generally the case that our churches provide us with a moral anchor and impress upon us a severity in morals. Most of the mainline Protestant sects now fiercely advocate a toleration and compassionate embrace of that which they once regarded as abhorrent: if sanctimony is sustained, it is solely in offering succor to sin. Those Catholic priests and evangelical Protestant ministers who are genuinely unsympathetic with the culture of self-indulgence all too frequently lack the moral authority required for persuasion. In our day, as in Tocqueville's time, they fear their flocks, and they tailor their sermons to accommodate current fashion.[2]

---

2   Paul A. Rahe, *Soft Despotism, Democracy's Drift,* (New Haven &

Still, *the path back from the abyss must be charted by those fathers in office and blood.*

However, the mutually reenforcing seven deadly values are centered on **Individualism**, and, as Gillespie observes,
> Such a focus on the individual was unknown in the ancient world. The ideal for the Greek artist and citizen was not the formation of individual character or personality but assimilation to an ideal model. Petrarch and his humanist followers did not put the human per se at the center of things but the *individual* human being, and in this respect they owed a deeper ontological debt to nominalism than to antiquity. For humanism, the individual is not a rational animal standing at the peak of creation. Like Ockham the humanists were convinced that human beings have no natural form or end.[3]

Lacking a "natural form or end"—in reality, a divinely-given form and end, as Scripture clearly teaches—man sought to make himself into a god who could establish his own form and end. But the result of this endeavor has been not deification, but dehumanization. **Scientism** has sought nothing less than to deprive him of his soul and reduce him to nothing more than a chemically-compelled, instinct-driven animal. **Democratism** has not given a voice to the individual; it has silenced him by depriving him of the dignity of the Estates in which the Lord has established a place for him, and subjected him to the crushing weight of public disapprobation if he sinned by transgressing against the will of the majority. This is the end of man's vaunted **"Progress"**—a fall more shameful than that of the prodigal son.

London: Yale University Press, 2009) p. 266.
3   Gillespie, p. 31.

Is the plight hopeless? Certainly not. And it is the calling of fathers in blood and office to resume their callings and lead those entrusted to their care in the way of repentance. The errors—the tragic end—of the seven deadly values of contemporary society is becoming increasingly apparent as material prosperity declines, as institutions fail, and as various political 'messiahs' prove vacuous idols. The ideology of **Progress** is a lie, and needs to be treated as such. Again, in the words of Bury:

> In achieving its ascendency and unfolding its meaning, the Idea of Progress had to overcome a psychological obstacle which may be described as *the illusion of finality*. ...
>
> But if we accept the reasonings on which the dogma of Progress is based, must we not carry them to their full conclusion? In escaping from the illusion of finality, is it legitimate to exempt the dogma itself? Must not it, too, submit to its own negation of finality? Will not that process of change, for which Progress is the optimistic name, compel "Progress" too to fall from the commanding position in which it is now, with apparent security, enthroned? Ἔσσεται ἧμαρ ὅταν ... A day will come, in the revolution of centuries, when a new idea will usurp its place as the directing idea of humanity. Another star, unnoticed now or invisible, will climb up the intellectual heaven, and human emotions will react to its influence, human plans respond to its guidance. It will be the criterion by which Progress and all other ideas will be judged. And it too will have its successor.[4]

Confronting the whole constellation of deadly deceptions which frame the ideologies of our modern age, one must strike at the root and repent of the striving for self-definition which is behind the rebellion against divine order. The root problem is

---

4   p. 351–352.

the sinful **Individualism** which has reigned in the heart of fallen man since the Garden of Eden. Individualism brought death to man in the garden, and, joined to the deadly values of this age, it has brought death to our civilization.

That Man is not simply an animal is established by the divine Word alone—and that Word also defines the relationship between men. One simply cannot have the one without the other: acknowledging the divine authorship of our very being confesses that He alone defines who we are as men formed in the image of Adam. Beholding that image set forth in the Word, we are called to repent—and the damage wrought by the deadly values of our age demonstrates to those who have eyes to see and ears to hear that we have much of which we must repent.

Fathers in blood and office need to lead in this repentance, and trusting in the One who bought them with His precious blood, stand fast in the duties of their God given Estates. Such men know Who has fashioned and called them to their holy calling, and they know the End to which He has called them. The world does not know such consolation as that which is revealed to the children of God. Our citizenship is in a Kingdom which knows no end, and our King has won the victory for us, delivering us from the snares of the evil one and with a Word casts out the spirits of the age.

The Thousand Year Descent
of the West

CHAPTER 1: THE DESCENT OF THE WEST?

he provocative title of this final portion of our examination of the concepts of sacred and secular history and myth may cause some readers to wonder precisely what intention is guiding us. In speaking of a descent, our concerns are neither economic nor geopolitical. There are many fine works by experts in various fields who are quite able to speak to such topics.

The intention in this final third of our task of exploration is to look at several of the myths which have entered the mind of Western man in the past thousand years, and have come to dominate his understanding of his place in the world. While the Sacred Scriptures have ostensibly been subjected to various notions of demythologizing, and while modern man indulges the vainglorious notion that his is the first generation to be freed from the slavery of mythology, the dark myths of the Gnostics have crept in unawares and converted many within the heart of Christendom.

The descent which has taken place is thus directly juxtaposed to the imagined ascent which Gnostics set forth as their doctrine of salvation: rather than man ascending, transcending the flesh and uniting himself with God, man has descended to ideologies of systematized murder and rapine. The tale of the past thousand years has been one marked by dark doctrines which have seduced souls, and given birth to hydra-headed idolatrous ideologies. It is a tragic history. And it is one into which we have been born.

CHAPTER 2. THE RETURN OF THE GNOSTICS—
THE CATHAR HERESY

In our generation, there are many people who are gravely concerned by the threat posed by militant Islam, and rightly so.[1] The Jihad is not a modern, or extraneous, aspect of Islam; rather, there is no Mohammedan religion without the Jihad. But Islam was not the only enemy confronting Christendom—in fact, a foe at least as dangerous as Mohammed's armed doctrine began to resurface not long after *anno domini* 1000—but while it began to resurface, it is clear that it never entirely went away. This enemy of the faith had once been well-known, and it was— and remains—as treacherous as Islam was and remains just as violent. But while Islam threatened destruction from without, Gnosticism endeavored to subvert Christendom from within.

One of the great academic 'footballs' which gets kicked around every time Gnosticism is mentioned is what relationship existed between the Christian faith and the origins of Gnosticism. Although it has been the politically expedient argument to maintain that Gnosticism originated on its own and not (as the Church fathers maintained) as a Christian heresy, in truth the churchly origin of Gnosticism remains the most plausible origin. As Pétrement wrote in his study of the origins of Gnosticism:

> Given the fact that all the forms of non-Christian Gnosticism seem to be attested later than Christian Gnosticism—not counting the fact that properly Gnostic ideas are less pronounced and less distinctive in the former

---

1   For the author's views on the dangers posed by the Jihad, and the West's theological confusion in the face of that danger, please see James Heiser and Jerald Dulas, *The One True God, the Two Kingdoms and the Three Estates*, (Malone, Texas: Repristination Press, 2011).

than in the latter—one cannot be sure that Gnosticism was not initially Christian. It seems to me that the theory according to which the Gnostics were originally and essentially Christian heretics, which in no way excludes the possibility that their ideas subsequently penetrated into traditions outside Christianity, is a theory that can still be upheld, and that it can even be upheld by arguments that are better founded than the opposite opinion, and that it is still the best explanation that can be given for this phenomenon and that there really is not another. For if Gnosticism is not explained by Christianity, it is difficult to see it as anything but a collection of bizarre doctrines, seemingly arbitrary and more or less absurd.[2]

Such an argument regarding the origins of Gnosticism thus remains tenable, and certainly the conflict between the Church and the various Gnostic sects of the early Church and Middle Ages is well-summarized by the words of Kurt Rudolph: "One can almost say that Gnosis followed the Church like a shadow; the Church could never overcome it, its influence had gone too deep."[3]

Gnosticism opposes the Christian verity in many ways, but not least in terms of epistemology and soteriology. The Gnostic substitutes *gnosis*—knowledge—in the place of the Christian's *pistis*—faith—and he maintains that salvation is obtained by the arcane knowledge which one possesses, rather than received by grace through faith in Christ. The Christian believes that which Jesus declared in John 18: "I spoke openly to the world. I always taught in synagogues and in the temple,

2   Simone Pétrement, *A Separate God—The Origins and Teachings of Gnosticism,* (New York: HarperSan Francisco, 1984) p. 4.

3   Kurt Rudolph, *Gnosis—The Nature and History of Gnosticism,* trans. by Robert McLachlan Wilson (New York: HarperSanFrancisco, 1987) p. 368.

where the Jews always meet, and in secret I have said nothing." However, the Gnostic seeks after hidden meaning, secret interpretations of Scripture, and private revelations. The gnosticizing mentality is well-summarized in the words of Giovanni Pico della Mirandola, who wrote in his *Oration* of 1486:

> Openly to reveal to the people the hidden mysteries and the secret intentions of the highest divinity, which lay concealed under the hard shell of the law and the rough vesture of language, what else could this be but to throw holy things to dogs and to strew gems among swine? The decision, consequently, to keep such things hidden from the vulgar and to communicate them only to the initiate, among who alone, as Paul says, wisdom speaks, was not a counsel of human prudence but a divine command.[4]

Furthermore, the salvation which the Gnostics seek is not redemption, but release from the created world. That the soul is joined to matter is the great agony of human existence in their system; the Gnostic desires to be freed from the flesh and to ascend to an essential unity with God.

Two other crucial aspects of Gnosticism for our consideration of its return in our modern age are its Dualism and Syncretism. The "Dualism" of the Gnostics refers to their belief that there are equal, and opposing, forces of good and evil, reigning over all things in this created world which are expressed in various ways mythologically within the diverse systems of the Gnostics. (For example, it was a common, blasphemous Albigensian belief that Satan was the firstborn child of God, while the Christ was the second born—with the two sons thus in eternal conflict.) As for Gnostic Syncretism, we must remember that

---

4   Giovanni Pico della Mirandola, *Oration on the Dignity of Man,* trans. by A. Robert Caponigri, (Washington, D.C.: Regnery Publishing, Inc., 1956) p. 60.

Gnosticism always seeks to subvert any and all religious literature into its system; any holy text can (and will) be reinterpreted
to give it a Gnostic sense.

Each of these aspects of Gnosticism brought it into
fundamental conflict with the Christian faith, and the battle of
beliefs went on for generations. In time, however, Gnosticism
declined, and generally faded away—in the West. As Stoyanov
notes in his book, *The Other God*, overtly Gnostic doctrine was
virtually expelled from the confines of Christendom by the time
of the early Middle Ages:

> Following the explosion of religious and spiritual
> creativity during late antiquity, traces and actual trans-
> mitters of Gnostic and dualist teaching in the early Mid-
> dle Ages become increasingly difficult to discern and
> identify. In the Near East such teachings enjoyed an un-
> interrupted historical prevalence within the still existing
> small religious group of the Mandaeans in southern Iraq
> and Khuzistan in Iran, rightly considered the last survivors
> of the great Gnostic movement of late antiquity.[5]

However, this did not mean that Gnosticism had been
eliminated from within the borders of Christendom; instead, the
movement had gone "underground," and had done so primarily within the territories of Eastern Orthodoxy. In Stuyanov's
analysis, it was primarily within certain limited circles that the
writings of the Gnostics were preserved:

> In the early Middle Ages traces and elements of
> Gnostic and dualist teaching in varying degrees of in-
> tensity were also preserved in diverse apocryphal works
> from late antiquity which despite being banned, were
> preserved and maintained their circulation, mainly in the

5   Yuri Stoyanov, *The Other God,* (New Haven and London: Yale
University Press, 2000) p. 124.

east Christian world, in heterodox, sectarian or simply learned circles. In the right circumstances these Gnostic or dualist residues in apocryphal works could stimulate a revival of related attitudes through simple borrowing of their themes or through creative interpretation spreading from these works to the canonical scriptures, with all the possibilities for the formulation of new heterodoxies and heresies.

A number of such apocryphal texts was [sic] preserved in Byzantium where the process of the creation of new apocrypha, such as apocalyptic revelations about the course of world history, also continued throughout the early Middle Ages.[6]

The return of Gnosticism to the Latin Church is a story of the effluence of such heresy washing out of the East, first from within the Monophysite territories, such as Armenia, and later from the Neoplatonic circles within Constantinople.

According to Lambert in his book, *Medieval Heresy*, no heretics were burned in the West since the execution of Priscillian of Avila in 383 until the death of the Orléans Gnostics in 1022.[7] When heresy erupted in the West, it suddenly appears in a full-grown state, Gnostic in content and conspiratorial in methodology:

It turned out to be a thoroughgoing heresy, traces of which in Orléans apparently went back to about 1015. The core of the heretics' beliefs lay in a *gnosis*, entry to which was conferred by a ceremony of laying-on of hands. Initiates, relieved of the stain of all sin, were filled by the gift of the Holy Spirit, which gave them full un-

6   Stoyanov, p. 125.

7   Malcolm Lambert, *Medieval Heresy—Popular Movements from the Gregorian Reform to the Reformation,* 2nd ed., (Cambridge: Blackwell Publishers, 1992) p. 12.

derstanding of Scripture. Orthodox doctrines connected with Christ's possession of a human body were denied in the group: 'Christ was not born of the Virgin Mary. He did not suffer for men. He was not really buried in the sepulchre and was not raised from the dead.' There was wholesale denial of the validity of the sacraments of the Church. ... The 'heavenly food' Paul [of Saint-Père de Chartres] interpreted as meaning a devilish viaticum made of the ashes of a murdered baby, the child of the group's nocturnal orgies, in which each of the men 'grabbed whatever woman came to hand'.

... And yet, for all Paul's emotive terminology, his description of the manner in which the leaders of the Orléans circle carried Aréfast step by step toward their inner secrets corresponds so well to the technique of a Gnostic, illuminist sect, in which the core of doctrine is only revealed to a select few, taken on 'from the Charybdis of false belief' until illumination is attained and the neophyte has begun 'to open his eyes to the light of the true faith'. The approach is well known, both from the history of the Gnostic sects of the early centuries and that of the Cathar movement in the twelfth and thirteenth centuries in the West.[8]

Such a heresy was able to emerge in the West so suddenly because the system of doctrines had been preserved and cultivated in the East, and then exported. As Stoyanov explains, Armenia apparently proved a particularly fertile environment for a variety of false doctrines:

Although the Good Religion of Ahura Mazda declined in Iran, Zoroastrian traditions survived in Armenia into the Middle Ages and indeed might have persisted into the modern era, even until the early twentieth

---

8   ibid., p. 10–11, 14–15.

century. Moreover, with the establishment of Christian orthodoxy in the Roman Empire, Armenia became a refuge for heretics and heterodox sectarians. Marcionite and other Gnostic groups, perhaps including Manichaeans, certainly lingered in Armenia well into the fifth century, while the Paulicians, who appeared in the following century, still present numerous problems in the study of eastern Christianity and medieval dualism.[9]

Obviously, attempting to reconstruct the history of a group which went to great lengths to conceal itself because of its status as a banned heresy is quite difficult. Still, enough occasions exist in which the Church issues specific condemnations of various Gnostic groups to leave one with the impression that Gnostic groups continued to exist in Armenia and elsewhere in the East, and that such groups provided the start to later heretical groups. Thus, for example, Stoyanov observes that two such Gnostic sects—the Massalians (which first arose in Syria in the fourth century) and Paulicians (a group native to Armenia)—were active for centuries in Armenia:

> The heretics condemned in 719 by a council of the Armenian Church as 'sons of Satan' and 'fuel for the fire eternal' may or may not have been actual Paulicians but earlier, in the mid fifth century, it was still the Massalians who were perceived as the greatest heretical threat in Armenia. In 447 a special council announced sweeping measures against the Massalian heresy. The Massalians (the praying people), also called Enthusiasts were an anti-clerical, pietist sect about whose actual teachings not enough is known. Their main belief was underlain by a peculiar type of anthropological dualism, according to which from birth in every man dwells a demon, who cannot be banished by baptism alone, but

---

9   Stoyanov, p. 126.

through continuous, zealous prayer and spiritual 'baptism by fire'.[10]

But these heretical groups were not content to remain within the confines of one nation; the actively conducted efforts to spread their beliefs:

Historical links between the early Massalians and the Manichaeans in Mesopotamia and Byzantium are not implausible but they have not been established and the repeated allusions to the Massalians after the eleventh century indicate that their name was used as a label for the new heretics, namely the Bogomils, rather than to refer to a genuine revival of the ancient sect.

It is possible that some Massalians were resettled along with the Paulicians during the eighth century in the Byzantine campaigns whereby Syrian and Armenian heretics were sent to the Balkans.[11]

According to one piece of anecdotal evidence, it would appear that the Armenian heretics were quite well-travelled. In fact, they may have travelled to the very limits of European civilization during the eleventh century. The *Íslendingabók* (*Book of the Icelanders*) was composed by Ari Þorgilsson in the early twelfth century, and it contains a reference to a number of genuine bishops who traveled to Iceland both before and after the conversion of the country in A.D. 1000; but Ari also refers to others who "styled themselves bishops" including "three Armenians, Petrus, Abraham, and Stephanus."[12] The strange journey of the "three Armenians" has generated its own literature discussing their identity, but the fact that Ari challenged their episcopal cre-

---

10   ibid., p. 128–129.
11   ibid., p. 129–130.
12   Gwyn Jones, *The Norse Atlantic Saga,* 2nd ed., (Oxford and New York: Oxford University Press, 1986) p. 151.

dentials—even in an era when Icelandic identification with the Roman Church was somewhat nebulous—speaks volumes regarding the dubious nature of the ministry of the three Armenians.

As noted previously, although Armenia provided a bastion, after a fashion, for Gnostic heresies, such movements were unwilling to remain within one nation's borders, and began to spread their influence, beginning with the Bulgarian empire (A.D. 632–1018), but also gradually spreading through the areas under the control of Constantinople. Again, in the Stoyanov's words:

> Conversely, the early Bulgarian empire provided perfect conditions for the revival and continuation of pagan cults and traditions which had been suppressed earlier throughout the Byzantine-controlled parts of the peninsula. The very foundation of the Bulgarian domain coincided with the convocation of the Third Ecumenical Council of Constantinople (680–1) which condemned and took measures against the remains of Dionysian and other mysteries, apparently still active in the Balkans. ...
>
> ...In Byzantium itself paganism might have been defeated but besides colouring Christian beliefs and practices pagan residues endured in certain areas of the empire and as late as the early tenth century Emperor Leo VI had to lead a crusade against the still strong paganism in the Peloponnesus region of Mani. Heterodox and heretical traditions also existed and were in force in the Byzantine world, particularly in Anatolian regions like Phrygia, where the enigmatic Judaizing sect of the Athingani synthesized the observances of the sabbath with astrological and magical beliefs and practices.[13]

The East thus began to function as an incubator of heresy. The intermittent struggle against various Gnostic and Neo-

---

13   Stoyanov, p. 149–150.

platonic movements in the East was without parallel in the West because such heresies were utterly extirpated within Latin Christianity. The emergence of Gnostic sects such as that found at Orléans, or which arose in the form of Albigensianism/Catharism roughly a century later, was without precedent in the West. As Lambert observed, "Heresy had reappeared in the West after a long gap. … Heresy of the old pattern virtually ceased to exist, its place being taken by the resistance to Christianity of paganism and superstition."[14] In *The Albigensian Crusades*, James Strayer also noted that heresy was a very rare phenomenon in the West: "It is less easy to see why Occitania was so receptive to heretical doctrines. … in the twelfth and thirteenth centuries, the only other country that was seriously infected with heresy was northern Italy. In Germany and northern France there were only small groups of heretics and in England there were almost none."[15] Strayer notes that Occitania was near the center of the Waldensian heresy, but mere proximity to an unrelated heresy seems a poor explanation for succumbing to a Gnostic doctrine. Lambert's assessment—that the Cathar heresy spread into the West in a very deliberate fashion—is more credible. If Lambert is correct, then the first Cathars in the West were Franks who were converted at Constantinople, who then returned to the West and spread the heresy there:

> The contact in Constantinople was crucial. Here, we may reasonably surmise, Bogomilism was westernized; its ritual was translated, most probably directly into Latin, so that Frankish converts could compete in liturgical solemnity with the Catholic mass, or with Catholic services of ordination or consecration which they felt it was their destiny to supplant.
>
> A natural focus for early translations of any kind

---

14   Lambert, *Medieval Heresy*, p. 25.
15   James Strayer, *The Albigensian Crusades,* (Ann Arbor, Michigan: The University of Michigan Press, 1992) p. 15.

would have been Constantinople, with the underground, heretical Latin Church to which Anselm alludes and natural access to bilingual elements in the population. … Constantinople is a city where one would expect to find the necessary scholarly expertise. Here, we may argue, Catharism evolved from Bogomilism and the missionaries were equipped who transmitted the heresy to the West. Westerners converted Westerners and this facilitated both the arrival of a Byzantine dualist heresy in Western Europe and its early successes.[16]

But for the Eastern export of Gnosticism into the West, the time was actually one in which the Western Church was knowing a period of growth and restoration. For example, at the moment when Gnosticism was creeping in from the East, various pagan peoples in the West—most notably the Scandinavians—were converting. Latin Christendom was certainly not moribund; in fact, the vibrant faith of the Western Church was continuing to proceed as the Lord so willed among those peoples who had fiercely, violently, opposed that faith only a generation or two earlier. The raid on the monastery of Lindisfarne in July 793 is usually noted as the beginning of the Viking era: by the early eleventh century, Sweden, Norway, Denmark, and Iceland had converted to the faith, and an archdiocese for all of Scandinavia was established at Lund, Sweden in the early twelfth century.

Latin Christendom also experienced victories against the Islamists who had invaded and occupied the Iberian peninsula—the *reconquista* of Spain and Portugal was not without setbacks, but gradually the Mohammedans were pressed back. In 792, Hisham I of Córdoba declared a *jihad* against the Christian

---

16   Malcolm Lambert, *The Cathars*, (Malden, MA and Oxford: Blackwell Publishing, 1998) p. 37.

state of Asturias, for the Mohammedans were bent on driving back the Christian forces. Hisham's *jihad* was a failure and the *reconquista* was victorious in Córdoba in 1236 and the inhabitants of the peninsula witnessed the gradual advance of Christian kingdoms which reached its completion with the fall of the last Muslim stronghold—Granada—in 1492.

Warfare—spiritual and military—against paganism and Islam was an ongoing reality of life in the West during the Middle Ages, but it was a warfare which witnessed many Christian victories, and the faith spread to more of the lands of the West. However, the eruption of Catharism in Italy and France took the Roman Church by surprise, and combating it took the creation of an entirely new teaching order, the Dominicans.

The new Gnostic heresies were also more dangerous than those of antiquity because they did not limit their expanse to a supposed intellectual 'elite'; rather, they were popular in form, and both perpetuated and exacerbated a propensity toward anti-clericalism which sporadically emerged during the Middle Ages. In his extensive study of Catharism, Lambert notes:

> Isolated and idiosyncratic as they were, the eleventh-century heresies are an overture to the much more substantial heretical movements of the twelfth and thirteenth centuries and share some characteristics with them: ethical considerations predominate over intellectual ones, in contrast to the classic heresies of early centuries. The laity are demanding a greater share in religious life and are prepared to break with ecclesiastical authority to secure it; growing literacy and awareness of texts and precedents create the conditions for an appeal to the New Testament, above all to the pattern of the life of the apostles, in opposition to the Church; monastic reform, spilling over into the lay world, helps to create a demand

for ascetic communities not under existing Rules, which carry renunciation to the limits of orthodoxy.[17]

Given the overlap between the life of Joachim of Fiore (1135–1202) and the emergence of Catharism (first emerging in the West in the 1140s), the common appeal to a life of ascetic monasticism—one which was also markedly disinterested in the hierarchical church of the Second Age—should not be ignored. To the extent that Joachim appealed to trends within the 'orthodox' Church, those same avenues were exploited by the Cathars in various ways.[18]

That which would be known in the West as the Albigensian or Cathar heresy began within the confines of the Bulgarian Empire, and then spread more broadly in the East. As Stoyanov wrote:

> While the first steps of Bogomilism largely remain uncharted, it is beyond dispute that by the mid tenth century it had already assumed the shape of an organized and rapidly spreading heretical movement. In the face of the rising heresy, [Tsar] Peter had to write twice to the princely patriarch of Constantinople, Theophylact Lecapenus, who was, however, said to spend more time

---

17   Lambert, *The Cathars*, p. 12.

18   Lambert agrees with this assessment: "Finally the appearance of Joachimism on the thirteenth-century scene contributed to popular religious feeling a set of myths that rivalled in their appeal the myths of the Cathars, and yet were more optimistic in tone. As in Cathar eschatology, there was to be a profound struggle with evil, but it would issue in a state of bliss here on earth, a foretaste, after spiritual warfare, of the pleasures of paradise. For those who had taste for such things, these myths were more positive: dualist myths of creation and the End faded in competition with them. All was not gain for the Catholics; there were dangers in Joachimism, and heresies fed on it. But it was another factor against Catharism. In a word, Italian dualism was in part eradicated by force and in part simply outgrown." (*Medieval Heresy*, p. 145–146.)

in ministering to his many horses than in the cathedral. The patriarch, none the less, was able to recognize this 'ancient and newly appeared heresy' as 'Manichaeism mixed with Paulicianism' and urged Peter to burn the 'bitter and evil roots' of their teachings in the 'holy fire of truth', arming the Tsar with a list of twelve anathemas.[19]

Although some within the Eastern Church clearly recognized the rising danger posed by Bogomilism, the East's difficulties in resisting such doctrines was on full display in its failure to suppress the new sect: "Less than a century after Basil [Emperor Basil II (976–1025)] sanctioned these Bulgaro-Byzantine marriages, Bogomilism was said to have affected the 'great houses' in Constantinople and it is possible that the Bulgarian influx into the Byzantine aristocracy might have facilitated the spread of the heresy among the Byzantine social elite."[20] Having gained such influence, and the power to export its doctrines by means of Western converts, Bogomilism in the East became Catharism (or Albigensianism) in the West.[21]

Strayer offers a summary of the doctrines which were thus transmitted by the Cathars, which demonstrates that their doctrine was filled with typical Gnostic dualism[22] and docetism[23]:

Satan or Lucifer, the highest of the angels, perhaps even a son of God, led by pride and ambition, departed from the realm of pure spirit and created the material world.

---

19   Stoyanov, p. 159.

20   ibid., p. 168.

21   "That there was a substantial transmission of ritual and ideas from Bogomilism to Catharism is beyond reasonable doubt." (Lambert, *The Cathars*, p. 31.)

22   Dualism sets forth the notion that creation is a balance of the work of 'good' and 'evil' forces.

23   Docetism maintains that Christ only appeared to be a man, and that His incarnation was thus illusory.

He made man and woman from clay, but these miserable beings had no soul. According to one version, God took pity on these victims of Satan and gave them souls; another source says that Satan used the souls of the angels who fell with him. In either case the first woman was tempted to commit the sexual act and so the human soul was lost, perpetually imprisoned in the body, which was material and evil. Cathar doctrine on the source of new souls is not clear; some Cathars believed in the transmigration of souls, others that Satan constantly drew on the stock of souls of fallen angels. In any case, sexual intercourse was the greatest sin, for it either condemned an existing soul to another period of imprisonment in matter or it involved a new soul in this evil world.

God again took pity on the wretched human race and sent his son Jesus to show men how to escape from the power of Satan. Jesus was an emanation from God, but he was not God. Neither was he man; his apparent body was merely an illusion, for pure spirit could have no contact with matter. Thus, Jesus did not suffer on the cross and the cross was not to be venerated; it was evil, as all material things were evil; it was a sign of the attempt of Satan to defeat the plans of God. In fact, Satan had failed, but his wicked cunning enabled him to postpone the inevitable, final catastrophe. The saving truths that Jesus had revealed were misinterpreted and falsified, and the orthodox Christian Church was built on these errors. It was a creature of Satan; it worshiped Satan in revering the God of the Old Testament, who was the creator of the material world. Fortunately, the real message of Jesus had been preserved among the Cathars, and more and more people were accepting the truth. The Cathars, the purified, would reduce their contacts with the material world to an inescapable minimum and so they would be saved. Eventually all souls would be saved and Satan and his world would come to an end. The process would be slow, but on the other hand there was no need for purgatory or for an eternal hell. Purgatory and hell were here on earth; it was punishment to have to live in the body, and some souls would have to endure that punishment for many generations.[24]

Such a doctrinal core would have been fundamentally acceptable to the ancient Gnostics. Certainly, the Church Fathers had confronted such heresies in ages past and had done so, by God's grace, to great effect. However, the movement of such doctrines from the realm of elites to a more popular doctrine, with the establishment of a parallel church structure, allowed the new Gnostics an influence in the West which the early Gnostics had failed to achieve.

It is, of course, not our intention to tell the details of the rise and fall of the Cathar heresy; the *fact* of the heresy—and the implications of its existence for the West—are our concern here. From 1208 until 1255—nearly 50 years—crusades were sent against the Cathars. This was, from a certain perspective, a rather brief period of time; after all, the crusades in the Middle East lasted significantly longer. Nevertheless, the suppression of the Cathars brought about important changes in the Church. Certainly, the Fourth Lateran Council (1215) was conducted in the context of the war against the Cathars, and the establishment of the Dominican order took place in the context of this struggle. As Strayer noted, St. Dominic began his order in the effort to combat the Cathars:

> Gregory IX saw, with increasing clarity, that heresy could be repressed only by establishing an institution designed specifically for this task and staffed with

---

24   Strayer, p. 28–29.

men who had expert knowledge of the problem. The experts were ready at hand: the friars of the Dominican Order. St. Dominic had begun his mission by attempting to convert the heretics of western Occitania; his first foundation, the nunnery of Prouille (1207), was created to receive women who had been reclaimed from Catharism. The Dominicans themselves were to be the Order of Preachers, men who would recall the ignorant, the careless, and the sinful to the true faith. … They knew more about heresy and more about the behavior of the masses than did most bishops. They were ideal instruments for Gregory's plans.[25]

The Dominicans, in turn, became the instruments of a new Papal institution: the Inquisition:

Before 1233 the bishops had the chief responsibility for discovering and investigating cases of heresy, even if they were assisted from time to time by agents designated by the pope. After 1233 the responsibility fell more and more on specially appointed inquisitors, usually drawn from the Dominican Order. The bishops naturally resented this interference with their jurisdiction and tried to keep the inquisitors subject to their authority or even to prevent them from acting. But while the bishops gained some temporary victories, and some face-saving forms of procedure, by the second half of the thirteenth century they had definitely lost control of heresy prosecutions in France.[26]

By divorcing the investigation of heresy from the bishops who were charged with shepherding their diocese, a vital step on the way to Papalism had clearly been taken. And the

25   ibid., p. 146.
26   ibid., p. 147–148.

institution of the Inquisition would have severe, deleterious effects on the Roman Church for hundreds of years. Long after the Albigensian Crusade had come to a conclusion, the trials of the Inquisition continued to successfully seek out surviving Cathar circles.

Generations after the political might of the Cathars had been broken, a final major effort was made to revive the movement, and the architect of this effort was Pierre Autier, who was active in Languedoc in southern France from 1299 until 1310. Even at the end, the Cathars did not break with their core beliefs; in Lambert's words, "Autier's revival cannot in any way continue to be classed as decadent or aberrant: it deserves to be analysed as part of mainstream Catharism surviving under harsh circumstances."[27] And Autier, like Cathars before him, continued the two-fold approach of appealing to the 'ethical' superiority of their religion (supposedly living more piously than did Catholics) and to a rationalism which is strikingly modern in some of its formulations:

> In his second sermon to the Peyre family, Pierre Autier used the ancient *mot* about Christ's body needing to be as big as a mountain to feed the priests. Defendants most commonly denied transubstanstiation and said that the host was only dough. … The mass came under especially heavy fire because of its central role in Catholic devotional life. Catharism had no substitute for it, although the blessing of bread had a liturgical significance. The object of the Cathar leadership was to de-mystify it and destroy its hold.
>
> Other sacraments underwent similar attack. …
>
> In this process of destruction, the leaders made use of scepticism rather than their own underlying doctrines. Cathar Docetism was incompatible with the doctrine of

---

27   Lambert, *The Cathars*, p. 230.

the mass, and bread and wine were in any case part of the evil creation of Satan, but in practice the mass was denigrated on grounds of a generalized rationalism.[28]

In time, the Cathar movement was virtually exterminated; as Lambert records,[29] the last Cathar bishop was arrested in 1321, the last Cathar in Florence was found in 1342, and a final 15 heretics were executed in 1412. But dualistic heresy was by no means destroyed; it lived on in Bosnia, which was "the promised land of heresy, the ultimate outpost of the dualists, ... one may fairly speak of an heretical State Church."[30] Located on the theological border between East and West, Bosnia provided a safe haven for such teaching. But, as we will see, our concern for the continuing revival of Gnosticism in the West is not particularly interested in such historical survivals at the theological fringes. Instead, the next wave of Gnostic doctrine to strike the West would have the same point of origin as the Cathar Church: Constantinople.

---

28   ibid., p. 248–249.
29   ibid., p. 289, 296.
30   ibid., p. 297.

CHAPTER 3. THE RETURN OF THE GNOSTICS— HERMETICISM AND THE SYNCRETISTIC MYTH.

The next wave of Gnostic teaching arrived roughly a century after the last known Cathars had been uprooted, and it came, once again, from Constantinople. Whereas the Cathar heresy slipped in unexpectedly through the missionary endeavors of Bogomil heretics converting Westerners who were temporarily residing in Constantinople, the next wave began through the travels of an Easterner to a Church Council held in the West. The first wave of Gnosticism was of the 'negative' form of Gnosticism: Cathar doctrine was dualistic, and contained the reviling of the created order typical of many ancient forms of Gnosticism. In short, the material world was seen as evil—a prison to be fled. The new wave of Gnosticism was of a more 'positive' form, a body of doctrine known as "Hermeticism." Hermeticism still sought to flee the world—but it also sought to *transform* it.

In his classic study, *The Gnostic Religion,* Hans Jonas did not hesitate to identify these Hermetical works as being "Gnostic":

> This literature, not as a whole but in certain portions, reflects gnostic spirit. The same goes for the closely related *alchemistic* literature and some of the Greek and Coptic *magical papyri,* which show an admixture of gnostic ideas. The Hermetic *Poimandres* treatise itself, in spite of some signs of Jewish influence, is to be regarded as a prime document of independent pagan Gnosticism.[1]

---

1   Hans Jonas, *The Gnostic Religion*, third ed., (Boston: Beacon Press, 2001) p. 41. It should be noted that Jonas devoted an entire chapter to analyzing Hermeticism as a form of Gnosticism.

Like other forms of Gnosticism, Hermeticism links *knowledge* with salvation—a salvation which is by means of ascension from this world. The astrological component of Hermeticism is concerned with various corruptions of the soul which supposedly take place as it descends into a body through the various heavenly spheres and then ascends again through those same spheres.[2]

Hermeticism takes its name from Hermes Trismegistus—"thrice-great Hermes"—who was purported to be the author of a variety of philosophical, theological, alchemical and magical writings. The writings attributed to the mythical figure of Hermes Trismegistus have been a troublesome form of Gnosticism which the Church has confronted since the days of the early church fathers.[3] Various legends grew up around Hermes Trismegistus—the more tame of which portrayed him as an Egyptian who was a contemporary of Moses.[4] However, other traditions provided him with an even more grand identification:

> In Hellenistic Egypt Hermes Trismegistus arose from a merging of the figures of Thoth and Hermes. ... In the fifth century Herodotus wrote that Hermes and Thoth corresponded to each other, for both were considered to be tricksters, and sometimes even thieves, who equipped with magical capabilities, were messengers of the gods and conductors of the dead. ...

> Was there only a single Hermes Trismegistus? A text attributed to Manetho, an Egyptian priest of the third century B.C.E., tells of two figures who bore the name

2   ibid., p. 157 and 165.

3   See, for example, Florian Ebeling, *The Secret History of Hermes Trismegistus—Hermeticism from Ancient to Modern Times* trans. by David Lorton (Ithaca and London: Cornell University Press, 2007) p. 38–44.

4   For a comprehensive study of the changing 'face' of Hermes, see Antoine Faivre, *The Eternal Hermes—From Greek God to Alchemical Magus* (Grand Rapids: Phanes Press, 1995).

Hermes. The Egyptian Thoth was the first Hermes; prior to the Flood he recorded his knowledge in hieroglyphs. After the Flood the knowledge was translated from the "sacred language" into Greek and placed in the temples by the second Hermes, the son of "Agathodaimon" and father of Tat. Cicero took multiplicity to the limit, reporting in his *On the Nature of the Gods* that there were five gods called Hermes, the last of whom was Hermes Trismegistus.

God, prophet, or sage? In any event, writings bearing the name of Hermes Trismegistus were handed down, and these works established the Hermetic tradition.[5]

While some fathers such as Clement of Alexandria and Lactantius were somewhat favorable in their assessment of Hermes' writings, St. Augustine of Hippo recognized that Hermetic prophesies—and Hermetic magic—were irreconcilable with the Christian verity, and following the time of Augustine, the one known work attributed to Hermes—the *Asclepius*—was little threat to Christian orthodoxy. Generally speaking, from the time of Augustine until the fifteenth century, Hermes was virtually forgotten in the West.

In his introduction to his new translation of the *Hermetica,* Copenhaver notes that the means of transmission for the Hermetic writings may have been through a community living within the sphere if Islam, in Harran in upper Mesopotamia (now Turkey), where the people took the name "Sabi'an" "and for their prophet they chose Hermes, whom they identified with the Quranic Idris and the biblical Enoch."[6] Copenhaver writes:

Forced conversion intensified in the early ninth century,

---

5   Ebeling, p. 6–7.

6   *Hermetica*, trans. and ed. by Brian P. Copenhaver, (Cambridge: Cambridge University Press, 1992) p. xlvi.

yet the Hermetic Sabi'ans held out until the middle of the eleventh century, producing several important scholars, of whom the greatest was Thabit ibn Qurrah in the ninth century. Noting that the end of Sabi'an Hermeticism in Harran roughly coincided with the new Byzantine interest in Hermes represented by Michael Psellus, Walter Scott speculated that the dispersal of the Sabi'ans might have stimulated a Hermetical revival in Byzantium.[7]

If this speculation is correct, the Sabi'an influence in Constantinople would have been indirectly connected with the later explosion of interest in Hermeticism in the West—a Gnostic sect within the borders of Islam may have influenced various thinkers in Constantinople at the same time that Bogomilism was sweeping into the city from Bulgaria. At the same time, Gnostic doctrine was to be found in the Iberian Peninsula, in the Mohammedan territory of Córdoba, where Ismailist doctrine had certain similarities both to the succession of teachers propounded by Ficino and the inauguration of a last age which sounds similar to Joachim's hopes for a *dux de Babylone* who would initiate the Third Age of Man:

> While the caliphate of Cordoba was a stronghold of Sunni Islam, the official creed of the Fatimid dynasty was Ismailism, a major Shia branch which enriched Shia traditions with Neo-Platonic and Gnostic doctrines but was condemned by its Sunni opponents as a revival of Zoroastrianism, and even Manichaeism, in Islamic garb. Ismailism achieved one of the most striking medieval religious syntheses, in which the universal religious history was seen as comprising seven great prophetic cycles of revelation, six of which had already been initiated by Adam, Noah, Abraham, Moses, Jesus and Mohammed and the last one was to be inaugurated by the advent of

---

7   ibid.

the final Mahdi (or Qaim), the expected seventh Imam of the Ismaili movement.[8]

However, for Muslims, Hermes Trismegistus was more overtly a figure associated with occultism. As Kevin van Bladel explains in his magisterial treatise on the topic, *The Arabic Hermes*:

> The philosophical dialogues of Hermes Trismegistus, although so influential in Europe, were practically unknown in premodern Arabic. Instead, Hermes was famous more strictly as a teacher of astrology, alchemy, and talisman making. This is reflected in the hundreds of Arabic manuscripts of works on these subjects attributed to Hermes extant today. …
>
> What these authors were *not* is "Hermeticists." Their references to Hermes demonstrate not membership in a Hermetic school or sect, but merely their shared participation in and knowledge of Arabic scholarship concerned with the recovery and preservation of ancient science and wisdom. In this Eastern classical tradition, rooted in late antiquity, Hermes Triplicate-in-Wisdom came to play an important role as a figure of legend, an ideal of wisdom to be emulated, the founder of learning, a master of the spirits, the prophet of science who had touched the stars and heard the words of angels, the first sage.[9]

Hermes Trismegistus took on a new life in the days of the fifteenth century Italian Renaissance. Gemistos Plethon (1355–

---

8   Yuri Stoyanov, *The Other God,* (New Haven and London: Yale University Press, 2000) p. 155–156.

9   Kevin van Bladel, *The Arabic Hermes—From Pagan Sage to Prophet of Science,* (Oxford and New York: Oxford University Press, 2009) p. 237, 239.

1454)[10]—a neopagan who served as a member of the Greek delegation to the Council of Ferrara-Florence—was in Florence in 1438 and 1439, and inspired Cosimo de'Medici with the idea of founding a Platonic Academy. In fact, the meeting of Gemistos and Cosimo is among the more significant events of the Renaissance era, the ramifications of which extend down to this day.

Despite his official role as a member of the Greek delegation to the Council of Ferrara-Florence, Gemistos was secretly a pagan who desired to see the ancient Greek gods once again venerated. One who personally knew Gemistos, George Trapezuntius, related in 1455 the comments of Plethon during the council:

> I myself heard him at Florence—for he came to the Council with the Greeks—asserting that the whole world would in a few years adopt one and the same religion, with one mind, one intelligence, one teaching. And when I asked: 'Christ's or Muhammad's?' he replied: 'Neither, but one not differing from paganism.' I was so shocked by these words that I hated him ever after and feared him like a poisonous viper and I could no longer bear to see or hear him. I heard, too, from a number of Greeks who escaped here from the Peloponnese that he openly said, about three years before his death, that not many years after his death both Muhammad and Christ would be forgotten and the real truth would shine through on all the shores of the world.[11]

In his study of Gemistos, C.M. Woodhouse observes that there is reason to believe Trapezuntius' story is accurate:

> Gemistos' heterodoxy was by no means an impossible

10   For Plethon's neopagan views, see C.M. Woodhouse, *Gemistos Plethon—The Last of the Hellenes* (Oxford: Clarendon Press, 2000).
11   quoted in Woodhouse, p. 168.

243

outcome of his study of Neoplatonism … Hence, Gemistos, who had no idea of the comparative antiquity of religions, looked to Zoroaster, Moses, and various legendary Greeks as the nominal sources of his system. But he formulated its content in terms of what he believed to be the oldest surviving religion, and also the best known to him, which was the Olympian religion of his ancestors, including its pre-Olympian core. This reversion to paganism on his part was deliberately provocative, but it was not mere foolishness.[12]

And Trapezuntius was not the only witness to the influence of paganism in the thought of Pletho; another of his contemporaries and a fellow delegate to the Council of Ferrara-Florence—Gennadios Scholarios—maintained that Gemistos was converted to paganism by an apostate Jew named Elissaeus:

The climax of his apostasy came later under the influence of a certain Jew with whom he studied, attracted by his skill as an interpreter of Aristotle. This Jew was an adherent of Averroes and other Persian and Arabic interpreters of Aristotle's works, which the Jews had translated into their own language, but he paid little regard to Moses or the beliefs and observances which the Jews received from him.

This man also expounded to Gemistos the doctrines of Zoroaster and others. He was ostensibly a Jew but in fact a Hellenist [pagan]. Gemistos stayed with him for a long time, not only as his pupil but also in his service, living at his expense, for he was one of the most influential men at the court of these barbarians. His name was Elissaeus. So Gemistos ended up as he did.[13]

---

12   ibid., p. 168–169.
13   quoted in ibid., p. 24.

While Gemistos was in Florence, he took the opportunity to urge the humanists of that city toward agreement with his Platonic/ Neoplatonic (the distinction did not exist at his time) doctrine; his neopagan views remained a more private affair.

For a scholar dedicated to the revival of Platonism, mid-fifteenth century Florence must have seemed idyllic. Humanists had been afforded a status in Florence which they had yet to attain in other cities; with Cosimo de'Medici at the center of the circle of Florentine humanists, a great deal of wealth and power was at their disposal, and there remained a circle of scholars who had gained at least a working knowledge of Greek, and were therefore in a position to understand, and presumably profit from, Gemistos' influence. As a result, Plethon threw himself into the task of initiating a Platonic revival:

> Gemistos found himself immediately at home in this environment. … So Gemistos spent his time … among the Florentine humanists, discussing philosophy and correcting their misunderstandings of Plato and Aristotle. Eventually the discussions seem to have taken the form of lectures by Gemistos, which he later embodied in a summary version entitled *On the Differences of Aristotle from Plato* (literally, 'with regard to Plato'), commonly known as *De Differentiis*.[14]

Still, even in Florence, "only a handful" of Italians were "competent to study Plato in Greek,"[15] and thus the intersection of the lives of Gemistos and Cosimo was highly significant. Although to this day, a great deal of speculation swirls about regarding the precise roster of attendees at Gemistos' lectures, the one person whose attendance mattered the most had both the means and the will to follow through on the Platonic inspiration

---

14   ibid., p. 155–156.
15   ibid., p. 157.

which the visitor from Constantinople had to offer.

The task of establishing the academy fell to the man chosen by Cosimo de'Medici: a young scholar by the name of Marsilio Ficino (1433–1499). Cosimo personally procured a collection of manuscripts now known as the *Corpus Hermeticum*, which he made Ficino's top priority for translation:

> Leonardo de Pistoia, a monk who worked for Cosimo as an agent, purchasing any interesting scholarly works he came across, had discovered an item in Macedonia that he was sure his boss would appreciate. It was a near complete edition of a collection of texts whose existence was suspected, but which had been lost to the west since late antiquity and the beginning of the Dark Ages. ... The work de Pistoia brought back to Florence from the land of Alexander the Great was the *Corpus Hermeticum*, and its author was, depending on your sources, a god, a magician, or something in between: the fabled Hermes Trismegistus, 'thrice-great Hermes'.[16]

The text which fell into Ficino's hands may have owed its existence to the Sabi'an influence in Constantinople which was noted previously. As Lachman writes:

> The collection that reached Ficino itself was incomplete, containing only fourteen of the fifteen texts making up the corpus. This was more than likely put together by a Byzantine scholar, sometime in the tenth or eleventh century; at least there is no mention of the *Corpus Hermeticum* as a specific collection prior to that time, and the eleventh century Byzantine Platonist Michael Psellus is the first to refer to it as such.[17]

---

16   Gary Lachman, *The Quest for Hermes Trismegistus,* (Edinburgh: Floris Books, 2011) p. 11–12.
17   ibid., p. 15.

According to Woodhouse, this same Psellus (Psellos) was one of the few "theologians of recent times" to have any influence on Gemistos Plethon:

Psellos also tried to reconcile paganism with Christianity, but he was otherwise a man more after Gemistos' heart. ... Psellos himself sought to illustrate the truths of Christianity from the 'omnifarious thought' of Plato and Plotinus. Like the 'admirable Proclus' before him and Gemistos after him, he wrote a commentary on the Chaldean Oracles, but not without references to the Fathers of the Church. ...

The classical revival in the eleventh and twelfth centuries, tinged like that in Gemistos' time with Neoplatonism and paganism, was in some ways even more marked, because it affected the arts as well as philosophy. In the eleventh century classical themes reappeared in miniatures, ivories, and enamel work; but these did not recur in the fourteenth century, when the new classical revival seems to have been confined to literature and philosophy.[18]

In time, Ficino also translated works which were purportedly written by Orpheus and Zoroaster—a further sign of the lingering influence of Plethon over the course of the Florentine Renaissance. Ficino also attempted a harmonization of Christian and Neoplatonic doctrine, a work which he entitled, *Theologia Platonica.*

Ficino believed that Zoroaster and Hermes Trismegistus were the first teachers in a succession of *Prisci Theologi,* "ancient theologians" whom he thought were divinely inspired, and who thus led the Gentiles in the way of salvation. D.P. Walker,

18   Woodhouse, p. 70–71.

one of the most significant scholars of the Renaissance concept of *prisca theologia*, defines the "ancient theology" as follows:

> By the term 'Ancient Theology' I mean a certain tradition of Christian apologetic theology which rests on misdated texts. Many of the early Fathers, in particular Lactantius, Clement of Alexandria and Eusebius, in their apologetic works directed against pagan philosophers, made use of supposedly very ancient texts: *Hermetica, Orphica,* Sibylline Prophecies, Pythagorean *Camina Aurea*, etc., most of which in fact date from the first four centuries of our era. These texts, written by the Ancient Theologians Hermes Trismegistus, Orpheus, Pythagoras, were shown to contain vestiges of the true religion: monotheism, the Trinity, the creation of the world out of nothing through the Word, and so forth.[19]

In the promotion of the notion of such *Prisci Theologi,* Ficino was joined by Giovanni Pico della Mirandola (1463–1494), whose *Oration on the Dignity of Man* and *900 Theses* were written in defense of the divine inspiration of such ancient pagan teachers, and promoted the study of a form of medieval Jewish gnosticized mysticism known as Kabbalah as a key to understanding the true meaning of Scripture.[20]

Prior to Ficino's translation of the *Corpus Hermeticum,* only one work attributed to Hermes was known—the *Asclepius*—and that treatise only existed in a Latin edition. Ficino's publication of a collection of Hermetic writings in 1471—fourteen treatises—was an important part of his effort to establish a succession of pagan teachers who had been divinely inspired. As

19   D. P. Walker, *The Ancient Theology,* (Ithaca: Cornell University Press, 1972) p. 1.

20   For an extended examination of Ficino's and Pico's theological systems, see Heiser, *Prisci Theologi,* (Malone, Texas: Repristination Press, 2011).

Ficino wrote in the preface to his *Corpus Hermeticum*:

> At the time when Moses was born flourished Atlas the
> astrologer, brother of the natural philosopher Prometheus
> and maternal grandfather of the elder Mercurius, whose
> grandson was Mercurius Trismegistus. ... They call him
> Trismegistus or thrice-greatest because he was the great-
> est philosopher and the greatest priest and the greatest
> king. ... Thus he was called the first author of theology,
> and Orpheus followed him, taking second place in the
> ancient theology. After Alaophemus, Pythagoras came
> next in theological succession, having been initiated
> into rites of Orpheus, and he was followed by Philolaus,
> teacher of our divine Plato. In this way, from a wondrous
> line of six theologians emerged a single system of an-
> cient theology, harmonious in every part, which traced
> its origins to Mercurius and reached absolute perfection
> with the divine Plato. Mercurius wrote many books per-
> taining to the knowledge of divinity, ... often speaking
> not only as philosopher but as prophet. ... He foresaw
> the ruin of the old religion, the rise of the new faith, the
> coming of Christ, the judgement to come, the resurrec-
> tion of the race, the glory of the blessed and the torments
> of the damned.[21]

With time, Ficino modified his list of six theologians, omitting
Philolaus and adding Zoroaster as a theologian who preceded
Hermes—maintaining six such theologians was of profound significance to Ficino because of the mystical significance of the
number as the first 'perfect' number and first 'nuptial' number.[22]

Ficino's promotion of Hermeticism, and his pagan suc-

---

21   Quoted in *Hermetica*, trans. and ed. by Brian P. Copenhaver,
(Cambridge: Cambridge University Press, 1992) p. xlviii.
22   see Heiser, *Prisci Theologi*, p. 44.

cession of teachers bequeathed to the West a most pernicious legacy: *the Myth of Syncretism.* Catharism was a Gnosticism of a different stripe: Cathar teachers shared with the orthodox a belief in the exclusivity of truth. One could either believe that Cathar doctrine or the Catholic verity was the one, true faith. Hermeticism teaches that *all* religions are divinely inspired. This teaching is known as a doctrine of multilinear inspiration. Prior to Ficino's hermetical doctrine of the *prisca theologia,* teachers of the Church had maintained that any knowledge which pagans might possess of the divine was either gained from natural revelation (that which may be known of God from the study of nature, and the study of the conscience) or was gained by a borrowing from the Scriptures. As Moshe Idel observes in his essay, "Prisca Theologia in Marsilio Ficino":

> There were two main theories that allowed the adoption of these doctrines [the teachings of the *prisci theologi*] into a Christian monotheistic framework: the first contends that they agree with Christian theology because they were influenced by a primeval tradition which included or at least adumbrated the tenets of Christianity; the alternative argues that the affinity between these two bodies of thought has no historical explanation but is a result of a revelation or a series of revelations imparted separately to both pagan and monotheistic spiritual leaders.[23]

Ficino and Pico promoted the second theory, maintaining that each of the ancient theologies was divinely inspired and thus independent of the Christian verity. Again, in Idel's words:

> The Christian Renaissance thinkers seem, however, to have been fascinated more by another theory,

---

23   Moshe Idel, "Prisca Theologia in Marsilio Ficino," in *Marsilio Ficino: His Theology, His Philosophy, His Legacy*, ed. by Michael J. B. Allen and Valery Rees with Martin Davies, (Leiden, Boston, Köln: Brill, 2002), p. 138–139.

which I should like to designate 'multilinear'. This latter theory seems to have been influenced in part by the views of a mid fifteenth-century Byzantine author who had strong pagan proclivities, George Gemistos Plethon. ... Ficino embraced some views of Plethon, which contributed to the turning away in the West from the earlier traditions concerning the unilinear theory to embrace the hypothesis of two or more lines of transmission. The multilinear version of *prisca theologia* assumes the possibility of more than one source of valid religious knowledge and more than one line of transmission. Though the contents of this knowledge are identical in the two or more lines of transmission, their literary or terminological expressions differ from one case to another.[24]

Not only did Ficino treat his pagan succession of *prisci theologi* as divinely inspired, he also received even the pagan sibyls as equivalent to the prophets: "However divine truth has told no lie; for divine truth, from the very beginning of the world, inspired a great many prophets and sibyls, who had no knowledge of astronomy, to foresee and foretell the Christian law by divine providence."[25] And Ficino hardly hesitated even to interpret Socrates as a type of Christ:

If I did not fear, excellent Paolo, that there would be some who through perversity of their nature or through narrow-mindedness, would contrive to take everything in a sense other than the one we intend, I would show that Socrates was, so to speak, a forerunner of Christ, the author of salvation. He was not like Job and John the Baptist, yet perhaps in a way he foreshadowed Christ ...
But what can I say? He could easily have defend-

24   ibid., p. 141.
25   *The Letters of Marsilio Ficino*, vol. 6, (London: Shepheard-Walwyn Publishers, 1999) p. 24. (Letter 14)—6 January 1482.

ed himself in court, but he did not; nor did he excuse himself, but accused the judges. While he could have escaped from prison he refused, and he most willingly suffered an unjust death, giving to posterity an example of supreme steadfastness and patience.

For now, I pass over the sum of thirty pieces of silver offered for Socrates, as well as the prophecies of Socrates himself and the divine vindication which followed immediately after his death. I pass over the act of bathing undertaken by Socrates in the evening shortly before his death, and his exhortation, at the hour of supper to revere the divine. But what about the wine-cup and the blessing at that same hour, and the mention made of the cock at the very time of his death?

Furthermore, I pass over the many deeds and words of Socrates which are recorded not by him but chiefly by his four disciples and which mightily confirm the Christian faith in opposition to Lucian. For there are many things, very important things, that are recounted about the divine qualities poured into this man, his withdrawal of the mind from the body, and his apparent transfiguration.[26]

Giovanni Pico della Mirandola built on the work of Ficino and expanded it; his *Oration on the Dignity of Man* and his *900 Theses* are dedicated to building on the concept of a unity among the *prisci theologi* which Pico believed to be absent in the writings of the Scholastic theologians. In fact, Pico (like Ficino) sought to reform the Church by moving from the divisions between warring Dominicans, Franciscans, and Augustinians to the unity of the *prisci theologi*. As S. A. Farmer wrote in his introduction to the *900 Theses*:

---

26   *The Letters of Marsilio Ficino*, vol. 7, (London: Shepheard-Walwyn Publishers, 2003) p. 12, 13.

The emanations of wisdom in Pico's historical theses expresses a parallel movement [from multiplicity to unity in his cosmological systems], reflected in the conflicting theses of *gentes* and *heresiarchae* in Pico's reverse genealogy of thought. These conflicts are sharpest and most frequent at the beginning of the text with the corrupt Latins and Arabs and, after gradually diminishing, disappear totally at the end, in the harmonious concord of the *prisci theologi* and Cabalists.[27]

The inclusion of Gnosticizing Jewish Cabala (or Kabbalah) within the body of the *prisca theologia* was part of Pico's 'contribution' which would have significant implications for the future of humanist thought. In Pico's words:

... I have not been content to repeat well-worn doctrines, but have proposed for disputation many points of the early theology of Hermes Trismegistus, many theses drawn from the teachings of the Chaldeans and the Pythagoreans, from the occult mysteries of the Hebrews and, finally, a considerable number of propositions concerning both nature and God which we ourselves have discovered and worked out.[28]

As in his use of Medieval, Classical, and Hermetic source material, Pico's appropriation of Kabbalistic materials was hardly that of a dilettante. As Chaim Wirszubski observed in his crucial study of Pico's use of the Kabbalah:

Pico is the first Christian by birth who is known to have read an impressive amount of genuine Jewish Kabbala.

27   Giovanni Pico della Mirandola, *Syncretism in the West: Pico's 900 Theses (1486)—The Evolution of Traditional Religious and Philosophical Terms,* trans. by S. A. Farmer (Tempe, Arizona: Medieval & Renaissance Texts & Studies, 1998), p. 35.
28   Giovanni Pico della Mirandola, *Oration on the Dignity of Man,* (Washington, D.C.: Regnery Gateway, 1956) p. 49.

The Kabbala passed not only through Latin translation, but also through the creative mind of a Christian thinker who was trained in the schools of philosophy. As might be expected, Kabbala was transformed in the process. But the Kabbala that Pico read is still recognizable in the Kabbala that Pico wrote.[29]

As we will see later, Pico's importation of Kabbalah into Christian theology would have profound implications for centuries to come. But so would his revival of the elitism of the ancient Gnostics. Having absorbed the belief in a Gnostic ascension of the more 'worthy' souls of men, Pico sneeringly dismissed the less worthy. Thus he places the following words in the mouth of "the Supreme Maker" (who he also calls "Mightiest Architect"):

> We have made you a creature neither of heaven nor of earth, neither mortal nor immortal, in order that you may, as the free and proud shaper of your own being, fashion yourself in the form you may prefer. It will be in your power to descend to the lower, brutish forms of life; you will be able, through your own decision, to rise again to the superior orders whose life is divine.[30]

On the basis of this supposed divine decree than man may ascend or descend according to his will, Pico declared:

> Whichever of these a man shall cultivate, the same will mature and bear fruit in him. If vegetative, he will become a plant; if sensual, he will become brutish; if rational, he will reveal himself a heavenly being; if intellectual, he will be an angel and the son of God. And if, dissatisfied with the lot of all creatures, he should recollect

29   Chaim Wirzubski, *Pico della Mirandola's Encounter with Jewish Mysticism,* (Cambridge and London: Harvard University Press, 1989) p. 64.
30   *Oration on the Dignity of Man,* p. 7–8.

himself into the center of his own unity, he will there, become one spirit with God, in the solitary darkness of the Father, Who is set above all things, himself transcend all creatures.[31]

In fact, Pico found it possible to state such an ascent in even more blasphemous and egocentric terms:

If you see a man dedicated to his stomach, crawling on the ground, you see a plant and not a man; or if you see man bedazzled by the empty forms of the imagination, as by the wiles of Calypso, and through their alluring solicitations made a slave to his own senses, you see a brute and not a man. If, however, you see a philosopher, judging and distinguishing all things according to the rule of reason, him shall you hold in veneration, for he is a creature of heaven and not of earth; if, finally, a pure contemplator, unmindful of the body, wholly withdrawn into the inner chambers of the mind, here indeed is neither a creature of earth nor a heavenly creature, but some higher divinity, clothed with human flesh.[32]

Considering Pico's self-identification as a philosopher, one may recognize that he is far from lacking in self-esteem. An elitism is at work in the heart of the Hermeticists which would make a Valentinian blush; certainly he gives voice to the Gnostic distinction between Hylics, Psychics, and Pneumatics—between those men who are merely material, the 'spiritual,' and the truly ensouled. And Pico gave free expression to the fact that the secret core of Scripture and all revelation—that which was to be known by the Kabbalistic arts—must be concealed from the unworthy:

Not famous Hebrew teachers alone, but, from among those of our own persuasion, Esdras, Hilary and Origen

---

31   ibid., p. 9.
32   ibid., p. 10–11.

all write that Moses, in addition to the law of the five books which he handed down to posterity, when on the mount, received from God a more secret and true explanation of the law. They also say that God commanded Moses to make the law known to the people, but not to write down its interpretation or to divulge it, but to communicate it only to Jesu Nave who, in turn, was to reveal it to succeeding high priests under a strict obligation of silence. ... Openly to reveal to the people the hidden mysteries and the secret intentions of the highest divinity, which lay concealed under the hard shell of the law and the rough vesture of language, what else could this be but to throw holy things to dogs and to strew gems among swine? The decision, consequently, to keep such things hidden from the vulgar and to communicate them only to the initiate, among whom alone, as Paul says, wisdom speaks, was not a counsel of human prudence but a divine command.[33]

Thus we see the hermetical myth take shape—a belief that all religions (regardless of blatant contradictions between them) teach the same salvation, and lead to the same "Mighty Architect," but at the same time, the profound truths concealed within such a syncretic faith are to be hidden from the unworthy and retained for the spiritual elite. Discernment of the truth belongs to the spiritual elite—this is one of the dominant myths of our age. Its spirit is manifest in the technical elitism which predominates most fields of knowledge, but especially in those areas of study which seek to change the world—and man.

---

33   ibid., p. 59–60.

CHAPTER 4. THE RETURN OF THE GNOSTICS—KABBALAH AND ALCHEMY.

he Hermetic Reformation inaugurated by Marsilio Ficino and Giovanni Pico was not long contained to Florence; the effects of their efforts to change the theology of the Church quickly spread north of the Alps, and to the innermost circles of the Church in Rome. One of Ficino's students—Giovanni de'Medici (1475–1521)—declined the office of canon of the Cathedral in Florence in 1487 so that Ficino could receive the benefice.[1] In 1513, Giovanni de'Medici was elected and proclaimed pope, taking the name of Leo X. The new Pontiff dreamed great things concerning his rule, and imagined that his reign would initiate a new Golden Age. Given the contrast between a Christian understanding of the Edenic Paradise and the pagan belief in a cycle of history which led to Golden Ages, the peril for Christendom which is posed by popes believing in a fundamentally pagan understanding of history should be readily apparent. As Mebane wrote in his book, *Renaissance Magic and the Return of the Golden Age*:

> The theme of "The Golden Age Restored" was a favorite in courtly entertainments and civic pageantry from the time of the Medici in Florence through the reigns of Elizabeth and James I in England. When Lorenzo de Medici's son became Pope Leo X, the celebration in Florence included a symbolic representation of the birth of a new era: "From the center of the car rose a great globe in the form of the world," an observer recorded, "upon which a man lay prostrate on his face as if dead,

---

1   Peter Serracino-Inglott, "Ficino the Priest" in *Marsilio Ficino: His Theology, His Philosophy, His Legacy,* ed. by Michael J. B. Allen and Valery Rees with Martin Davies (Leiden, Boston, Köln: Brill, 2002) p. 9.

his armor all rusted, and from the open fissure of whose sundered back emerged a small boy all naked and gilded, representing the revival of the golden age and the end of the iron age, which expired and was reborn through the election of the pope" …

It would be easy enough to dismiss all instances of such spectacular praise as mere flattery. If we examine closely the careers of the artists and intellectuals who offer such homage, however, we often find that their work springs from genuine confidence in a ruler or a system of government and from sincere hopes for social and cultural progress.[2]

Another student of Ficino's—Egidio da Viterbo[3] (1469–1532)—was named by Leo X to be a cardinal "and took a prominent part in the Lateran Council…"[4] In his biography of Egidio, Francis Martin notes that "his natural element was in a Platonic Academy such as flourished under Ficino at Florence."[5] This is probably not a surprise, since some of the most formative time in Egidio's life was spent as a student of Ficino's Platonic, Hermetical theology:

> From Padua Giles [Egidio] went to study Plato under Marsilio Ficino at Florence; thence after some months he was appointed to lecture on theology at Capo d'Istria. The effect of his visit to Florence remained, and whenever he had a free moment at Capo d'Istria he gave

2   John S. Mebane, *Renaissance Magic and the Return of the Golden Age,* (Lincoln and London: University of Nebraska Press, 1989) p. 13.

3   Also known as Giles of Viterbo.

4   Charles Trinkhaus, *In Our Image and Likeness—Humanity and Divinity in Italian Humanist Thought*, 2 vols. vol. 2, (Notre Dame, Indiana: University of Notre Dame Press, 1995) p. 526.

5   Francis X. Martin, *Friar, Reformer, and Renaissance Scholar— Life and Work of Giles of Viterbo (1469–1532),* (Villanova, Pennsylvania: Augustinian Press, 1992) p. 17.

himself to a study of Plato. There was a natural affinity of soul between Marsilio and Giles; their common interest was Plato. Marsilio was not merely an intellectual fashion in the Europe of his day but was the leader of a group at Florence who were formulating a new exposition of Christianity, the *theologia platonica,* to counteract what they condemned as the insidious errors of Averroistic Aristotelianism. Giles' concept of reform, infused with the spirit of Marsilio and the Platonic Academy, embraced a whole outlook on life and not merely a disciplinary rejuvenation of the Augustinian Order.[6]

The selection of Giovanni de'Medici as pope in 1513, and the prominent role which both he and Egidio played at the Fifth Lateran Council (1512–1517) provided the Hermetic Reformation with an opportunity to begin shaping the doctrine of the Western Church. In 1943, P. O. Kristeller (the father of modern study of Ficino) raised the question of what role the Platonic/Hermetic doctrine of the essential immortality of the soul[7] might have had on council's dogmatic declaration of the immortality of the soul. As Kristeller noted, the Lateran Council was "the first time the traditional ecclesiastical doctrine of immortality" was expressed "in dogmatic form."[8] However, Kristeller noted at that time, "We cannot decide whether the theologians of the council, Giles of Viterbo, among others, were directly influenced by Ficino's work or whether they were led to similar conclusions by the nature of the situation."[9] Ongoing research has confirmed the Hermetical influence on the council.

---

6   ibid., p. 14–15.
7   That is, the notion that the soul is immortal because of its inherent properties, being a fragment of the Deity.
8   O. P. Kristeller, *The Philosophy of Marsilio Ficino,* (New York: Columbia University Press, 1943) p. 347.
9   ibid.

As Martin observes, Egidio was known for preaching funeral sermons on the hope of eternal life "in Platonic terms": "... he expounded doctrine in Platonic terms so that his audience might lift their eyes to life beyond the grave."[10] Such a deviation from sound, biblical preaching led Martin to ask, "Where does this get us to understanding Giles as a scripture scholar? Plato is not holy writ." Indeed. In fact, Plato—and, more specifically, Hermetical Syncretism—provided a mythological framework for reinterpreting all of Christian doctrine. It had already played such a role for Ficino and Pico,[11] and in the generations to follow, it played a growing role in the theology of Western Christendom, regardless of whether or not its direct influence was recognized. For Egidio, the Hermetic hope of the return of the soul to God was the hope which drove him:

> In the same spirit in which he had written to Brandolini, Giles exhorted Pontano to reflect on immortality and on the fact that he was numbered among "the sons of God." Pontano took the point and in replying to Giles developed the concept of divine sonship. This inner life, Pontano argued, is gradually frittered away during our passage through this world, until in old age we turn once more to God *as we prepare to rejoin him in heaven.* [emph. added] The Platonic concept of the return of the soul to God was one which Pontano freely acknowledged he had received from Giles.[12]

Thus, when the Fifth Lateran Council dogmatized the immortality of the soul, there is reason to see the hand of Ficino's doctrine at work when one of his students was Pontiff and another was one of the chief theologians of the council. As one

---

10   Martin, p. 156.
11   see Heiser, *Prisci Theologi and the Hermetic Reformation in the Fifteenth Century* (Malone, Texas: Repristination Press, 2011).
12   Martin, p. 156.

historian of the council has written:

> Whether or not the bull is seen as a dogmatic pronouncement on immortality, it can nevertheless be established that Florentine Platonism and its doctrine on the soul was probably a major factor in the creation of *Apostolici regiminis*. From the work of Giles of Viterbo by John O'Malley and from John Monfasani's work on philosophical liberty in pre-Reformation Italy, it is possible to reconstruct much of the process through which *Apostolici regiminis* was drafted and promulgated. This reconstruction confirms Kristeller's suggestion by demonstrating, independently of any interpretation of the bull's content, that the decree was likely profoundly influenced by Platonism and particularly by Ficino's doctrine of the soul.[13]

It is worth noting, at least in passing, that it was in the house of Egidio that Martin Luther could have had his first encounter with the Hermetical doctrine, for Luther "was a visitor in the house of the Augustinian Order in Rome during the time when Egidio was its Prior General."[14] As Egidio's biographer is quick to point out, both men were to spend their years of service to the Church in various efforts at 'reformation' of the Church, but the reformation which Egidio sought was dramatically different from that of the Lutheran Reformation:

> Alphons Müller attempted in a number of studies to prove that the unorthodox ideas which distinguished Lutheranism from the traditional teachings of the Church were to be found in the writings of Augustinian theologians of the fourteenth and fifteenth centuries. A French theolo-

---

13   Eric A. Constant, "A Reinterpretation of the Fifth Lateran Council Decree *Apostolici regiminis* (1513)," in *Sixteenth Century Journal*, XXXIII:2 (2002), p. 357.
14   Trinkhaus, p. 529.

gian, Jules Paquier, following out this line of thought, set himself the task of comparing Luther's theological principles with those of Giles. His conclusions, published in 1912, showed that there was no convergence of ideas between the two Augustinians. Paquier, in the process of his lucid demonstration, expounded how Giles' neoplatonic treatment of the *Sentences* was in the manner of Marsilio Ficino.[15]

In point of fact, it was Egidio who was the unorthodox innovator who sought to smuggle in strange doctrines as a part of his Syncretic approach to the Catholic verity.

The errors of men such as Egidio of Viterbo may seem someone esoteric, but those of other men influenced by the Hermetic Reformation are more marked in their deviation from the teachings of Christianity. In the words of one scholar:

> The impact of this body of doctrine upon the continental Renaissance deserves notice. Unlike references to astrology, witchcraft, magic, and alchemy, allusions to philosophical or theological Hermetism may slide across the readers mind without attracting much attention. The system itself is not widely known, and what has little meaning is quickly forgotten. …
>
> … the tendency in some quarters was to regard the *Hermetica* as nearly, or occasionally quite, equal in authority to Holy Writ. The vogue reached its height in the fifty years on either side of 1500, but continued strong well into the late sixteenth century and regained prominence form time to time until the 1650s, after which it subsided.[16]

---

15   Martin, p. 138.

16   Wayne Shumaker, *The Occult Sciences in the Renaissance—A Study in Intellectual Patterns,* (Berkeley, Los Angeles, London: University

In truth, however, it did not so much subside, as transform.

As noted previously, one of Giovanni Pico's 'contributions' to the Hermetic Reformation was his effort to include Jewish Kabbalah in the body of the *prisca theologia*. Pico's claims concerning the Kabbalah helped to lead to his condemnation by the pope. Pico made quite expansive claims concerning the Kabbalah in his *900 Theses*, especially as pertains to magic. As one scholar has noted:

> Forty-seven of his propositions were directly taken from Cabalistic sources, and seventy-two more reflected his own conclusions from his research on the Cabala. Most striking among these 119 theses was his claim that 'no science can better convince us of the divinity of Jesus Christ than magic and the Cabala'. ...
>
> In advancing such claims, Pico was much bolder than Ficino. ... For Pico also insisted that pure Cabala could go beyond Ficino's natural magic. It could go immediately to the first principle, to God himself.[17]

Of course, Pico's advocacy of Kabbalistic studies did not die with him; far from it. In fact, study of the Kabbalah led to the study of Hebrew north of the Alps. When it came to the Kabbalah, Johannes Reuchlin (1455–1522) was the student who advanced beyond his master, and brought its pernicious influence into Germany.

Lutheran Reformation historian Lewis Spitz refers to Reuchlin as "Pythagoras reborn,"[18] while a scholar of the Re-

of California Press, 1979) p. 232.

17   Stefan Rossbach, *Gnostic Wars—The Cold War in the Context of the History of Western Spirituality*, (Edinburgh: Edinburgh University Press, 1999) p. 136.

18   Lewis W. Spitz, *The Religious Renaissance of the German*

naissance revival of Gnosticism calls him "the most important representative of their [Ficino's and Pico's] syncretistic Neo-Platonism north of the Alps."[19] Reuchlin first met Ficino in 1482 during a trip to Florence with the duke of Württemberg; on his second trip to the city, in 1490, "he met Pico and perhaps saw Ficino again, an event of the greatest moment for his intellectual development."[20] Reuchlin began his study of Hebrew in 1486 and twenty years later published "the first fairly reliable manual of Hebrew grammar by a Christian scholar".[21] In the years following publication of his Hebrew grammar, Reuchlin was drawn into an Imperial controversy over the question of whether or not various Jewish books should be destroyed on account of blasphemy; when, in 1509, an Imperial commission sought guidance from major universities on the question of whether such books should be destroyed, Johann Pfefferkorn (a converted Jew who led the movement for banning such books) declared, "All, with the exception of Johann Reuchlin, unanimously declared and wrote for Christ, inspired by the Holy Spirit. His report alone … supported the perfidy of the Jews rather than the apostolic See and the most holy cause of our faith."[22] Nevertheless, the movement to ban and burn such books failed the next year.

Reuchlin's work with the Hebrew language was driven by the study of Kabbalah; in the words of Spitz, "Reuchlin considered the Cabala, not Hebrew for its own sake, his major concern."[23] Thus, when his massive study of the Kabbalah —*De arte cabalistica*—was published in 1517, he dedicated the work to Leo X, the most influential of all of Ficino's students. And

Humanists, (Cambridge: Harvard University Press, 1963) p. 61.

19   Rossbach, p. 137.

20   Spitz, p. 61.

21   ibid., p. 62.

22   Erika Rummel, *The Case Against Johann Reuchlin,* (Toronto, Buffalo and London: University of Toronto Press, 2002) p. 11.

23   Spitz, p. 68.

Reuchlin's theology was dominated by a Gnostic/Kabbalistic approach to the Word; the Name of Jesus was thus seen as a "wonder-working word" through which miracles could, and had been, performed:

> Reuchlin's Christology remains more a matter of gnosis than atonement.

> There is an unmistakable tendency in Reuchlin toward a religious universal theism. By the very nature of the evidence which he adduces to support Christian truth he lends a measure of authority to his non-Christian sources. The cabalists, Neoplatonists, Pythagoras, nature philosophers, Philo, Plato, Aristotle, and Mohammed are called upon to testify on such questions as immortality, miracles, and the nature of God. But he clearly used them to buttress the Catholic faith.[24]

Here one may readily see the Hermetic Syncretic mythology in operation. Using pagan teachers to supposedly "buttress the Catholic faith" is to endeavor to make the Christian verity in some fashion dependent on such pagan theologies. But then, the decision to dedicate a work of Kabbalistic theology to the pope demonstrates that the Myth of Syncretism had already taken root in Rome.

One of the few positive developments to come from the work of Reuchlin was his impartation of the knowledge of Hebrew to his nephew, Philip Melanchthon. (Indeed, it was Reuchlin who recommended Melanchthon for his position at the University of Wittenberg.[25]) However, although Reuchlin and Melanchthon had been exceptionally close, they were alienated by Melanchthon's adherence to the Lutheran Reformation. Re-

---

24   ibid., p. 76.
25   John Schofield, *Philip Melanchthon and the English Reformation*, (Burlington, Vermont: Ashgate Publishing Company, 2006), p. 3–4, 9.

uchlin aligned himself with one of Luther's greatest opponents, Johann Eck, and ended his days in Ingolstadt, living in Eck's home. Given the history of the revival of Hebrew studies—one which is inextricably bound up with Kabbalistic interpretations of Scripture and magic—it is a wonder to see the way in which the Lord used Philip Melanchthon to restore Hebrew studies to their proper usage, the faithful interpretation of God's Word.

Another continuation of the Hermetic Reformation is found in the writings of Theophrastus Bombastus von Hohenheim (1493–1541)—a man who renamed himself "Paracelsus." Although much of what needs to be said regarding Paracelsus will be addressed in the next chapter, for the moment it is largely sufficient to address him as one who consciously continued Marsilio Ficino's lead. Ficino's Hermetic Reformation not only unleashed Hermetic Gnosticism, it expanded the influence of a range of occult sciences: "The translation of the *Corpus hermeticum* by Ficino in 1463 added one more factor that was to affect the chemistry of the Renaissance. Fostering occult learning of all kinds, alchemy was shortly brought to the attention of all learned men as an area of study that had not received proper attention in the past."[26] In short, Ficino made Paracelsian alchemy possible. Alchemy was a constant influence in the development of Paracelsus' thought: his father (who was also a physician) dabbled in alchemy and he was instructed in alchemy by Johannes Trithemius (1462–1516) as a child.[27]

Whereas traditionally, all of nature was thought of in terms of four classical elements (earth, water, air, and fire), Paracelsus spoke in terms of three "principles" of sulphur, mercury

---

26   Allen G. Debus, *Man and Nature in the Renaissance,* (Cambridge: Cambridge University Press, 1978) p. 18–19.
27   ibid., p. 19.

and salt.[28] Shumaker explains that the sources of Paracelsian medicinal theory fall outside the bounds of the Christian verity:

> The three principles derived from Islam, and the medicinal implications of the cosmology had a Hermetic and Neo-Platonic origin. For example, the teaching that the various human organs were governed by separate "rulers" is obviously indebted to the Hermetic *daimones* which had similar responsibilities. Pythagorean or cabalistic numerology also plays a role, as it had done in the theories of Raymond Lull and Geber; and the "empiricism" sometimes hailed as a precious step toward modern scientific methods actually appears to have included a wholly uncritical acceptance of old wives' tales, which Paracelsus believed to have been tested by experience.[29]

As Weeks observes in his biographical examination of Paracelsus, it was precisely the Hermetical magical writings of Ficino which had the greatest appeal to Paracelsus: "As Pagel stated the matter: 'Paracelsus's whole life and work seems to be an attempt at implementing the ideal of Ficino's priest-physician.' Pagel indeed went beyond the importance of Ficino as an ethical model: 'It is from Ficino as the exponent of Neo-Platonism that Paracelsus derives his inspiration.'"[30] And, if anything, the Hermetical inclination was even stronger among Paracelsus' intellectual heirs:

> Above all, they sought to overturn the traditional, dominant Aristotelianism of the universities. ...
> The Paracelsians hoped to replace all this with a Christian neo-Platonic and Hermetic philosophy, one

28   Wayne Shumaker, *The Occult Sciences in the Renaissance—A Study in Intellectual Patterns,* (Berkeley, Los Angeles, London: University of California Press, 1979) p. 183.
29   ibid., p. 185.
30   Andrew Weeks, *Paracelsus—Speculative Theory and the Crisis of the Early Reformation,* (Albany: State University of New York Press, 1997) p. 57.

that would account for all natural phenomena. They argued that the true physician might find truth in the two divine books: the book of divine revelation—Scripture—and the book of divine Creation—nature. …

The early Paracelsians spoke harshly of Aristotle and Galen (if not always Hippocrates) and they turned instead to the recently translated Hermetic, alchemical, and neo-Platonic texts. A vitalistic universe founded on the macrocosm–microcosm analogy and the divine office of the physician was the basis for a new Christian understanding of nature as a whole.[31]

What began with Ficino's obsession with a relationship between various earthly elements and the celestial spheres transformed into a macrocosm–microcosm relationship between the universe and the body of man.[32] What Ficino deemed to be natural magic fairly easily transitioned into the alchemical medicine of Paracelsus.

The enumeration of the students of Ficino and Pico could easily fill a volume all on its own. Before concluding this chapter, however, one last individual needs to be identified: Giordano Bruno (1548–1600). Bruno has the distinction of being the most prominent Hermeticist to have been executed for his beliefs; having earned the disfavor of the papacy, Bruno was burned at the stake in the Camp de' Fiori ("Square of Flowers") for his paganism.

Earlier in his life, Bruno might have seemed an unlikely figure to end up being executed for his heresy. In his earlier years, Bruno was a Dominican (and thus of the order which was born to

---

31   Debus, p. 21, 32.
32   For more on Ficino's view of natural magic, see Heiser, *Prisci Theologi and the Hermetic Reformation in the Fifteenth Century,* (Malone, Texas: Repristination Press, 2011), p. 178–198.

fight against the Gnostic Cathars) but he abandoned the Catholic faith and committed himself to a restoration of the 'Egyptian religion': Hermeticism and magic. For thirteen years—from 1563 until 1576—Bruno was a Dominican, but his aberrant beliefs led him to finally flee his order, moving from place to place, being received as a lecturer at various universities—most of which he eventually either fled, or was driven from, because of his bizarre doctine and insufferable egotism.

Ficino and Pico believed that they were endeavoring to bring Neoplatonism and Hermeticism to the service of the Church; Bruno had no such illusions—or desires. As Frances Yates declares in her magisterial examination of Bruno's doctrine: "Thus Giordano Bruno, magician, had a Hermetic religious mission. He is the *enfant terrible* among religious Hermeticists, and yet he *is* a religious Hermeticist."[33] Bruno was utterly dismissive of the Jewish and Christian religions—and thus rejected the value of even the Kabbalah. In Bruno's words:

> Do not suppose that the sufficiency of the Chaldaic magic derived from the Cabala of the Jews; for the Jews are without doubt the excrement of Egypt, and no one could ever pretend with any degree of probability that the Egyptians borrowed any principle, good or bad, from the Hebrews.[34]

Unlike Ficino, who cautiously presented his teachings regarding magic in terms of natural magic, Bruno has no such scruples. Instead, black magic—talismanic magic and incantations—are, in his assessment, the very essence of Hermeticism.[35] In Yates' words:

---

33   Frances A. Yates, *Giordano Bruno and the Hermetic Tradition,* (Chicago and London: The University of Chicago Press, 1964) p. 231.
34   ibid., p. 223.
35   ibid., p. 230.

We have indeed come a long way from the Magia and Cabala system of the Christian Magus, with its safeguards in natural magic and its Hebrew-Christian angels as guarantees for religious magic. Nevertheless Giordano Bruno is the direct and logical result of the Renaissance glorification of Man as the great Miracle, man who is divine in his origin and can again become divine, with divine Powers residing in him. He is, in short, the result of the Renaissance Hermeticism. If man can obtain such powers through Hermetic experiences, why should not this have been the way in which Christ obtained his powers? Pico della Mirandola thought to prove the divinity of Christ through Magia and Cabala. Bruno interpreted the possibilities of Renaissance Magic in another way.[36]

Bruno was truly the logical extension of Renaissance Hermeticism—but he was not the only such extension. The extremity of his viewpoint should not be seen as having spent the force of Hermetical ideas; in fact, the slow progression of Hermeticism went on long after Bruno had been reduced to ashes. The Myth of Hermetical Syncretism was firmly in place. Men had begun to seek out the 'good' in all religions, and to seek all 'paths' as leading to true knowledge of the divine. Bruno's rabid anti-Christian rhetoric almost seems a throwback to the negativity of the Cathars.

Another aspect of the legacy of Giordano Bruno was the sowing of dragon's teeth in Lutheran Germany: the hidden cabal of his followers, who were called "Giordanisti." Dame Yates hints quite darkly at the connection between the Giordanisti who remained abroad in 1600—and beyond—and the horror which would be unleashed in Europe in 1618 when Rosicrucians helped spark the Thirty Years War; in Yates' words: "It has oc-

36   ibid., p. 266.

curred to wonder whether these rumoured 'Giordanisti' could have any connection with the unsolved mystery of the origin of the Rosicrucians who are first heard of in Germany in the early seventeenth century, in Lutheran circles."[37] Be that as it may, one need not establish an organic connection between the Giordanisti and the Rosicrucians to know that they were fruit from the same tree, and that tree was Hermeticism.

Thus, in this brief outline, the reader may begin to grasp some small measure of the influence of Gnostic Hermeticism in the Renaissance and Reformation era. In evaluating the transformation of human thought which began with the intersection of Hermeticism and Joachimism—the eruption of the new Syncretistic Myth—Rossbach concludes:

> Hermeticism and Cabalist mysticism provided fifteenth-century thinkers with precisely such a framework within which Joachim's books obtained a new meaning. Renaissance concerns such as the expectation of an imminent 'Golden Age', the celebration of the human being as a terrestrial god, as a co-creator and *magus* who, through alchemy, magic and science, acts upon the world to shape it according to his liking, derived from the amalgamation of these three ingredients: Joachimism, Hermeticism and Cabalist mysticism. Their intersection marks the beginning of the modern epoch.[38]

This is our assessment, as well: the amalgamation of these elements has forged the modern era. As one of the great historians of the Renaissance, Eugenio Garin, declared: "After Ficino there is no writing, no thought, in which a direct or indirect trace of his activity may not be found. Without Ficino that renewed sense of inner life and those new tones which moral and religious life ac-

37   ibid., p. 312–313.
38   Rossbach, p. 104.

quired in the European culture of the sixteenth and seventeenth centuries would be incomprehensible."[39]

39   Eugenio Garin, *Portraits from the Quattrocento*, trans. by Victor A. and Elizabeth Velen, (New York: Harper & Row, 1972) p. 156.

CHAPTER 5.
CHILIASM AND JOACHIMISM.

As with many aspects of the history of the modern West, a full account of the various strains of Chiliasm is far beyond the scope of the current work. Instead, we will focus on some aspects of this history which pertain to our theme. Chiliasm is linked to the Joachimite myth which has shaped so much of the modern age: *the Myth of the Third Age of Man*. By this point, of course, a great deal of attention has been devoted to this linchpin of Modernism, and this has been by design, because it is almost impossible to overstate its significance. The doctrine of Progress and the attendant hope for a coming Utopia are dependent on this myth. When we examine the *Myth of Socialism*, for example, we will see that its modern form is utterly dependent on Joachimism. Utopia has been sold in many forms—even before Thomas More wrote his book of the same name, Utopianism was called by other names, and pursued in different ways. For the classically educated, the pursuit of a Golden Age as a backdoor return to Paradise was the goal. Beliefs concerning the Thousand Year Reich and the final state of Communism owe their existence to Joachimism. And the Chiliastic fantasies which have brought bloodshed and sorrow time and again across the centuries owe their existence in no small part to this new doctrine. Although Chiliasm antedated Joachimism, the doctrine taught by the abbot of Fiore fundamentally transformed such movements and equipped them with a militancy and sense of immediate expectation which had not been as fully realized previously.

Norman Cohn's classic, *The Pursuit of the Millennium*, is still as valuable a resource now as when it was first published in 1957; when the third edition was published in 1969, Cohn

274

could rightly boast that it was "still the only book on its subject, i.e. the tradition of revolutionary millenarianism and mystical anarchism as it developed in western Europe between the eleventh and the sixteenth centuries."[1] Cohn's work and Robin Bruce Barnes' *Prophecy and Gnosis*,[2] will be utilized throughout our reflections on the development of this myth.

Prior to Joachim of Fiore's momentous prognostications, some of the most important extra-biblical influences for Millenarian fantasies came from the pseudo-Sibylline Oracles.[3] J. B. Hare notes that the texts were imagined to be the ancient Sibylline Oracles, but were in fact forgeries from late antiquity:

The texts which are presented here are forgeries, probably composed between the second to sixth century C.E. They purport to predict events which were already history or mythological history at the time of composition, as well as vague all-purpose predictions, especially woe for various cities and countries such as Rome and Assyria. They are an odd pastiche of Hellenistic and Roman Pagan mythology, including Homer and Hesiod; Jewish legends such as the Garden of Eden, Noah and the Tower of Babel; thinly veiled references to historical figures such as Alexander the Great and Cleopatra, as well as a long list of Roman Emperors; and last but not least, Gnostic and early Christian homilies and eschatological writings, all in no particular order. There may be actual residue of the original Sibylline books wedged in here

1   Norman Cohn, *The Pursuit of the Millennium*, 3rd ed., (Oxford, London, New York: Oxford University Press, 1970) p. 9.

2   Robin Bruce Barnes, *Prophecy and Gnosis—Apocalypticism in the Wake of the Lutheran Reformation,* (Stanford, California: Stanford University Press, 1988). Thomas Molnar's *Utopia, the Perennial Heresy,* (New York: Sheed and Ward, 1967) is also a useful work to consider.

3   An 1899 English translation of the 'Sibylline Oracles' can be referenced online at http://www.sacred-texts.com/cla/sib/

and there, but this is dubious.[4]

However, despite the dubious origins of the pseudo-Sibyllines, they exerted a powerful influence on the Western mind; in Cohn's words:

> Throughout the Middle Ages the Sibylline eschatology persisted alongside the eschatologies derived from the Book of Revelation, modifying them and being modified by them but generally surpassing them in popularity. For, uncanonical and unorthodox though they were, the Sibyllines had enormous influence—indeed save for the Bible and the works of the Fathers they were probably the most influential writings known to medieval Europe. They often dictated the pronouncements of dominant figures in the Church, monks and nuns such as St Bernard and St Hildegard whose counsel even popes and emperors regarded as divinely inspired.[5]

In short, the influence of the pseudo-Sibyllines could be considered roughly analogous to the influence of pseudo-Dionysius in the Eastern Church. But while the millennial expectations influence by the 'oracles' were inclined to deviate from the teachings of Scripture, the deviations were not as radical of departures from the revealed truth as would be manifested under the influence of the Joachimite doctrine, and the Sibylline prophecies of a "great, last World Emperor" would take on a whole new significance when viewed through the lens of Joachim's *dux e Babylone*. Furthermore, the eruption of millennial movements greatly expanded in the historical context which saw the emergence of the new teaching. As Cohn observes, lay preachers who announced the end was at hand had certainly been around for centuries; "Such people were known already

---

4   ibid.
5   Cohn, p. 33.

in sixth-century Gaul; and they continued to appear from time to time until, from about 1100 onwards, they suddenly became both more numerous and more important."[6]

> In Cohn's assessment, Millennialist expectations increased as the manifest corruption of the papacy became something which was known to a broad segment of the laity:
>> ... at least from the thirteenth century onwards, the Papacy itself was decidedly worldly. Popes tended to be primarily statesmen and administrators. ...
>> ... The founding of the new monastic orders of the eleventh and twelfth centuries, the innovations of St Francis and St Dominic in the thirteenth century, the conciliar movement of the fifteenth century, even the 'evangelical' movement which was spreading on the very eve of the Reformation, are only a few examples out of many of the capacity of the medieval Church for facing up to its many shortcomings.
>> Judged by the norms of medieval Latin Christianity, which were accepted in principle by all alike, the record of the Church was in reality far from being wholly black. But it looked wholly black to millenarians who, at once terrified and enthralled by the imminence of the Second Coming, applied those norms with absolute intransigence and a total refusal to make allowances.[7]

Of course, one finds a similar mindset which is very active in Millennialist circles today—which is to say, in the mindset of the average American 'Conservative Evangelical.' However, while the Millennialist sects of the Middle Ages tended to be anti-Semitic, their modern successors are obsessed with the secular state of Israel, and various confusions of doctrine which

---

6   ibid., p. 38.
7   ibid., p. 82–83.

imagine the nation of Israel (and its temple) will be restored—a delusion which serves the geopolitical aims of the Neoconservative movement.

Although many Millennialist sects arose, it was only following the the spread of the Joachimite prophecies—and especially after the outbreak of the Black Death beginning in 1348[8]—that such sectarians began to develop into widespread movements of increasing strength and violence. The effects of the Death on the course of Western society were undoubtedly severe, and when combined with various theologies which looked for either the imminent end of the world, or the radical transition to a New Age of Man, the impact was quite profound; a portion of the Franciscan Order—the so-called Spiritual Franciscans—saw themselves as the fulfillment of Joachim's prophecy:

> By the middle of the [13th] century they had disinterred Joachim's prophecies (which hitherto had attracted little attention) and were editing them and producing commentaries upon them. They were also forging prophecies which they successfully fathered upon Joachim and which became far better known and more influential than Joachim's own writings. In these works the Spirituals adapted the Joachite eschatology in such a way that they themselves could be seen as the new order which, replacing the Church of Rome, was to lead mankind into the glories of the Age of the Sprit.[9]

Other Joachimite prophecies centered on Emperor Frederick II (1194–1250), who was among the most powerful of the medieval rulers of the Holy Roman Empire. The fact that he not only engaged in conflict with the Papacy, but even went on Crusade and was able to recapture Jerusalem—making himself king

---

8   ibid., p. 87.
9   ibid., p. 110.

of that city[10]—served to build the myth which surrounded him, a myth which death only enhanced: "All this helped to fit him for the role of chastiser of the clergy in the Last Days; and the pseudo-Joachite *Commentary on Jeremiah*, which was written in the 1240's, did in fact foretell that Frederick would so persecute the Church that in the year 1260 it would be utterly overthrown."[11] Although an almost-forgotten figure today, Frederick assumed an almost 'Arthurian' status; for centuries following his death, Millennialists lived in expectation of his return, after the fashion of similar expectation surrounding King Arthur. The violent mischief worked by followers of the dead Frederick was so great over the centuries that, as one chronicler recorded in 1434, "a new heresy arose which some Christians still hold to in secret; they believe absolutely that the Emperor Frederick is still alive and will remain alive until the end of the world, and that there has been and shall be no proper Emperor but he. ... The Devil invented this folly, so as to mislead these heretics and certain simple folk...".[12] And, as Cohn records:

> How seriously the clergy took this heresy and how alert they were to detect it is shown by the curious story of a Greek philosopher who ventured in 1469 to divulge in Rome the conviction which he had derived from long study of the Greek Sibyllines—which was that the Last Emperor would shortly be converting all peoples to Christianity. In this as in other Byzantine prophecies the coming of the Last Emperor in no way implied a massacre of the clergy or social upheavals of any kind. But this was so inconceivable to the ecclesiastical authorities in Rome that they imprisoned the unfortunate man and confiscated his belongings.[13]

---

10   ibid., p. 111.
11   ibid.
12   quoted in ibid., p. 117.
13   ibid., p. 117–118.

Such a reaction to the poor Greek philosopher is not surprising given the mayhem worked by the Joachimites. Thus, for example, the Brethren of the Yellow Cross—a name which eerily anticipates the equally conspiratorial Brethren of the Rosy Cross (Rosicrucians)—set forth the goal of slaughtering the ungodly:

... the route to the Millennium leads through massacre and terror. God's aim is a world free from sin. ... The most urgent task of the Brethren of the Yellow Cross is therefore to eliminate sin, which in effect means to eliminate sinners. The Brotherhood is portrayed as a crusading host led by an elite—the author calls it 'a new chivalry'—which in turn is subordinate to the eschatological Emperor himself. ... To achieve that end assassination is wholly legitimate: 'Whoever strikes a wicked man for his evildoing, for instance for blasphemy—if he beats him to death he shall be called a servant of God; for everyone is bound to punish wickedness.' In particular the Revolutionary calls for the assassination of the reigning Emperor, Maximilian, for whom he had an overwhelming hatred. But beyond these preliminary murders lies the day when the new Emperor from the Black Forest, together with the Brotherhood, will 'control the whole world from West to East by force of arms'—an age of ubiquitous and incessant terror, in which the hopeful prophecy was to be amply justified: 'Soon we will drink blood for wine!'

... The fanatical layman never tires of portraying—and in the most lurid possible colours—the chastisement which the coming Emperor, that is he himself, will inflict on those children of Satan, the friars and monks and nuns. In particular, he rages against priests who break their vow of chastity and set up households. Such priests, he cries, should be strangled or burnt alive, or else driven with their concubines into the hands of the Turks; their children—true children of Antichrist—should be left to starve. But indeed the whole clergy must be annihilated: 'Go on hitting them,' cries the Messiah to his army, 'from the Pope right down to the little students! Kill every one of them!' He foresees that 2,300 clerics will be killed each day, and that this massacre will continue for four and a half years.[14]

When the violence unleashed by Millennialists proved inadequate to bring about the fulfillment of their Joachimite dreams, the Roman Church persecuted them, and the heretics developed a habit of conspiratorial secrecy—a tactic which would be pursued by other heretical movements (e.g., the followers of Giordano Bruno, the Giordanisti) in the centuries to come. The reasoning was simple: *those who would conspire to transform the world must become adept at hiding their intentions, tactics, and strategy from those who have not been initiated into their mysteries.*

Among the Gnostic religions which arose during the late Middle Ages, the Free Spirit heresy remains the least well-known, but while it enjoys less familiarity than, for example, the Cathar abomination, its heretical teachings were at least as widespread—and as dangerous. In the assessment of Norman Cohn, the Gnostic heresy of the Free Spirit was widespread, and yet remained well-hidden:

> … in the social—as distinct from the purely political—history of western Europe the heresy of the Free Spirit played a more important part than Catharism. The area over which it extended was, by medieval standards, a vast one. … And this movement had an extraordinary capacity for survival; for, constantly harassed by perse-

---

14   ibid., p. 120–121.

cution, it persisted as a recognizable tradition for some five centuries.[15]

The salvation which the Free Spirit sought was a gnosis of "quasi-mystical anarchism"—"an affirmation of freedom so reckless and unqualified that it amounted to a total denial of every kind of restraint and limitation."[16] As with the Cathars, there are indications that this cult developed in the East, and demonstrated some of the pernicious influence of Islamic Sufism.[17] Having perhaps entered the West in secrecy, the heretical movement continued to live in secret; although it is believed to have entered the West around the year 1200, all such estimates must remain approximate. What one finds is that a form of antinomian Gnosticism was able to survive for centuries in the West, and—despite an Inquisition dedicated to its eradication—continued to spread its teachings:

> By 1320 persecution had driven the movement of the Free Spirit underground; and thereafter the heretical Beghards seem to have done less begging and to have relied rather on a conspiratorial understanding which they were able to develop with certain of the Beguine communities. ... The Millennium of the Free Spirit had become an invisible empire, held together by the emotional bonds—which of course were often erotic bonds—between men and women.[18]

The flagellant movement which arose in the years following the outbreak of the Black Death was allegedly involved in such a conspiracy against the clergy,[19] and one of its fanati-

15 ibid., p. 148.
16 ibid.
17 ibid., p. 151.
18 ibid., p. 162.
19 ibid., p. 137.

cal leaders—Konrad Schmid of Thuringia—built on the combination of anti-Roman, Apocalyptic, and Joachimite thought to justify violent suppression of those deemed to be 'ungodly.' Although the Inquisition was not slow in responding to the flagellants, this did not stop more such groups from arising generation after generation in Thuringia, and beyond. As Cohn records:

> Early in the fifteenth century a chronicler of Thuringia noted how vigorously the 'secret heresy' concerning the sleeping Frederick was flourishing there—how firmly simple folk were persuaded that the Emperor really did appear from time to time among men and how confidently they were awaiting his return as the Emperor of the Last Days; and it was surely no coincidence that it was in the towns around Kyffhäuser that the clandestine flagellant movement persisted. For the rest, these secret flagellants were still very conscious of their link with the predecessors. They had preserved the rites of the movement of 1349 and were still defending their practices by appealing to the Heavenly Letter [of 'the Revolutionary,' cited above]. ...
>
> ... Eighty or ninety flagellants were burnt in 1414 and, it seems, 300 on a single day in 1416—certainly a startling expression of the fear which this movement inspired in 'the great.' Even that failed to put a stop to the movement. A generation later, in 1446, a dozen flagellants were discovered at Nordhausen, the town where Schmid himself had probably been burnt. In this case, too, even those who recanted were burnt—a course of action which could only have been adopted by the secular authorities without sanction from the Church; it is probably not irrelevant that the one victim whose trade is known was a weaver [a profession often linked with spreading heresy]. In 1454, again, a couple of dozen flagellants, men and women, were burnt at Sonderhausen; and it was

as late as the 1480s that the last (so far as is known) of the secret flagellants were tried and burnt—again at the instigation of the local prince.

If thereafter no more is heard of the sect, it is still of some interest that the district where it had flourished most was the district which was to witness the exploits of Thomas Müntzer. The village where, in 1488 or 1489, the *propheta* of the Peasants' War was born lies within a few miles of Nordhausen, and so does the scene of the massacre which overwhelmed his peasant army.[20]

In fact, such knowledge presents the Peasants' War (1524–1525) in an entirely new light. Even a casual perusal of the writings of Müntzer reveals a rabid character of anti-clerical, proto-communist sentiment which certainly was in keeping with the doctrines of the old flagellant ideologues. The notion that their heresy preserved itself secretly for many generations, and could easily have provided an influence (at least in terms of doctrinal content) which led to one of the more horrifically violent uprisings of the sixteenth century bespeaks the deadly character of the heresies haunting Europe in the aftermath of the eruption of Joachimite and pseudo-Joachimite prophecy.

The interaction of Millennial-Joachimite expectations with the various forces of the Reformation is a complicated topic, to say the least. In the sense of the Hermetic Reformation of Ficino, Pico, Reuchlin and Bruno, certainly there is a sense of such expectation inherent in their interest to establish a new Golden Age.[21] However, such Millennial expectations were not

20   ibid., p. 146–147.
21   In Barnes' words: "The goal of recovering lost truth or spiritual insight appealed to zealous preachers and classical scholars alike. The pursuit of occult wisdom among Renaissance Platonists drew much of its inspiration from the sort of prophetic hope nourished by Joachimism and related trends. But as usual, there were two sides to this coin: although many Florentine

absent from the true Reformation; in fact, Barnes contends that:

> Indeed, Luther's Reformation, in appropriating and imaginatively reconstructing the prophetic world-view, actually reinforced an inherited sense of expectancy, and helped to produce in sixteenth-century Germany a level of apocalyptic expectation that finds few parallels in Western history. Moreover, as the sixteenth century progressed, apocalyptic thinking in Lutheran areas tended to become more explicit, more reasoned, and more comprehensive.[22]

In Barnes' assessment, Luther himself was responsible for such a "sense of expectancy" because "More effectively than any previous interpreter, he gave a world-historical, indeed a world-transcending significance to contemporary events by placing them in an eschatological framework; everything pointed to the coming Day of Redemption."[23] But Luther was no Joachimite: there was no Third Age, and certainly no Golden Age in such an expectation; in short, he was most certainly not a Millennialist. Instead, Lutheran apocalypticism was an anticipation that in an age in which the Antichrist has been made known, the end is near at hand. In point of fact, in *Luther's View of Church History*, Headley maintains that Luther's apocalyptic understanding of history precludes a worldly victory for the Lutheran Reformation; in Headley's words: "Yet so grave is the condition of the Church and so real the presence of the Antichrist that Luther despairs of any general reformation".[24] In Headley's assessment, Luther's view of the present age thus remains fundamentally <u>Augustinian, not Joachimite, in its orientation; that is, there is</u> no

intellectuals drank in Savonarola's promise of a *renovatio mundi*, they were equally moved by his terrifying warnings of divine chastisement." (p. 28–29)

22   Barnes, p. 2–3.
23   ibid., p. 4.
24   John M. Headley, *Luther's View of Church History*, (New Haven and London: Yale University Press, 1963) p. 61.

new glorious age which is about to burst forth into the world— all that remains is the world's senescence, until the events of the end of the age reach their terminus in the Last Day. Again, to cite Headley:

> The true Church is hidden not because it is persecuted but because it has the Word, which reveals itself only in terms of opposites. By its very nature the Word creates a community that is unknown and rejected by the world; moreover, it introduces division and strife into any humanly devised order. The Church's sufferings and tribulations are consequences of the fact that it has only the Word and must appear to the world as dispossessed, heretical, and powerless. Therefore, the idea of the hidden Church is intimately related to the double aspect of the Church in which adherence to the Word struggles with possession of the name and the external trappings of authority. In all times, Luther tells us, we are either Jacobites or Esauites. ...

This enduring conflict between two peoples presents an essentially Augustinian pattern to Church history. In fact, Luther claimed to be following Augustine and a basic agreement was inevitable. Nevertheless, within the general framework of the two societies and their continuing struggle, significant differences appear. For Augustine the two opposing lineages originate and persist more as a result of a previous election than as a consequence of a contemporary act on God's part. Because of the nature of the Word and the hiddenness of the Church, Luther saw the ensuing dualism and struggle as inhering to the Church rather than being imposed from outside. Secondly, Augustine's two cities are distinguished preeminently by two different loves. They are not divided by the impact of the Word and according to faith. ... Despite the grandeur of Augustine's view, it lacks the coherence, focus, and intensity which Luther achieved through his doctrine of the Word and his definition of the Church as a people of faith.[25]

Luther's understanding of the relationship between religious and secular history—rooted as it was in the divine Word—thus preserved him from falling into the apocalyptic errors which consumed some of his contemporaries. Nevertheless, even within the circles of the Lutheran Reformation, there were currents of thought less salutary in nature; less than entirely confident in the ultimate sufficiency of the Word in such matters, they sought confirmation of their apocalyptic expectations elsewhere:

> Prophetic research blossomed in the later sixteenth century as professors, pastors, and laymen sought to achieve assurance in an increasingly confused world. Searching more intently for signs that could bolster their eschatological faith, Luther's followers increasingly turned the intellectual methods of Renaissance humanism toward the goal of apocalyptic understanding. Evidence from history was used more and more to complement and support biblical prophecies, as ever more serious efforts were made to discern the outlines of the divine plan. … Astrologers, like preachers and theologians, were generally convinced that universal changes would soon occur, and many Lutherans sought eagerly after their forecasts. Mathematics and other nontheological tools were used with growing boldness in serious efforts to seek out clear answers to the mysteries of the Last Days.[26]

Intriguingly, Barnes notes that Calvinism is *not* immune to Millennial thinking (a fact readily on display in these United

---

25   ibid., p. 67–68.
26   ibid., p. 7.

States) and that the sentiment was present from the time of the Reformation era:

> Calvin did agree with Luther in emphatic rejection of chiliasm or millenarianism. The idea that Christ would return to rule on Earth for a thousand years, or that a truly godly kingdom could be established in his name, was a gross vulgarization in the eyes of both reformers. But far more clearly than the German Reformer, Calvin held out the possibility that God's plan allowed real hope for the earthly future. Indeed, despite Calvin's Augustinian avoidance of historically oriented eschatology, the hint of progressivism in his thought left the way open for the frank meliorism and chiliasm of many later Calvinist thinkers.[27]

Leaving the door open to any form of Progressivism has proven deadly to most confessions; it must necessarily war against belief in the doctrine of original sin, and, in fact, opens the door to various forms of Utopianism.

As stated before, Luther was certainly not a Millennialist, but he was a Reformer who firmly believed certain apocalyptic expectations were being fulfilled. He had no use for the nonsense of astrology, but he was—for a time—influenced by the Sibylline Oracles (imagining Frederick the Wise was "the emperor of the Last Days"[28]) and perhaps saw himself fulfilling prophecy:

> Again, while denying that he possessed special prophetic powers, he was not entirely opposed to the notion that he was the long-awaited prophet through whom God would effect the final reformation of the church. Though unwilling to see himself—or anyone else—as the second

---

27   ibid., p. 33.
28   ibid., p. 47.

Elijah sent explicitly to announce the return of the Christ, he did believe that his role was a prophetic one, and he seems to have believed that a few predictions pertained to his own life. One was that of the Franciscan visionary Johann Hilten, who decades earlier had foreseen the rise of a great reformer.[29]

Luther's teaching that the Papacy is the Antichrist, and the belief that Hilten prophesied the coming of Luther are two aspects of the Reformer's apocalypticism which are specifically taught in the Book of Concord.

The identification of the Papacy as Antichrist is a point which is affirmed at several points in the confessional documents, but never more adamantly than in an article of Luther's Smalcald Articles, "Of the Papacy." Luther upheld the equality of all bishops, citing the words of St. Jerome, who "writes that the priests at Alexandria together and in common governed the churches, as did also the apostles, and afterwards all bishops throughout all Christendom, until the Pope raised his head above all." (§9) It was this action by the Pope which demonstrated the Antichristian character of his office:

> This article clearly shows that the Pope is the very Antichrist, who has exalted and opposed himself against Christ, because he does not wish Christians to be saved without his power, which nevertheless is nothing, and is neither established nor commanded by God. This is, properly speaking, to "exalt himself above all that is called God," as Paul says, 2 Thess. 2:4. This indeed neither the Turks nor the Tartars do, although they are great enemies of Christians, but they allow whoever wishes to believe in Christ, and they receive bodily tribute and obedience from Christians.

29   ibid.

The Pope, however, prohibits this faith, saying that if any one wish to be saved he must obey. This we are unwilling to do, even though on this account we must die in God's name. This all proceeds from the fact that the Pope has wished to be considered the supreme head of the Christian Church according to divine law. Accordingly he has made himself equal to and above Christ, and has caused himself to be proclaimed the head, and then the lord of the Church, and finally of the whole world, and simply God on earth, until he has attempted to issue commands even to the angels in heaven. ... Wherefore just as we cannot adore the devil himself as Lord and God, so we cannot endure his apostle, the Pope or Antichrist, in his rule as head or lord. For to lie and to kill, and to destroy body and soul eternally, is a prerogative of the Papal government, as I have very clearly shown in many books. (Part II, Article IV, §10–13, 14)

The Apology of the Augsburg Confession contains the prophecy of John (Johann) Hilten, and it seems to lend a certain measured credibility to the purported prophecy:

In the town of Eisenach in Thuringia, there was, to our knowledge, a monk, John Hilten, who thirty years ago was cast by his fraternity into prison, because he had protested against certain most notorious abuses. For we have seen his writings, from which it can be well understood what the nature of his doctrine was. And those who knew him testify that he was a mild old man, and serious indeed, but without moroseness. He predicted many things, some of which have thus far transpired, and others still seem to impend, which we do not wish to recite, lest it may be inferred that they are narrated either from hatred toward one or from partiality to another. ... "But another one," he said, "will come in A. D. 1516, who will destroy you, neither will you be able to resist him." This very opinion concerning the downward career of the power of the monks, and this number of years, his friends afterwards found also written by him in his Commentaries, which he had left, concerning certain passages of Daniel. But although the issue will teach how much weight should be given to this declaration, yet there are other signs which threaten a change in the power of the monks, that are no less certain than oracles. (§1–4)

The text of the Apology seems willing to admit the possibility of the genuinely prophetic character of Hilten's declaration, without placing absolute trust in such an assertion; however, the dogmatic assertion that the Papacy fulfills the marks of Antichrist is a declaration of an entirely different character. In short, the apocalypticism of the Lutheran Reformation is most certainly present—at least in part—in the Book of Concord. The Lutheran Reformation avoided the Millennialism of many movements of its age, and largely avoided the pernicious influence of Joachimism. But, as we will examine, this is not to say that all who lived under the auspices of the Lutheran Church were free from such influences.

CHAPTER 6. PARACELSUS, WEIGEL, ROSICRUCIANISM, AND THE LUTHERAN RESPONSE.

fter the death of Martin Luther in 1546, the sheer quantity of apocalyptic writings generated in Lutheran circles only increased—both in terms of collections of what were seen as Luther's prophetic utterances, and in works intended to build on the accuracy of prophetic prognostication.[1] The propensity to issue such writings did not, interestingly enough, follow the usual late-Reformation divisions between Gnesio-Lutherans and Philippists; rather, "Gnesio-Lutherans, Philippists, and other factions did not differ in their central eschatological teachings. … The typical Lutheran pastor probably went about his work with little direct involvement in these quarrels, but was likely to take refuge from confusion in the comforting belief that the end was very near."[2] According to Barnes, however, it would appear that the one Lutheran theologian who endeavored to interpret the Reformation in Joachimite terms was Matthias Flacius Illyricus, who was willing to see Luther's Reformation in conjunction with the abbot's prophecies.[3]

---

1   "In the 1550s, collections of Luther's prophecies began to appear regularly. Some of these were brief pamphlets such as the *Several Prophetic Statements of Doctor Martin Luther, the Third Elias*, issued by a preacher in Nordhausen in 1552. But Luther had much to say to worried times, and his dark warnings and forecasts could fill tomes. In 1557 Peter Glaser of Dresden published 120 of the Reformer's collected prophecies; by 1576 the number had grown to 200 in a work of well over 300 pages. The first edition, explained Glaser in his preface to the 1574 edition, had long ago sold out and now almost nowhere to be purchased." (Robin Bruce Barnes, *Prophecy and Gnosis—Apocalypticism in the Wake of the Lutheran Reformation,* [Stanford, California: Stanford University Press, 1988] p. 61.)

2   ibid., p. 65–66.

3   ibid., p. 77. Barnes maintains Flacius "used only what suited his

The Lutherans earnestly expected the end of the Age was imminent, and even theologians such as Andreas Musculus (1514–1581)—one of the authors of the Formula of Concord—relied upon astrology and medieval prophecies to bolster the understanding that the end was near:

> In 1577 Andreas Musculus pointed to the recent discovery and publication of several old vaticinations supporting the common assertion that the world could not last much longer. These forecasts had been written three or four hundred years earlier, according to Musculus, but they applied directly to the present age. They complemented the prediction of the astrologers—"our astrologers" he called them—who foresaw nothing but misery and affliction until 1580 or even 1588 unless the world came to an end before then.[4]

What saved the Lutheran theologians from fanaticism was, in no small part, the Scriptural doctrine of original sin, which prevented them from looking for any improvement in human nature, and the fixed character of the biblical revelation:

> Lutherans conceived of the Reformation not as an unveiling of new truths but as a return to old ones. The essence of divine revelation, once preached openly, had been obscured for centuries; Luther had simply rediscovered it. …
>
> Ultimately, even the wildest prophetic schemes that emerged among Luther's heirs—and some were wild indeed—looked not to any gradual working out of God's plan, but to some sudden cosmic transformation.[5]

---

purposes," raising doubts as to whether Flacius actually believed Joachim's speculations, or whether it simply suited his apologetic purposes.

4   ibid., p. 79.
5   ibid., p. 95–96.

The last point is of great significance, because it marks a delineating line between the Lutheran Reformation and those who sought to subvert that reformation: Paracelsus, Valentin Weigel, and the Rosicrucian movement. As such men—and many others who had absorbed some of the teachings of the Hermetic Reformation—continued their Progressive speculations and search for a Gnostic ascension of the soul and Hermetic transformation of nature itself, several of the Lutheran theologians began to fight back against the "prophetic quest":

> The Lutheran opposition to the prophetic quest we have examined had become organized into a well-defined doctrinal front by the time Nicolaus Hunnius issued his *Comprehensive Account of the New Prophets* in 1634. Hunnius's work was essentially an attack on chiliasm as a thoroughly satanic notion, invented, he said, by Jews and heretics, that had seduced many souls away from the true church. For Hunnius, chiliasm epitomized virtually the whole range of theological error. The chiliast had forgotten the essential Christian virtue, humility, and from this one failing derived every intellectual perversion of the Weigelians, the Boehmists, and all other fanatics. By this lumping together almost all forms of unorthodoxy and discussing them as a single enemy, Hunnius was helping to establish a position that would characterize orthodoxy for many decades to come. He was joined in this view by Johann Gerhard, who also worked to formulate a general concept of illegitimate future expectations.[6]

But Hunnius' contribution to the struggle against the Gnosticizing tendencies of the fanatics began well before the publication of his 1634 work. In fact, Hunnius was fully com-

---

6   ibid., p. 247.

mitted to the struggle while he was still a member of the faculty of the University of Wittenberg in 1619. We will now turn our attention to a work which he published in that year, *Principia Theologiæ Fanaticæ*, as an interpretive key to understanding the danger posed by the fanatics, and the Lutheran response to that threat.

Nicolaus Hunnius (1585–1643) was the third son of Aegidius Hunnius (1550-1603), another notable Lutheran theologian, who was the superintendent of Saxony and a professor at the University of Wittenberg. An instructor in philosophy and theology by the age of 24, Nicolaus Hunnius went on to receive his doctorate in 1612 and was called by the elector of Saxony to serve as superintendent of Eilenburg. Hunnius returned to academia in 1617 when the elector of Saxony called him to the University of Wittenberg to fill the vacancy left by the death of Leonard Hütter (1563–1616). However, Hunnius did not remain in academia for long; in 1623, he accepted the call to serve as superintendent of Lübeck. Hunnius has the distinction of being the only major theologian of the Age of Lutheran Orthodoxy to leave the university not only once, but twice, to serve an altar and pulpit in the ministry of Word and Sacrament.

The work under consideration at present—Hunnius' *Principia Theologiæ Fanaticæ (1619)*—belongs to the second period of its author's service at the University of Wittenberg, and its brevity belies its significance. Although little more than a tract,[7] Hunnius' work constitutes the first formal response by one of the Lutheran fathers to the growing threat of late-Reformation/post-Reformation Spiritualism. Specifically, the "theological fanatics" which are the focus of Hunnius' examination are the followers of Theophrastus Bombastus von Hohenheim

---

7   The work is only 60 pages long, which would not be an unusual length for an introductory chapter in the books of that period.

(1493–1541)—remembered today by his chosen sobriquet, "Paracelsus"—and Valentin Weigel (1533–1588). Paracelsus is remembered not only for his contributions to the field of medicine, but above all for his mystical theology—and it was, of course, this latter Paracelsian influence which was of interest to Nicolaus Hunnius.

The name of Valentin Weigel is undoubtedly less familiar today than that of Paracelsus, but his influence was profoundly significant in the realm of mystical theology[8]—an influence made all the more galling to a theologian of Hunnius' caliber, in that Weigel was a Lutheran pastor who had publicly subscribed to the Book of Concord (1580), at the same time that he generated a vast, private literature which directly attacked the theology confessed in the *Concordia*. Regarding the hypocrisy of his position, Weigel sets forth what is presumed to be an autobiographical passage in a 1584 work entitled, *Dialogus de Christianismo:*

> I did not subscribe to their teaching or human books, but rather since their intention was aimed at the apostolic Scripture and the same is to be preferred to all human books, as it should be, I could suffer it. But had they placed one single other book above the Scriptures of the prophets and apostles, I would not have agreed to it. Besides, it all [happened in] a rush or an overhastening, so that one wasn't permitted to think it over for several days or weeks. Instead, in a single hour they read off the entire convolute and demanded a signature right away. Third,

---

8   "Weigel's existence has suffered eclipse in the tradition in which his work is a pivotal landmark. In the history of German mysticism, he stands halfway between Paracelsus (1493–1541) and Sebastian Franck (1499–1542) who were his dissenting forerunners and Jacob Boehme (1575–1624) who was the most important dissenter to follow after and resemble him." (Andrew Weeks, *Valentin Weigel—German Religious Dissenter, Speculative Theorist, and Advocate of Tolerance,* [Albany: State University of New York Press, 2000] p. 5)

I poor Auditor didn't see fit to prepare and serve a feast for the devil, [knowing] that the whole lot would have cried out: "There, there, we knew it all along: he is not in conformity with our doctrine!"[9]

Weigel's example is proof that the phenomenon of pastors taking a *quatenus*[10] subscription to the Book of Concord is nothing new. Whatever the reservations Weigel maintained within his conscience, he served as the pastor of the Lutheran congregation in Zschopau, Saxony from 1567 until his death in 1588.[11]

The Principia *in the Context of the Thirty Years War*

While considering Hunnius' *Principia*, it is important to remember the broader context of both the work and its author. In a very real sense, one may briefly summarize the historical context of the *Principia Theologiæ Fanaticæ* of Nicolaus Hunnius as the end of Christendom, in the sense that it appeared in print just as the death knell was sounding for an era which began with Constantine's Edict of Milan (A.D. 313). Such an evaluation would, in fact, be accepted even within the sphere of secular historical study, for the *Principia* was published at the beginning of that momentous—though even now, poorly understood—period succinctly called the Thirty Years War (1618–1648). If 'Christendom' was still an operative concept at the beginning of that war, the same could not be said by its end.

Since the Peace of Augsburg in 1555, a truce had existed

---

9   Weeks, *Valentin Weigel—German Religious Dissenter,* p. 15.

10   A *quatenus* subscription—because it claims to only subscribe to the confessions *in so far* as they are in agreement with the Scriptures, is a meaningless subscription. One could have a *quatenus* subscription to the Koran or the New York phone book, for that matter. A *quia* subscription—confessing that one subscribes the confessions because they *are* the doctrine of Scripture—is an faithful subscription.

11   ibid., p. 11.

which permitted the appearance of Christendom to remain, albeit as a hollow shell. As Wilson observed in his recent history of the Thirty Years War:

> ... [T]he peace-makers of 1555 deliberately blurred the religious distinctions to maintain an element of the old universal ideal of a single Christendom. Lutherans were referred to as 'adherents of the Confession of Augsburg', without defining what that meant, while use of words like 'peace', 'religious belief' and 'reformation' were a deliberate attempt to incorporate values that all still shared, yet understood differently. For Lutherans, 'reformation' meant the right of legally constituted authorities to change religious practice in line with their founder's teachings. To Catholics, it confirmed their church's role in spiritual guidance.
>
> These ambiguities were carried over into the confessional element of the settlement. While France, Spain and the Dutch were still fighting to achieve victory for a single confession in their domains, the Empire agreed to recognize both Catholicism and Lutheranism at its territorial level. Contrary to the later impression, this did not leave the princes entirely free to choose between the two faiths. The formula 'he who rules, decides the religion' (*cuius regio, eius religio*) was not included in the text and emerged in debates about the treaty only after 1586. Rather than allowing perpetual change, the intention was to fix matters as they were mid-century.[12]

The Peace of Augsburg allowed the memory of Christendom to continue for a few generations, and it was not in vain. The Church of the Augsburg Confession had time to resolve its own controversies and make its own common confession in 1580

---

12   Peter H. Wilson, *The Thirty Years War—Europe's Tragedy,* (Cambridge, Massachusetts: Harvard University Press, 2009) p. 41–42.

against those errors which had erupted in the Church since the death of Martin Luther. The Roman Church also reached its own common confession, as that was imposed in the final sessions of the Council of Trent, which came to its conclusion in 1563. However, the presence of the two irreconcilable confessions within one empire required that either the unity of the empire or the integrity of the respective confessions would be sacrificed.

Again, as Wilson observes, the treaties at the end of the war did not programmatically terminate Christendom, but it did recognize the divisions as permanent, and began opening the door to further secularization of European society:

> Rulers retained the 'right of Reformation' granted in 1555, but only as supervision of their territorial churches. They were no longer able to impose their own theological beliefs on their subjects. Any subsequent conversion was to remain a private matter. Rulers gained personal freedom of conscience but lost a key aspect of their political authority. …
>
> Only the Habsburgs retained the full right of Reformation in its previous form, because the IPO [*Instrumentum Pacis Osnabrugense*] merely obliged them to respect the Protestant faith of the Lower Austrian nobility, the city of Breslau, and the Silesian princes and their tenants. Elsewhere, they remained free to suppress Protestant minorities, even if these had existed in 1624. … Whereas half of Europe had been under Protestant rule in 1590, that proportion fell to a fifth a century later under the most significant Catholic gains made in the Habsburg monarchy.[13]

The aftermath of the Thirty Years War was thus a time of growing confessional chaos. The Peace of Westphalia declared

---

13   Wilson, p. 759.

in 1648 not only legalized Calvinism[14]—it released the restraints which had previously suppressed an occult undercurrent which had haunted the Reformation and post-Reformation eras. The understanding of the relationship between Church and State which emerged from the ashes of thirty years of butchery unveiled a state with an attenuated interest in upholding the confession of the faith, even as the secular authorities saw their own authority in more 'divine' terms as the power of the Church waned. Louis XIV (1638–1715)—the "Sun King"—typified the absolutist pretensions of secular authority deified in the pages of Thomas Hobbes' book, *The Leviathan (1651)*. In this new world, the forces of orthodoxy found themselves suddenly bereft of the powers of the State to suppress Spiritualism and Occultism—and it was not long before the opponents of the faith were running rampant.

Hunnius' work gains added significance when one considers that, at the very moment when the armed might at the disposal of the Roman Church was threatening to sweep northward, he warned of a threat which was ultimately more dangerous than that posed by an invading army.

An Overview of the Structure of Hunnius' Principia

The structure of Hunnius' *Principia* is surprisingly complex, given the relative brevity of the work. Following a brief introduction, the remainder of the work is divided into five chapters which are, in turn, divided into various sub-points. In fact, it is relatively easy to become lost in the maze of subdivisions of the argument, if one is not familiar with the methodology of theological argumentation common to that era and a basic parallelism within the structure of the *Principia*.

While Hunnius' argumentation shows the careful attention to structure which is often rewarded with the charge of

---

14   ibid., p. 758.

"scholasticism," his introduction of the work in question makes it clear that he understood his topic to be far removed from dry academic pursuit:

> So then, it was not enough Satanic madness to oppress the Church through the frenzy of the Antichrist, the deceits of Calvinism and the tricks of Photinianism and in this way to sift the saints [Amos 9:9]; they also had to stir up some new breed, varied in its origin, hermaphroditic by profession, *alchemico-theological*, of pretended holiness, spiritual, united in essence with Christ, furnished with the direct inspiration of God and thus God-taught. For this reason, it was powerful in a profound knowledge of all things, with the ability of investigating the human heart, of foretelling the future, of interpreting Scripture, or performing miracles, and with the faculty of explaining whatever great thing has existed in the world. Finally, it overflowed with the riches of the entire world. Of these and other matters it boasts at great length in its published writings.

Hunnius believed the entirety of the fanatical theology to be permeated with "trifles" and "diabolic snares" (§II)—"a poisoned potion" mixed with "something quite pleasing" (§III). Hunnius' concern is that of a minister of the Word; the novelty of the Paracelsian/Weigelian doctrine is not something to be indulged, but "Satanic madness" to be openly opposed with all the means at his disposal. Contrary to the style of feigned ambivalence which has become quite common in academic writing today, Hunnius wrote as a steward of the mysteries of God, one who is "holding fast the faithful word as he has been taught, that he may be able, by sound doctrine, both to exhort and convict those who contradict." (Titus 1:9 NKJV)

In the first chapter ("On the origin and name of this

sect."), Hunnius demonstrates a thorough knowledge of the origins of this doctrine. He in knowledgable of the succession of teachers which has lead to the heresies of Paracelsus and Weigel:

> Comparatively speaking, he [Paracelsus] was the *primary* author, for we read of many authors who spread that poison, such as Albertus Magnus, H. Cornelius Agrippa, Aegidius of Rome, Gerhard of Sutphania, Johan Hagen de indagine, Johan Reuchlin, the Minorite Pietro Palatino, the Minorite Francisco Giorgio, Marsilio Ficino, William Postellus, Henry Horphius, Marco Antonio Mocenico, Stephan Conventanus. Some anonymous author relates to these the origin of cabalistic theology in the preface of his book *De Magia*. These men, I say, spread here and there the first seeds of their tares in the papist monasteries and schools, which were full of Satanic sorcery and diabolic arts, and they exerted themselves to infect their descendants with the rest of their writings. Paracelsus, however, used their works and by the productivity of his temperament, he sought out from them all their ideas with his eagerness for something new and stuffed his books with that material. In this way, those poisons which we could have hoped would die along with the writings of the ancients were vindicated by his death and came into the hands especially of those who used those works in their eagerness to learn medicine. (§III)

Hunnius understands the connection of Paracelsian doctrine to a succession of teachers reaching back into the thirteenth century, and his understanding of the influence of figures such as Johann Reuchlin (the greatest proponent of Kabbalistic studies in all of Germany), Marsilio Ficino (the father of the modern Hermeticism) and Cornelius Agrippa (made famous by his study of magic) is quite telling. So, too, he understood the connection between the Paracelsian doctrine and that of Reformation-era Enthusiasts: "At the same time, however, *Caspar Schwenkfeld, Carlstadt* and their associates, the *Anabaptists*, as well as other 'heavenly prophets,' each of whom drew something from the theology which was flowing into Paracelsus from one place or another, were producing their not dissimilar monster." (§V) Weigel, in turn, Hunnius recognized was not only shaped by these influences through Paracelsus, but was himself shaped by Ficino's most famous theologian of antiquity (*"Mercury Trismegistus"*) and also by the mystics of the Medieval and Reformation eras: "Tauler… Dionysius … and Thomas Müntzer" (§VII). And Hunnius connects the doctrine of Weigel to that of contemporary fanatics (Ezechiel Meth, and the Brotherhood of the Rosy Cross/Rosicrucians)—a theme which we will return to in our conclusion to this chapter. By identifying the close theological kin of the Paracelsians and Weigelians, Hunnius established the place of such theology in the context of condemnations which are already to be found in the Book of Concord. For example, the twelfth article of the Formula of Concord condemns numerous articles of the Anabaptists which cannot be tolerated in the Church, the State and the Home, and it condemns eight erroneous articles of the Schwenkfeldians. Luther's famous condemnation of Müntzer[15] in the Smalcald Articles sets the stage for condemning the Paracelsians and Weigelians for sharing Müntzer's contempt for the Scriptures. Much of the rest of the *Principia* is devoted to fleshing out the content of the fanatical traditions which Paracelsus and Weigel have received—and amplified.

---

15   "And in those things which concern the spoken, outward Word, we must firmly hold that God grants His Spirit or grace to no one, except through or with the preceding outward Word. Thereby we are protected against enthusiasts, i.e. spirits who boast that they have the Spirit without and before the Word, and accordingly judge Scripture or the spoken Word, and explain and stretch it at their pleasure, as Münzer did, and many still do at the present day; they wish to be acute judges between the Spirit and the letter, and yet know not what they say or propose." (SA III, VIII:3)

The second chapter ("On the primary efficient cause of the theological institution, which the school of Paracelsus has rejected.") is, as its title indicates, dedicated to the fanatics' rejection of the Scripture as the only source of theology, and the effort of the fanatics to interpret Scripture according to their own private judgment. Hunnius thus set forth Holy Scripture as the norm of all theology: "That theology in which the principles as well as dogmas of faith and godliness are not sound and are not in harmony with the canon of Holy Scripture is not a divine theology." (§II) The express intention which permeates Hunnius' *Principia* is that which is set forth in Section II.I:

> The very satisfactory and, in fact, infallible criterion for recognizing the false prophets has been revealed to us in Mat. 7:15: *You will know them by their fruits.* As we pay attention to this, we seek those fruits not in some external appearance of saintliness, but we believe that those fruits exist chiefly in their doctrines of faith and godliness and in the principles thereof. Accordingly we in such wise accuse them of Paracelsic idle chatter.

Hunnius maintained that the Paracelsians neglected the primary efficient cause by having disdain for the Word of God revealed in Holy Scripture; for Hunnius, "whoever in the business of faith does not bind himself entirely to Scripture does not hear as God teaches him, and overthrows the first foundation of sincere theology." (§XI) As for the Paracelsians, their theology "does not encourage the reading of the Bible but even disapproves of hearing it along with reading it." (§XIV) In place of the revealed word, the fanatics encourage their followers to learn the truth by examining their own hearts, based on the notion that all truth can be found within:

> The second effect is to *bestir that which lies in the heart* and to recall to memory that effect which Weigel appears

to assign to Scripture. Indeed, from the fact that he does not even say this seriously and that on the basis of the hypothesis of the same school that Scripture does not even stir the mind in any way, it is obvious therefrom that the Paracelsists are awaiting a divine revelation, a momentary illumination, an internal discourse, a divine inspiration, an angelic conference—which remedies will remind them of those things which naturally lie hidden within hearts, according to that statement: *A person hears with the internal eye of his soul but considers the truth without any external persuasion* (*philos. mystic.*, p. 206).

Scripture, the fanatics maintain, "*has a double meaning and is ambigious*" (in Weigel's words) and he "ponders the serious mistake that the preachers and academics command their hearers to be content with the Word as that is preached from pulpits and commentaries on the Bible so that nothing is necessary to fly up into the heavens after the manner of the 'heavenly prophets' nor to await the illuminations of the Anabaptists." (§XXV) As for any meaning to be drawn from Scripture, the fanatics declare that "*the literal meaning is foreign to a Christian* as it comes forth from the old man, from the natural spirit of the world, from the Old Testament, from the Antichrist" (§XXXVI)—instead, it is necessary to bring meaning *to* Scripture (§XXXVIII).

Hunnius observed that the fanatics not only attack Scripture, but also those men who have been divinely called to proclaim God's Word. Hunnius maintains that to hear the "faithful pastors" is to "hear Christ teaching"; as for the Paracelsians, "They disrespect the successors of the apostles either as preachers or as writers and forbid people to listen to them, as they even now teach." By neglecting—even attacking—both the divinely inspired Word and the ministry of that Word, the fanatic theology "does not permit the active principle of theological understanding to exist. As a consequence it rejects the true and primary cause of teaching." (§LIV)

As the second chapter addressed the Paracelsian/Weigelian rejection of the authority of Holy Scripture, and the office which Christ ordained for the proclamation of His Word, the third chapter turns to their rejection of the churches and schools in which that Word is proclaimed—the "organic and ordinary cause of theological instruction," as Hunnius termed it. Weigel declared ministers to be "mercenaries" (§VII) who lack that which he deemed necessary: an *immediate* call, and *immediate* divine instruction (§VIII), and such teachers must be sinless—a requirement which prompted Hunnius to retort, "If this is true, there will not be a single one of the mortal race who teaches theology fruitfully." (§XI) Not surprisingly, then, the fanatics "revile the churches because people bind themselves to them and torment themselves with the visiting of churches and listening to sermons" (§XIII), and they "curse vehemently the *academies* and their lecture halls as they claim that these are the enemies of Christ." (§XIV) The rejection of the preaching office is threefold, disparaging sermons (§XVI), "the reading of books" (§XVII), and "the exercises of debate" (§XVIII). All of this, Hunnius observed, was not because of "some abuse but also *per se.*" After all, Hunnius did not deny that there are abuses— immoral ministers, poor teachers, etc.—but the scandal of the fanatical theology is that it rejects the entirety of the office of the ministry and its work.

Having rejected both the substance of Christian theology (the doctrine revealed in Holy Scripture) and the means by which the theology is taught to the Church (the office of the ministry), upon what does Paracelsian theology rest? The fourth chapter is paired with the second chapter: if the fanatics have taken away the Word of God as the source of doctrine, what have they put in its place? Hunnius summarized their foundation at the beginning of chapter four:

> We find these foundations to be of two classes: some are *primary* and some *secondary*. We say that the former ones are, first, *the internal word which is innate in a person*; second, *divine revelation*; third, *the conversations of the angels*; fourth, *heavenly philosophy* which they pawn off as divine truth on the basis of, first, *the Cabala*; second, *astrology*; third, *alchemy*; and fourth, *mystic numbers*. (§II)

It is in chapter four that one begins to see more clearly the degree to which Hermeticism and Kabbalistic studies have thoroughly permeated the entire theology of the fanatics. Hunnius devoted the chapter to refuting each of these foundations, demonstrating that each was utterly inadequate as a basis for sound teaching. Again and again, the emphasis in the *Principia* is on the inadequacy of such foundations to sustain faith and hope in the heart of believers; thus, for example, Hunnius noted regarding the inadequacy of natural revelation: "How shamefully, however, this begs the question and how dangerously they build faith on the sand (Mat. 7:26) and upon no rooted foundation we leave to each godly person for his upright investigation." (§VI) The notion that immediate inspiration can be relied upon as a source of doctrine was rejected by Hunnius, and he dismissed their purported conversation with angels with the argument that the testimony of Holy Scripture utterly opposes such a reliance. And Hunnius did not mask his open contempt for their reliance upon alchemy and the Kabbalah: "We justly wonder at that wisdom from beyond the sea because it scarcely appears that this comes forth from human talent, unless one's brain is attracted by the satanic arts." (§XXXIV)

The fifth chapter ("On a student's requirements which

the school of Paracelsus prescribes for those who are learning") parallels the third chapter: If the fanatics have taken away the pastoral office and the regular call, what have they put in its place? Hunnius identified a three-fold abnegation on the part of the student which a Paracelsian teacher demands of him: (1) all worldly knowledge must be rejected, (2) the student can never argue with his teacher, and (3) the doctrine of *Gelassenheit* ("that abandonment of oneself" [§XXIII], is required. In essence, the student is to utterly surrender himself to his teacher, offering no resistance at all to the new doctrine, and forsaking all biblical knowledge which he had acquired previously (§II), and even abandon his sense of self, so that he may be reshaped. Hunnius thus concluded his *Principia* with the declaration:

> We are agreed, however, on the basis of these very brief samplings, that *even the passive principle of theology*, that is, *the learner*, is transformed and corrupted in so ugly a fashion by the Paracelcists that he comes out as totally unsuitable for grasping theological instruction. From this there emerges the general conclusion:

Therefore, the theology of Paracelsus is not divine.
This is what we had to prove.

The overt substitution of hidden doctrines, supposedly drawn from oneself, but which is imparted—without question—by the teacher who claims immediate inspiration is far removed from that Christian doctrine drawn from the divine Word and taught by those whom Christ has sent, mediately, to teach His Church.

However, by the time of the publication of Hunnius' *Principia* in 1619, the doctrine of the fanatics was already bringing havoc to the Church and State. As Frances Yates observed in her book, *The Rosicrucian Enlightenment*,[16] such a doctrine drove the decision of Frederick V, the elector Palatine, to initiate the chaos of the Thirty Years War by means of his willingness to accept the crown in Bohemia after the Defenestration of Prague. Already under the rule of Emperor Rudolph II, the city had become haven for the fanatics:

> [Rudolph II] moved the imperial court from Vienna to Prague, which became a centre for alchemical, astrological, magico-scientific studies of all kinds. Hiding himself in his great palace at Prague, with its libraries, its 'wonder rooms' of magico-mechanical marvels, Rudolph withdrew in alarm from the problems raised by the fanatical intolerance of his frightening nephew. Prague became a Mecca for those interested in esoteric and scientific studies from all over Europe. … Jews might pursue their cabalistic studies undisturbed (Rudolph's favourite religious adviser was Pistorius, a Cabalist) and the native church of Bohemia was tolerated by an official 'Letter of Majesty.'[17]

When the new emperor, Ferdinand, brought all of this to an end with his rise to power, the Bohemian Brethren and those allied with them brought about a temporary change. The bordering Duchy of Württemberg was similarly inclined to support mysticism, for "The alchemical and esoteric interests encouraged by Rudolph II had represented a more liberal, Renaissance atmosphere than that which the Reaction wished to impose, and such studies were popular at German courts, particularly those of Hesse and Württemberg."[18] Indeed, the "Rosicrucian manifestos"—bearing the stamp of a theology influenced by the same teachers who shaped the doctrine of Paracelsus and Weigel and

---

16   (London and New York: Routledge, 1972).
17   ibid., p. 16–17.
18   ibid., p. 27.

possibly Bruno—were written by an influential pastor of Württemberg, Johann Valentin Andreae.[19] The Joachimite expectations of the forces behind the short-lived reign of Frederick
V—perhaps alluded to by Hunnius (4:XVII) and certainly very
much in the minds of the men behind the Rosicrucian movement[20]—led to an overconfidence that victory was fated to the
rebellion. Thus, in Yates' assessment:

> A culture was forming in the Palatinate which
> came straight out of the Renaissance but with more re-
> cent trends added, a culture which may be defined by the
> adjective 'Rosicrucian'. The prince around whom these
> deep currents were swirling was Frederick, Elector Pala-
> tine, and their exponents were hoping for a politico-reli-
> gious expression of their aims in the movement towards
> the Bohemian adventure. As I begin to see it, all the mys-
> terious movements of former years around such figures
> as Philip Sidney, John Dee, Giordano Bruno, were gath-
> ered to a head in the Anhalt propaganda for Frederick.
> The Frederickian movement was not the cause of these
> deep currents, and it was far from being the only expres-
> sion of them. *But it was an attempt to give those currents
> politico-religious expression, to realize the ideal of a
> Hermetic reform centred on a real prince. The movement
> tried to unite many hidden rivers in one stream, the Dee
> philosophy and the mystical chivalry from England were
> to join with German mystical currents.* The new alchemy
> was to unite religious differences, and found a symbol in
> the 'chemical wedding' with its overtones of allusion to
> the 'marriage of the Thames and the Rhine'. We know
> that this movement was to fail disastrously, was to rush

19   Marshall rightly describes the manifestos as "strongly Hermetic
and alchemical" (Peter Marshall, *The Magic Circle of Rudolf II*, [New York:
Walker & Co., 2006] p. 234.)
20   Yates, p. 35.

over a precipice into the abyss of the Thirty Years War.[21]

Thirty years of crushing warfare would be the lasting monument to the scale of their error.

As the war progressed and Hunnius served as superintendent of Lübeck, he continued to combat the pernicious influence of the Paracelsian and Weigelian fanaticism. In Erdmann Rudolph Fischer's *The Life of John Gerhard*, a 1625 letter from Gerhard to Hunnius is preserved which offers a window into Hunnius' continued research. The letter deals with Johann Arndt (1555–1621), whose magnum opus, *True Christianity*, would prove to be the pivotal work inspiring the later Pietist movement, and in it, Gerhard addresses the influence of the fanatic theology on Arndt:

> I have known the aforementioned Arndt for many years because he was the bishop for several years in my home town. He has always professed to have a great and heartfelt interest in our [Augsburg] Confession and in the symbolical books of our churches and he has borne public witness that we should understand his books according to their norm. I therefore cannot yet be persuaded to believe that some fanatic spirit has driven him to have confessed something with his lips but to have something else closed up in his heart, because he has always seemed to me to be a stranger to hypocrisy.
>
> Meanwhile, I do not deny that in his books *de vero Christianismo* there occur ambiguous phrases and, in fact, some of the type which one can draw easily into the meaning of Weigel. For this reason, when the very reverend and renowned prince and lord, Duke Christian of Brunswick and Luneberg, and the bishop of Minden sent our faculty the Latin version of the four books *de*

---

21   ibid., p. 90. Emphasis added.

vero Christianismo and sought either their censure or approval, I responded along with my esteemed colleagues in this vein: that we were prepared to explain the things which appeared in Books 1, 2 and 4, although with the substitution of more appropriate phrasing and heading off any corruption, to the extent that we could do that; but that he had arranged Book 3 in such a way that one could scarcely correct it without the loss of a greater part thereof. For this reason, we refused our approval of the book.

... I think there are two reasons for his inappropriate and dangerous phrasing: the first, that he was especially given to the study of medicine in the academies and had not yet shaped his judgment about theological controversies by listening to lectures and holding discussions; but the second, that the reading of the books of Paracelsus and Weigel pleased him, for an eyewitness testifies that Arndt brought from them many things into his books *de vero Christianismo.*[22]

Modern analysis of Arndt has demonstrated that he incorporated even more of the 'fanatic theology' than Gerhard had realized into the writing of *True Christianity.*[23] And the influence of the 'fanatic theology' remained clearly present in the theology of Arndt's theological descendants, the Pietists.[24] Thus, for example, the basis of the thought of Friedrich Christoph Oetinger (1702–1782) is described as follows:

22   E. R. Fischer, *The Life of John Gerhard,* trans. by Richard J. Dinda and Elmer Hohle, (Malone, Texas: Repristination Press, 2001) p. 425-426.

23   see Johannes Wallmann, "Johann Arndt" in *The Pietist Theologians—An Introduction to Theology in the Seventeenth and Eighteenth Centuries,* ed. by Carter Lindberg (Malden, Massachusetts: Blackwell Publishing, 2005) p. 30–31.

24   Peter C. Erb, *Pietists, Protestants, and Mysticism,* (Metuchen, New Jersey: The Scarecrow Press, 1989) p. 14.

The basis of his theological development rested on Lutheran Orthodoxy and piety; an intensified biblicism and chiliasm mediated by Bengel; a greater nearness to the Old Testament, Judaism, and the Cabbala; a profound sympathy to hermeticism, neoplatonic images, and German philosophy of nature; and a deferential joy of discovery in nature, science, human individuality and society.[25]

The influence of the 'fanatic theology'—both as it was transmitted through the writings of Arndt and as it was absorbed by direct exposure to Hermeticism, Kabbalah, Paracelsian, and Weigelian theology—remains in need of further exploration in the history of the Pietist movement. Given the profoundly detrimental effects of the Thirty Years War and Pietism on the survival of Lutheran Orthodoxy, the fanatical theology condemned in the *Principia* may be rightly held to have been a significant factor in the decline of the Lutheran Church in the seventeenth and eighteenth centuries. The existence of Hunnius' writings demonstrates that the danger posed by false doctrine could be recognized and refuted; the tragedy is that the warning went unheeded, and the Gnostic teachings which had already brought so much suffering to mankind, brought further war and death to Europe.

---

25   Martin Weyer-Menkhoff, "Friedrich Christoph Oetinger" in *The Pietist Theologians—An Introduction to Theology in the Seventeenth and Eighteenth Centuries*, p. 250.

CHAPTER 7. THE RISE OF THE NEW MYTHOLOGIES— SOCIALISM AND THE CHILIASTS.

he collectivist ideology now known as Socialism has long been inseparable from Gnostic and Hermetic fantasies aimed at the fundamental reform of human society. In his superb history of the Socialist ideology, Igor Shafarevich rightly points to Aristophanes' *Ecclesiaszusæ* as containing the first known example of a Socialist system; Aristophanes links the collectivist mentality to a secret cabal of women to seize power. The imposition of a more 'ideal' form of government—in the minds of the female conspirators—involves collectivism, 'free love,' communal meals and life, and the wearing of androgynous clothing. The specific ideological contexts for Socialism may change, but its overall content—and its goals—remain the same. As Shafarevich explains:

> All such doctrines (and as we shall see, there were many of them) have a common core—they are based on the complete rejection of the existing social structure. They call for its destruction and paint a picture of a more just and happy society in which the solution to all the fundamental problems of the times would be found. Furthermore, they propose concrete ways of achieving this goal. In religious literature such a system of views is referred to as belief in the thousand-year Kingdom of God on earth—chiliasm. Borrowing this terminology, we shall designate the socialist doctrines of this type as "chiliastic socialism."[1]

---

1   Igor Shafarevich, *The Socialist Phenomenon,* trans. by William Tjalsma, (New York: Harper & Row, 1980) p. 3.

The other form of Socialism which Shafarevich identifies—state socialism—is not primarily our focus at this point, except to say that the Socialist Myth simply metastasizes into that latter form at its appointed hour. As Shafarevich observes:

> It therefore seems impossible to draw any firm theoretical distinction between the doctrines of chiliastic socialism and the practices of the socialist states. The only difference stems from the fact that in the first case we have a clearly formulated ideal, whereas the second presents a series of variants, stretching down through history, where no more than an attempt can be made to distinguish a certain trend. But this trend, if extrapolated to its logical conclusion, points toward the same ideal that is proclaimed by the socialist doctrines.[2]

The Joachimite movements often carried a quite overt Socialist streak within their doctrine: hatred of the clergy, hatred of the rich, and the forced redistribution of wealth were commonplaces of such fanatics long before the ravings of Thomas Müntzer during the lead up to the Peasants' War. The Socialist mindset was certainly present in the writings of the Revolutionary whose scribblings had a profound influence on the flagellant sect; his hatred of the clergy was only matched—perhaps—by his hatred of the rich:

> The Revolutionary is utterly convinced that God has ordered the great massacre of clergy and 'usurers' in order to remove such abuses for ever, the holocaust is to be an indispensable purification of the world on the eve of the Millennium. And one fact about the Millennium which emerges with great clarity is that it is to be strongly anti-capitalist. …
>
> …Nothing, he insists will do more to establish and protect the new order of equality and communal ownership

_____

2   Shafarevich, p. 253–254.

than this new type of justice.[3]

The Socialist doctrine—and its attendant violence—was certainly present in the teachings of the heresy of the Free Spirit; thus, in Cohn's words:

> In 1317 the Bishop of Strasbourg commented: 'They believe that all things are common, whence they conclude that theft is lawful for them.' ... The point was made clearly enough by John Hartmann, an adept who was captured at Erfurt at the same time as the flagellant messiah Konrad Schmid: 'The truly free man is king and lord of all creatures. All things belong to him, and he has the right to use whatever pleases him. If anyone tries to prevent him, the free man may kill him and take his goods.' ... Cheating, theft, robbery with violence were all justified.[4]

The violence inherently linked to the Socialist mentality was quickly asserted in the various Gnostic sects which sought to remake Christendom according to their own whims. And Joachim's doctrine of three ages played into the mythology of Socialism: Socialist doctrines preserve the notion of the medieval mystics about the *three stages* in the historical process, as well as the scheme of the *fall* of mankind and its return to the original state in a more perfect form. The socialist doctrines contain the following components:

> a. The *myth* of a primordial "natural state" or "golden age," which was destroyed by the bearer of evil called private property.
>
> b. A *castigation* of the way things are. Contemporary society is pronounced incurably depraved, unjust and

3   Norman Cohn, *The Pursuit of the Millennium*, 3rd ed., (Oxford, London, New York: Oxford University Press, 1970) p. 122–123.
4   ibid., p. 182–183.

meaningless, ready only to be scrapped. Only on its ruins can a new social structure be built, a structure that
would guarantee people every happiness of which they
are capable.

c. The *prophecy* of a new society built on socialist principles, a society in which all present shortcomings would
disappear. This is the only path for mankind to return to
the "natural state," as Morelly put it: from the unconscious Golden Age to the conscious one.[5]

As Molnar observes in his book, *Utopia, The Perennial Heresy,*
"Utopian systems never speak of the individual; they always
speak of mankind."[6] This was certainly the mindset of the sects
which we have examined, which viewed mankind according to
classes, and never beheld their individual victims. The Utopian
myopia made it possible for the Revolutionary to see only the
class of clergymen, and never the discrete individuals whom he
posited should be slaughtered by the thousands each day. As the
Paracelsian teacher demanded the utter surrender of self-will
and critical thinking on the part of his student as a necessary
condition for learning his Gnostic doctrine, so the Utopian sacrifices individuals for the sake of the species. In the words of
Shafarevich:

> We can see that all elements of the socialist ide-
> al—the abolition of private property, family, hierarchies;
> the hostility toward religion—could be regarded as a
> manifestation of one basic principle: the suppression of
> individuality. ... All this is inspired by one principle—the
> destruction of individuality or, at least, its suppression to
> the point where it would cease to be a social force. Dos-
> toyevsky's comparisons to the ant hill and the bee hive

5   Shafarevich, p. 130.
6   Thomas Molnar, *Utopia, The Perennial Heresy,* (New York: Sheed
and Ward, 1967) p. 113.

turn out to be particularly apt in the light of ethological classifications of society: we have constructed the model of the *anonymous society*.[7]

The individual thus loses his identity: He no longer knows *who* he is, *where* he is, and *when* he is. These things are replaced by the ideological constructs furnished by the Gnostic teacher. Those things which make a man an individual who is part of overlapping communities—that rich tapestry of human existence which weaves together strands of Home, State, and Church—are eliminated and replaced by a lie. The terrible simplifications of ideology require a man to ignore even the testimony of his own senses, his memory, his sentiment, his convictions, and to replace them with that which has been mass-produced for his new identity. The sacred gift of the Triune God—that one is born with, and grows into, a divinely-bestowed identity—is ripped away, and replaced with an idol fashioned by the grubby hands of Ideologists.

Joachim opened the door to a doctrine of Progress, and Socialism became an element of technique for implementing that progress. The dark myths of the Modern Age war against man's God-given place in the world, and demand that he become less than human. Socialism is a myth which teaches men to imagine themselves as nothing more than economic units—consumers and producers. Men have come to view themselves as mere machines; the biochemical puppets of the Darwinist Myth, the economic entities of the Socialist Myth.

But man is not such a mean thing. The eternal Son of God became Man that He might die for man and deliver him from death, and in the resurrection of the Christ to give hope to all who believe in Him. To know oneself to be thus redeemed

---

7   Shafarevich, p. 269.

is to transform all that we are, and to no longer loath the lingering vanity of life in this fallen world. The perfection of the machine is the god of the Socialist or the Darwinist. As John Ruskin observed in 1853, the works of men are glorious even in their imperfections, not in the slavish conformity to the empty perfections of the machines:

> But in the mediæval, or especially Christian, system of ornament, this slavery is done away with altogether; Christianity having recognized, in small things as well as great, the individual value of every soul. But it not only recognized its value; it confesses its imperfection, in only bestowing dignity upon the acknowledgment of unworthiness. That admission of lost and fallen nature, which the Greek or Ninevite felt to be intensely painful, and, as far as might be, altogether refused, the Christian makes daily and hourly, contemplating the fact of it without fear, as tending, in the end, to God's greater glory. Therefore, to every spirit which Christianity summons to her service, her exhortation is: Do what you can, and confess frankly what you are unable to do; neither let your effort be shortened for fear of failure, nor your confession silenced for fear of shame. ...
>
> ... And therefore, while in all things that we see or do, we are to desire perfection, and strive for it, we are nevertheless not to set the meaner thing, in its narrow accomplishment, above the nobler thing, in its mighty progress; nor to esteem smooth minuteness above shattered majesty; nor to prefer mean victory to honourable defeat; nor to lower the level of our aim, that we may the more surely enjoy the complacency of success.[8]

Living out our lives in the midst of a fallen world, those who

---

8   John Ruskin, *On Art and Life,* (New York: Penguin Books, 2005) p. 11–12, 13.

have been washed in the blood of the Lamb of God await the resurrection, when all will have been perfected by the hand of the Triune God. The striving in one's various vocations highlights the effects of the fall, and yet without despair. But the man that would seek worldly Perfection, the inauguration of a Golden Age by the hand of man, will make a hell in the midst of this world, and make men less then men. Again, in Ruskin's words:

> You must either make a tool of the creature, or a man of him. You cannot make both. Men were not intended to work with the accuracy of tools, to be precise and perfect in all their actions. If you will have that precision out of them, and make their fingers measure degrees like cog-wheels, and their arms strike curves like compasses, you must unhumanize them. All the energy of their spirits must be given to make cogs and compasses of themselves. All their attention and strength must go to the accomplishment of the mean act.[9]

As we shall see in the next chapter, even Ruskin could never have imagined how literally his imagery would come to pass under the powers of the dark myths of this age.

---

9   ibid., p. 14.

8. THE RISE OF THE NEW MYTHOLOGIES—
THE SINGULARITY.

ou must either make a tool of the creature, or a man of him. You cannot make both. Men were not intended to work with the accuracy of tools, to be precise and perfect in all their actions." More than a century and a half after John Ruskin penned these words, there are men and women eagerly desiring to bring to pass such a dehumanization of man. As is common with the ways of the Gnostics in each age, they seek to make man less than he is while claiming that they will make a god of him.

The Hermetic form of Gnosticism has sought to bring about a new Golden Age by means of technology—the Myth of Progress and the Myth of Darwinism combine with the ancient Gnostic desire to 'ascend' and become one with a god of our own making, and the lie is packaged in a new form: transhumanism (the ideology which teaches that man may achieve immortality and shed his biological existence through technological means). The old methodologies of the Gnostics have taken on new forms, but now it is not enough to wait for death to leave behind the prison of the flesh. In the quest for immortality and a deliverance from biological life, the modern Hermeticist wants to escape the body for a machine of his own making, thus Erik Davis wrote in *TechGnosis*:

> Obviously, an incalculable historical, cultural, and spiritual divide exists between the mystical aspirations of ancient dualists and the cultures and concepts that would come to surround information and its technologies in the twentieth century. But from a hermetic perspective, which reads images and synchronicities at least as deeply as facts, the mythic structures and psychology

of Gnosticism seem strangely resonant with the digital zeitgeist and its paradigm of information. As we'll see, Gnostic myth anticipates the more extreme dreams of today's mechanistic mutants and cyberspace cowboys, especially their libertarian drive toward freedom and self-divinization, and their dualistic rejection of matter for the incorporeal possibilities of mind. Gnostic lore also provides a mythic key for the kind of infomania and conspiratorial thinking that comes to haunt the postwar world, with its terror of nefarious cabals, narcotic technologies, and invisible messengers of deception.[1]

However, the desire to use technological means to 'perfect' nature is nothing new—it has existed for as long as Hermetic Gnosticism has influenced Western thought. William Newman notes the linkage uniting alchemy and Hermeticism:
> The full fruition of this grafting of Greek philosophical ideas onto the chemical technology of ancient Egypt did not occur, however, until somewhat later. We encounter it clearly in the writings of the mysterious and prolific alchemist Zosimos, evidently a native of Panopolis in upper Egypt, who flourished around 300 C.E. Zosimos was conversant with the revelations attributed to Hermes Trismegistus in the Greek *corpus hermeticum* and in various types of Gnostic literature. … No longer content with the goal of simulating natural products, Zosimos views alchemy as providing the means by which nature itself can pass from an imperfect state to a regenerate one. … He views evaporative processes as the conversion of a body into semimaterial spirit (*pneuma*) or as the release of such spirit from a body in which it has been trapped.[2]

---

1   Erik Davis, *TechGnosis,* (London: Serpents Tail Books, 2004) p. 97.
2   William R. Newman, *Promethean Ambitions—Alchemy and the*

Alchemy was treated as the most 'secretive' and 'elite' science until the later stages of the Modern Age—a 'science' which captured even the mind and imagination of Isaac Newton—thus from the very midst of the first Gnostic era, alchemy was combined with Hermeticism as a technological means of ascent from materiality, or at least as a means of achieving physical immortality:

> While Zosimos views the goal of alchemy as that of separating the pneuma of material substances from its restrictive matrix, this is not the end of the story. The pneuma is also to be rejoined with the body, presumably after the body has been purified. Elsewhere in his writings, Zosimos explains that this is a physical death followed by a reanimation of the body undergoing treatment. Alchemy, by providing the material key to this operation, reveals the method by which nature itself is not merely mimicked but transformed.[3]

Such an understanding of the linkage between Hermeticism and alchemy continued during the Reformation and post-Reformation eras. The medicinal alchemy of Paracelsus and the 'natural magic' of Marsilio Ficino are simple two examples among many of the blending of magical technique and mystical ends. And near the heart of the Hermetic dream of purifying—recreating—man was his desire to create a man-like creature in the image of man. Thus, the Hermetic dream of creating the homunculus or (in Kabbalistic terms) *golem*. The concept of creating life out of unliving matter was part of the alchemical dream from the time of that first Hermetical alchemist, Zosimos:

> Whenever the homunculus is mentioned by historians, one finds references to the work of Zosimos of Panapo-

Quest to Perfect Nature, (Chicago and London: The University of Chicago Press, 2004) p. 29.
3   ibid., p. 30.

lis ... The *anthrōparion* of Zosimos is not an example of artificial human life, but of the rich symbolism of alchemy, which employed every conceivable image to veil the exact nature of the processes being described. For this reason we can call the *anthrōparion* of Zosimos a "pseudohomunculus."[4]

That which Zosimos described in the imagery of alchemy, became an active pursuit of alchemy as practiced by Muslims and Jews during the period of the Christian Middle Ages. Thus, for example, *The Book of the Cow* (a Arabic forgery falsely attributed to Plato) describes an alchemical process whereby it was claimed that an artificial man could be created; it is perhaps no surprise that some scholars believe the work was written in Harran[5]—the Mesopotamian city where Hermeticism survived the longest, before that tragic legacy passed to Constantinople. The homunculus of Arabic and Paracelsian alchemy—being of a more overtly Gnostic character—is considerably more threatening that the Kabbalistic *golem*. In Newman's estimation:

> The rational animal of *The Book of the Cow* is a prophetic creature whose blood and body parts allow the magician to acquire paranormal powers. The homunculus of Jābir is also a prophetic being, at least in its most perfect state. All of these artificial creatures equal or surpass the products of ordinary generation, unlike the Jewish golem. ... the homunculus of Paracelsus was conceived precisely in the light of outdoing nature and was viewed as the final pinnacle of man's technological power. It could not be more distinct from the Hebrew golem, either in its mode of generation or in its relationship to the ordinary products of divine creation.[6]

---

4   Newman, p. 171, 173.
5   Opinion of David Pingree, cited in Newman, p. 179.
6   ibid., p. 186.

However, in either case, the goal is the creation of life—it is simply a question of how far from the truth, and how deeply into Gnostic error, the particular practitioner has slipped. Newman likened the relationship between the two forms in quite modern terms: "If it were not rash to draw a modern comparison, perhaps one could say that the golem belongs to the realm of 'hard' artificial life, the world of robotics, cybernetics, and artificial intelligence, where ordinary biological processes are obviated or simulated by nonbiological means. The homunculus proper is a child of the 'wet' world of in vitro fertilization, cloning, and genetic engineering, where biology is not circumvented but altered."[7] The comparison seems an apt one, given the mentality at work behind such modern pursuits; the Gnostic origins of such endeavors are often no longer recognized as such, but this is primarily because the Gnostic influence on modern civilization is so pervasive, and the capacity for the necessary theological reflection has been so atrophied in modern man.

Although the work is undoubtedly flawed in certain regards, David Noble's book, *The Religion of Technology*, tracks numerous aspects of the triumph of such Hermetic thinking. Noble links the chiliastic (thus Joachimite) search for Utopia with the Hermetical aims of fashioning man into a god in the pseudo-science of self-deification which is one of the primary legacies of both heresies in this age:

In the sixteenth century, inventors and mechanics had increasingly invoked the image of God as craftsman and architect in order, by analogy, to lend prestige to their own activities: in their humble arts, they were imitating God and hence reflecting his glory. In the seventeenth century, the scientists began to carry this artisanal analogy between the works of man and God somewhat

---

7   ibid., p. 187.

further, toward a real identity between them. ...

Increasingly, in the inspired imagination of the time, man's contribution to creation loomed ever larger in the scheme of things. Despite their caveats about the necessity of humility, and despite their devout acknowledgement of divine purpose in their work, the scientists subtly but steadily began to assume the mantle of creator in their own right, as gods themselves. Francis Bacon, for example, had insisted that man's mission to remake the world was in reality but "the footsteps of the Creator imprinted on his creatures." "God forbid that we should give out a dream of our own imagination for a pattern of the world," he declared. Yet, at the end of his life, in his *New Atlantis*, he predicted that men would one day create new species and become as gods—"the undeclared ultimate goal" of modern science, as Lewis Mumford put it.[8]

The odd world of artificial intelligence 'visionaries' provides some of the more explicitly Gnostic prognostications regarding the character of their craft. For example, Edward Fredkin—one of the early leading figures in the development of modern computer systems—has developed his own form of 'digital philosophy,' and (according to Noble) speaks of the rise of artificial intelligence in terms which harken back to the language of Joachim:

"I think our mission is to create artificial intelligence," Edward Fredkin boldly declared; "it is the next step in evolution." There have been three great events of equal importance in the history of the universe, he explained. The first was the creation of the universe itself; the second was the appearance of life; and the third

8   David F. Noble, *The Religion of Technology—The Divinity of Man and the Spirit of Invention,* (New York: Penguin Books, 1999) p. 65–66, 67.

was the advent of Artificial Intelligence. The last, according to Fredkin, is "the question which deals with all questions. In the abstract, nothing can be compared to it. One wonders why God didn't do it. Or, its a very godlike thing to create a superintelligence, much smarter than we are. It's the abstraction of the physical universe, and this is the ultimate in that direction. If there are any more questions to be answered, this is how they'll be answered. There can't be anything of more consequence to happen on this planet."[9]

There is a painful absurdity to Fredkin's assertions which tempts a reader to simply dismiss the man, and his muddled notions, out of hand. However, such a casual dismissal would be dangerous: the inherent egotism of the advocates of artificial intelligence and transhumanism is paired to a fatally flawed worldview, and the advocates of that worldview see themselves in godlike terms, destined to change the course of the human race and to shape the future of the universe itself. The citation of another of Noble's multitudinous sources —artificial intelligence 'guru' Earl Cox—demonstrates that such TechGnostics have a limitless confidence in their own divinity:

> We are thus already at the twilight of human civilization and the dawn of a new robotic "supercivilization," which will remake the entire universe in its digital image. Happily, he advises, *Homo sapiens* need not be completely left behind, as the dinosaurs were. "Technology will soon enable human beings to change into something else altogether" and thereby "escape the human condition." "Humans may be able to transfer their minds into the new cybersystems and join the cybercivilization," securing for themselves an eternal existence. "This is not the end of humanity," Cox explains, "only its physical ex-

---

9   quoted in Noble, p. 163–164.

istence as a biological life form. Mankind will join our newly invented partners. We will download our minds into vessels created by our machine children and, with them, explore the universe. ... Freed from our frail biological form, human-cum-artificial intelligences will move out into the universe. ... Such a combined system of minds, representing the ultimate triumph of science and technology, will transcend the timid concepts of deity and divinity held by today's theologians."[10]

Thus, one may see that transhumanism and the quest for artificial intelligence are connected to an impulse which seeks to create a perfect world through a simple solution which lies within the grasp of human competence, while simultaneously praising human ingenuity in terms which are, bluntly, absurd. While the advocates of such pseudoscience view their quest in terms of their incipient godhood, the din of their rhetoric has a familiar ring to it. As Thomas Molnar observed over four decades ago:

Perfectionism in our time is not essentially different from that of other ages. Invariably, some new invention, discovery or even—in expectation of the millennium, socio-political revolution, or new technological advances—offers the utopian his pretext for announcing the need of a new and final set of moral values worthier of a purified, sinless, mature, autonomous, perfected mankind than any previous set of moral imperatives. As Pope Pius XII viewed it, modern technology seems to communicate to man, kneeling at its altar, a feeling of self-sufficiency and satisfaction in his insatiable desire for knowledge and power. ...

The real issue, then, is not one of opposition between exaltation of and contempt for technology. The issue

10   ibid., p. 164–165.

is whether the laws of morality are likely to undergo and, in fact, ought to undergo fundamental changes because of technological progress or some startling development.[11]

The heart of Utopianism is always a dehumanizing sham. The quest for moral perfectionism, the search for a technological solution to the horrors of life in a fallen world, the armed doctrine of Socialism which justifies murder and rapine to create a more 'just' distribution of wealth are all ideological swindles—to borrow the language of Eric Voegelin—aimed at selling false wares to the philosophically and theologically ignorant. Such ideologies are expressed in terms of fanaticism because their adherents seem incapable of grasping the complexities of human history—or of daily human existence. Again, in Molnar's words:

> If the utopian seizes upon fashionable ideologies, scientific inventions and technical improvements to shorten the way toward the desired perfect state, it is because he holds all intermediary situations in contempt. He does not proceed, like the usual reformer, in piecemeal fashion because he lacks the patience to adjust concrete realities to new requirements. He is intent on abolishing every part of an existing situation because only in this way can he prevent the radically new from being contaminated by the necessarily old.[12]

Thus the advocates of transhumanism and artificial intelligence—having become bored, or terrified, by the details of actual human existence—seek to so fundamentally alter our existence that one may question whether the fruit of their labors (if successful) could be considered human in any meaningful sense. When men begin to speak publicly of the "twilight of human

---

11   Thomas Molnar, *Utopia, the Perennial Heresy,* (New York: Sheed and Ward, 1967) p. 48.
12   ibid., p. 49.

civilization" and an "escape" from the "human condition," even while claiming such a thing would not be the end of humanity, one is tempted to simply mock the absurdity of the self-contradictory character of the claims: How could there be a humanity which is not subject to the "human condition"? The purveyors of such ideologies have no room for a doctrine of redemption which would see a divine restoration of humanity to its initial human condition—and more—in Christ; rather, their objection is to life in the created order as that order is known to modern science. They reduce human existence to nothing other than a series of biochemically-stored memories and biochemically-induced reactions to experiences, and then claim that the new humanity will remain meaningfully human utterly apart from a biological context.

One of the more significant advocates of transhumanism and artificial intelligence is Ray Kurzweil, author of *The Singularity is Near*, among other works. It is Kurzweil's contention that ongoing advances in computer processing capacities and data storage will inevitably and inexorably lead to "the Singularity"—the breakthrough moment when our machines become self-aware. Hidden in the entire argument is the false axiom that self-awareness is simply a byproduct of processing speed and data storage. Once again, on a certain level it is hard to take Kurzweil's argumentation as a serious philosophy. Anyone who could subtitle his *magnum opus*, "When Humans Transcend Biology," is either lost in a haze of sophistry, or may well be incapable of serious philosophical and theological discussion. That "biology" is an inescapable aspect of the very definition of humanity is lost on Kurzweil. But, then, that fact was a stumbling stone to the ancient Gnostics, as well.

Kurzweil and other transhumanists are engaged in a sophistical game in which the very points which they endeavor to prove are already contained in the axioms of their argumentation. Thus, for example, they assume that self-awareness is a function of data processing. They assume that 'humanity' is a meaningful concept apart from biology. They assume that machines can reach self-awareness by making them more like transhumanists' flawed notion of what constitutes the basis of self-awareness.

However, in the words of John Searle, an insightful critic of Kurzweil's flawed logic, all of the talk about 'thinking' computers is fundamentally flawed: "Any pocket calculator can beat any human mathematician at arithmetic. Is this a blow to human dignity? No, it is rather a credit to the ingenuity of programmers and engineers. It is simply a result of the fact that we have a technology that enables us to build tools to do the things that we cannot do, or cannot do as well or as fast, without the tools."[13] Kurzweil's entire argument is irredeemable because it is logically incoherent, as Searle demonstrates in the following case of Kurzweil's chop logic:

> He confuses the computer simulation of a phenomenon with a duplication or re-creation of that phenomenon. This comes out most obviously in the case of consciousness. Anybody who is seriously considering having his "program and database" downloaded onto some hardware ought to wonder whether or not the resulting hardware is going to be conscious. ... He does not claim to know that machines will be conscious, but he insists that they will claim to be conscious, and will continue to engage in discussions about whether they are conscious, and consequently their claims will be largely accepted. People will eventually just come to accept without question that machines are conscious.

---

13   John Searle, "I Married a Computer," in *Are We Spiritual Machines?—Ray Kurzweil vs. the Critics of Strong A.I.,* (Seattle: Discovery Institute Press, 2002) p. 64.

But this misses the point. I can already program my computer so that I says that it is conscious—i.e., it prints out "I am conscious"—and a good programmer can even program it so that it will carry on a rudimentary argument to the effect that it is conscious. But that has nothing to do with whether or not it really is conscious.[14]

The TechGnostics have proven themselves to have swallowed whole the accumulated myths of a thousand years of flawed Hermetical thinking. For someone who believes in the Socialist Myth, the failure of every Socialist system to deliver on its promises is simply irrelevant. For someone who believes in the Joachimite Myth of Progress—of a Golden Third Age of Man—it does not matter that every prophet who has predicted that age has proven false, and that most of them have been harbingers of slaughter and chaos. Many more permutations of the myths that govern the modern age have already been offered in the second portion of this work. The deadly values of our culture have created an entire mythological structure to sustain them, and their advocates have gone to great lengths to hide the history of the failure of their myths. The false gods of modernity have been exposed as mere idols of men. It is time for the idols to be broken.

---

14   ibid., p. 65–66.

CONCLUSION.

he idolatry of the new Gnostics has failed to deliver the promised salvation of mankind. Instead, the legacy of Hermeticism and Joachimism has been a tale of human misery and loss. The technological 'gains' which have taken place in the Modern Age have often been perverted to serve the ignoble ends of the Gnostics, and it raises again the question, "For what profit is it to a man if he gains the whole world, and is himself destroyed or lost?" (Luke 9:25 NKJV) In the concluding pages of his book, David Noble wrote:

> A thousand years in the making, the religion of technology has become the common enchantment, not only of the designers of technology but also of those caught up in, and undone by, their godly designs. The expectation of ultimate salvation through technology, whatever the immediate human and social costs, has become the unspoken orthodoxy, reinforced by a market-induced enthusiasm for novelty and sanctioned by a millenarian yearning for new beginnings. ... Thus, unrestrained technological development is allowed to proceed apace, without serious scrutiny or oversight—without reason. Pleas for rationality, for reflection about pace and purpose, for sober assessment of costs and benefits—for evidence even of economic value, much less larger social gains—are dismissed as irrational. From within the faith, any and all criticism appears irrelevant, and irreverent.[1]

The myths of modernity have blinded modern man to his own nature. History has been perverted or forgotten. The an-

1   David F. Noble, *The Religion of Technology—The Divinity of Man and the Spirit of Invention,* (New York: Penguin Books, 1999) p. 206–207.

cient myths are subjected to ridicule, while the new myths are to be considered inviolable—as unto a message from God, if there was still a place for God in their ideological construct.

Where, in this conflict, is the Church? Over thirty years ago, Russell Kirk observed that "American churches are engaged in a kind of unconscious holding-action, as if awaiting an event which lies concealed in the hand of God."[2] The Remnant has not succumbed to the darkness of the fallen myths of modernity because the saints have been made partakers of the "myth that is fact." The idolatries of the Modern Age—the deadly values with which the Church must contend every day—cannot overcome the Christian verity. Often, refuting the lies of the enemy is as simple as exposing the errors which rest in the assumptions upon which fallen men rest their arguments.

This is a dark age, in the proper sense of the concept. It is an age in which those who claim to *know* are ignorant—ignorant of the sacred history, and thus ignorant of *who* they are, *when* they are, and *where* they are. The baptized child of the Triune God has that which the Gnostic lacks as long as the Gnostic remains in his error: a true identity, rooted in relationship to the world in which we all live—this vale of tears. In the will and timing of the Holy Trinity, the darkness of this age may be swept away. But in the midst of the darkness, we have the light of the knowledge of salvation. In the light of the risen Christ, we are bold to believe in the hope which abides in us. For we have been redeemed by the blood of the Lamb slain from the foundation of the world, and in His return we have an everlasting citizenship in the Kingdom of God.

—*soli Deo gloria*—

---

2   Russell Kirk, "America's Augustan Age?," in *The Wise Men Know What Wicked Things are Written on the Sky,* (Washington, D.C.: Regnery Gateway, 1987) p. 21.

Scriptural Index

336

Index of Names

www.ingramcontent.com/pod-product-compliance
Lightning Source LLC
LaVergne TN
LVHW051822080426
835512LV00018B/2689